Marketing

Marketing

Alexander Hiam

with Linda G. Rastelli

BICENTENNIAL
1807
WILEY
2007
BICENTENNIAL

John Wiley & Sons, Inc.

Credits

PUBLISHER
Anne Smith

ASSOCIATE EDITOR
Beth Tripmacher

MARKETING MANAGER
Jennifer Slomack

SENIOR EDITORIAL ASSISTANT
Tiara Kelly

PRODUCTION MANAGER
Kelly Tavares

PRODUCTION ASSISTANT
Courtney Leshko

CREATIVE DIRECTOR
Harry Nolan

COVER DESIGNER
Hope Miller

Material from chapters 3, 4, 7, and 8 from *Core Concepts of Marketing,* 2002, John Wiley & Sons, Inc. Used with permission of John Burnett.

Material from Chapter 13 from *The Ultimate Guide to Electronic Marketing for Small Business: Low-Cost/High Return Tools and Techniques That Really Work,* 2005, John Wiley & Sons, Inc. Grateful appreciation to Tom Antion for his contribution.

This book was set in Times New Roman, printed and bound by R.R. Donnelley.
The cover was printed by Phoenix Color.

To order books or for customer service please, call 1-800-CALL WILEY (225-5945).

ISBN-13 978-0-471-79079-2

ISBN-10 0-471-79079-6

Printed in the United States of America

10 9 8 7 6 5 4 3 2 1

PREFACE

College classrooms bring together learners from many backgrounds with a variety of aspirations. Although the students are in the same course, they are not necessarily on the same path. This diversity, coupled with the reality that these learners often have jobs, families, and other commitments, requires a flexibility that our nation's higher education system is addressing. Distance learning, shorter course terms, new disciplines, evening courses, and certification programs are some of the approaches that colleges employ to reach as many students as possible and help them clarify and achieve their goals.

Wiley Pathways books, a new line of texts from John Wiley & Sons, Inc., are designed to help you address this diversity and the need for flexibility. These books focus on the fundamentals, identify core competencies and skills, and promote independent learning. The focus on the fundamentals helps students grasp the subject, bringing them all to the same basic understanding. These books use clear, everyday language, presented in an uncluttered format, making the reading experience more pleasurable. The core competencies and skills help students succeed in the classroom and beyond, whether in another course or in a professional setting. A variety of built-in learning resources promote independent learning and help instructors and students gauge students' understanding of the content. These resources enable students to think critically about their new knowledge, and apply their skills in any situation.

Our goal with *Wiley Pathways* books—with their brief, inviting format, clear language, and core competencies and skills focus—is to celebrate the many students in your courses, respect their needs, and help you guide them on their way.

CASE Learning System

To meet the needs of working college students, *Marketing* uses a four-step process: The CASE Learning System. Based on Bloom's Taxonomy of Learning, CASE presents key marketing topics in easy-to-follow chapters. The text then prompts analysis, synthesis, and evaluation with a variety of learning aids and assessment tools. Students move efficiently from reviewing what they have learned, to acquiring new information and skills, to applying their new knowledge and skills to real-life scenarios. Each phase of the CASE system is signaled in-text by an icon:

▲ Content
▲ Analysis
▲ Synthesis
▲ Evaluation

Using the CASE Learning System, students not only achieve academic mastery of marketing topics, but they master real-world marketing skills. The CASE Learning System also helps students become independent learners, giving them a distinct advantage whether they are starting out or seek to advance in their careers.

Organization, Depth, and Breadth of the Text

Marketing offers the following features:

▲ **Modular format.** Research on college students shows that they access information from textbooks in a non-linear way. Instructors also often wish to reorder textbook content to suit the needs of a particular class. Therefore, although Marketing proceeds logically from the basics to increasingly more challenging material, chapters are further organized into sections (4 to 6 per chapter) that are self-contained for maximum teaching and learning flexibility.

▲ **Numeric system of headings.** Marketing uses a numeric system for headings (for example, 2.3.4 identifies the fourth sub-section of Section 3 of Chapter 2). With this system, students and teachers can quickly and easily pinpoint topics in the table of contents and the text, keeping class time and study sessions focused.

▲ **Core content.** Topics in the text are organized into four parts and thirteen chapters.

Part I: Business Marketing

Chapter 1, Making Marketing Happen, discusses the importance of having a program, knowing your customer, and finding innovative ways to make your product appealing. Influence points for different types of businesses, effective ways of improving your marketing, and the five Ps of the marketing matrix are presented.

Offers guidance on when to use an informational or an emotional approach, or a balance of the two, as well as how to focus your marketing efforts and be consistent.

Chapter 2, The Marketing Plan, describes how marketing strategies designed to reach a target audience are used to organize a marketing program, and how to use a marketing program to draw up a marketing plan. Different marketing strategies are reviewed, as are the components of a marketing plan and common methods for forecasting sales. Students will practice preparing a marketing program budget, writing marketing objectives and strategies for different stages of a company's growth, and assessing how well a given marketing program is working.

Part II: Analyzing Marketing Opportunities

Chapter 3, Knowing Consumers, outlines the internal and external sources of influence on buying; identifies the characteristics of reference groups, socialization agents, and opinion leaders; and distinguishes between consumer and organizational purchasing patterns. It also lays out the consumer and organizational buying decision process to help students analyze opportunities to influence buying decisions. Students learn how to assess the usefulness of buying factors, predict buying patterns based on the consumer life cycle, and estimate marketing effectiveness in buying situations.

Chapter 4, Segmenting and Targeting Markets, presents the advantages of segmenting markets, compares strategies and segmentation types, and highlights the bases for segmentation. Students differentiate between consumer and business segmentation, compare concentration strategies with undifferentiated strategies, and discriminate between key segmentation factors and less significant ones. Students also learn to use criteria to judge when a segment is a viable market and how to model a five-step process to target that market.

Chapter 5, Marketing Research, explains effective ways to conduct market research, including primary and secondary research methods, and quantitative and qualitative methods. Students learn to specify their information needs before doing research by first identifying research questions, analyzing the best way to obtain the needed information, and listening to their customers to determine whether market research is necessary.

Part III: Product and Distribution

Chapter 6, Developing and Managing Products, shows ways for devising new products and modifying old ones. The impact of product packaging and labeling upon sales, how to judge when to delete a product, and legal protections for products are all discussed, as are suggestions for choosing ideas that are legally permissible, assessing when a product is a good fit in a given product line, and ways to increase the breadth and depth of a product line.

Chapter 7, Marketing Channel Management, lays out how to make the most of marketing channels, whether by finding more distributors, streamlining channels, or using a new channel system. Market channel structure, direct vs. indirect channels, and the components of supply chain management are explained. Use of intermediaries to reduce transactions, strategies for finding distributors, and ways to predict potential channel management issues are also explored.

Chapter 8, Retailing, presents the different types of retailers, explains merchandising and direct marketing strategies, and outlines criteria for a strong POP display. Students learn how to apply an understanding of consumer behaviors, analyze the components of successful retailing concepts, choose retail locations with good potential, and assemble effective direct response ads.

Chapter 9, Pricing, discusses factors to consider when setting a price, including customers' price sensitivity and their perceptions of products and services. Students gain an understanding of discount structures and general pricing approaches, how to raise prices while increasing sales, the strategic use of special offers and discounts, and the importance of avoiding illegal pricing practices.

Part IV: Advertising and Promotion

Chapter 10, Marketing Communications and Personal Selling, helps students understand the process of personal selling and meeting customers' needs. Also offered are ways to pump up marketing communications and develop brand personality with great visuals, writing, and attention-getting strategies drawn from fiction and psychology, as well as strategies for finding, keeping, and managing effective salespeople.

Chapter 11, Advertising, reviews the types of advertising, from print ads, billboards, and brochures to signs and even media, such as radio, video, and television. How to choose from among these options based upon their relative advantages and how to design an effective ad or brochure are also presented.

Guidelines for estimating advertising costs, staying within budget, and measuring the effectiveness of an ongoing ad campaign are also provided.

Chapter 12, Publicity, Public Relations, and Sales Promotions, describes the different types of sales promotions and premiums, the role of publicity, and the elements of a good hook. How to handle public relations tasks, prepare reasonable impact scenarios, and use press releases to tell a story are also included. Students will learn to evaluate promotions to increase sales, manage word of mouth to their advantage, and develop mutually beneficial relationships with the press.

Chapter 13, Internet Marketing, explores the four marketing domains of internet commerce, and offers concrete ideas on how to design a robust, effective Web site and drive traffic to it. Ways to use online tools, banner ads, and e-mail to get sales are also included, as are guidelines for establishing a budget for Web marketing.

Pre-Reading Learning Aids

Each chapter of *Marketing* features the following learning and study aids to activate students' prior knowledge of the topics and orient them to the material.

▲ **Pre-test.** This pre-reading assessment tool in multiple-choice format not only introduces chapter material, but it also helps students anticipate the chapter's learning outcomes. By focusing students' attention on what they do not know, the self-test provides students with a benchmark against which they can measure their own progress. The pre-test is available online at www.wiley.com/college/Hiam.

▲ **What You'll Learn in This Chapter and After Studying This Chapter.** These bulleted lists tell students what they will be learning in the chapter and why it is significant for their careers. They also explain why the chapter is important and how it relates to other chapters in the text. "What You'll Learn . . ." lists focus on the subject matter that will be taught (e.g., what marketing research is). "After Studying This Chapter . . ." lists emphasize capabilities and skills students will learn (e.g., how to actually conduct marketing research).

▲ **Goals and Outcomes.** These lists identify specific student capabilities that will result from reading the chapter. They set students up to synthesize and evaluate the chapter material, and relate it to the real world.

▲ **Figures and tables.** Line art and photos have been carefully chosen to be truly instructional rather than filler. Tables distill and present information in a way that is easy to identify, access, and understand, enhancing the focus of the text on essential ideas.

Within-Text Learning Aids

The following learning aids are designed to encourage analysis and synthesis of the material, and to support the learning process and ensure success during the evaluation phase:

▲ **Introduction.** This section orients the student by introducing the chapter and explaining its practical value and relevance to the book as a whole. Short summaries of chapter sections preview the topics to follow.

▲ **"For Example" Boxes.** Found within each section, these boxes tie section content to real-world organizations, scenarios, and applications.

▲ **Self-Check.** Related to the "What You'll Learn . . ." bullets and found at the end of each section, this battery of short answer questions emphasizes student understanding of concepts and mastery of section content. Though the questions may either be discussed in class or studied by students outside of class, students should not go on before they can answer all questions correctly. Each Self-Check question set includes a link to a section of the pre-test for further review and practice.

▲ **Key Terms and Glossary.** To help students develop a professional vocabulary, key terms are bolded in the introduction, summary, and when they first appear in the chapter. A complete list of key terms with brief definitions appears at the end of each chapter and again in a glossary at the end of the book. Knowledge of key terms is assessed by all assessment tools (see below).

▲ **Summary.** Each chapter concludes with a summary paragraph that reviews the major concepts in the chapter and links back to the "What You'll Learn . . ." list.

Evaluation and Assessment Tools

The evaluation phase of the CASE Learning System consists of a variety of within-chapter and end-of-chapter assessment tools that test how well students have learned the material. These tools also encourage students to extend their learning into different scenarios and higher levels of understanding and thinking. The following assessment tools appear in every chapter of *Marketing*:

▲ **Summary Questions** help students summarize the chapter's main points by asking a series of multiple choice and true/false questions that emphasize student understanding of concepts and mastery of chapter content. Students should be able to answer all of the Summary Questions correctly before moving on.

▲ **Review Questions** in short answer format review the major points in each chapter, prompting analysis while reinforcing and confirming student understanding of concepts, and encouraging mastery of chapter content. They are somewhat more difficult than the Self-Check and Summary Questions, and students should be able to answer most of them correctly before moving on.

▲ **Applying this Chapter** questions drive home key ideas by asking students to synthesize and apply chapter concepts to new, real-life situations and scenarios.

▲ **You Try It** questions are designed to extend students' thinking, and so are ideal for discussion or writing assignments. Using an open-ended format and sometimes based on Web sources, they encourage students to draw conclusions using chapter material applied to real-world situations, which fosters both mastery and independent learning.

▲ **Post-test** should be taken after students have completed the chapter. It includes all of the questions in the pre-test, so that students can see how their learning has progressed and improved.

Instructor and Student Package

Marketing is available with the following teaching and learning supplements. All supplements are available online at the text's Book Companion Web site, located at www.wiley.com/college/Hiam.

▲ **Instructor's Resource Guide.** Provides the following aids and supplements for teaching an Introduction to Marketing course:

- *Diagnostic Evaluation of Grammar, Mechanics, and Spelling.* A useful tool that instructors may administer to the class at the beginning of the course to determine each student's basic writing skills. The Evaluation is accompanied by an Answer Key and a Marking Key. Instructors are encouraged to use the Marking Key when grading students' Evaluations, and to duplicate and distribute it to students with their graded evaluations.

- *Sample syllabus.* A convenient template that instructors may use for creating their own course syllabi.

- *Teaching suggestions.* For each chapter, these include a chapter summary, learning objectives, definitions of key terms, lecture notes, answers to select text question sets, and at least three suggestions for classroom activities, such as ideas for speakers to invite, videos to show, and other projects.

▲ **PowerPoints.** Key information is summarized in 10 to 15 PowerPoints per chapter. Instructors may use these in class or choose to share them with students for class presentations or to provide additional study support.

▲ **Test Bank.** One test per chapter, as well as a mid-term and a final. Each includes true/false, multiple choice, and open-ended questions. Answers and page references are provided for the true/false and multiple choice questions, and page references for the open-ended questions. Available in Microsoft Word and computerized formats.

BRIEF CONTENTS

Part I Business Marketing

1. Making Marketing Happen 1
2. The Marketing Plan 19

Part II Analyzing Marketing Opportunities

3. Knowing Consumers 47
4. Segmenting and Targeting Markets 71
5. Marketing Research 95

Part III Product and Distribution

6. Developing and Managing Products 118
7. Marketing Channel Management 145
8. Retailing 171
9. Pricing 195

Part IV Advertising and Promotion

10. Marketing Communications and Personal Selling 221
11. Advertising 248
12. Publicity, Public Relations, and Sales Promotions 276
13. Internet Marketing 296

Glossary 321

Index 335

CONTENTS

Part I Business Marketing

1. **Making Marketing Happen** 1

    Introduction 2

  1.1 What is Marketing? 2
      1.1.1   Getting to Know Your Customer 2
      1.1.2   The Marketing Mix 5

    Self-Check 8

  1.2 Focusing Your Marketing Program 8
      1.2.1   Finding Your Strengths 8
      1.2.2   Finding Your Influence Points 9
      1.2.3   Finding Your Markets 9

    Self-Check 10

  1.3 Improving Your Marketing Program 11
      1.3.1   Being Consistent 11
      1.3.2   Keep Moving 12

    Self-Check 14

    Summary 14

    Key Terms 14

    Assess Your Understanding 16

    Summary Questions 16

    Review Questions 17

    Applying This Chapter 17

    You Try It 18

2. **The Marketing Plan** 19

    Introduction 20

  2.1 Developing a Marketing Strategy 20
      2.1.1   Growing with a Marketing Expansion Strategy . 20
      2.1.2   Specializing with a Market Expansion Strategy . 21
      2.1.3   Developing a Market Share Strategy 22
      2.1.4   Considering Other Core Strategies 23
      2.1.5   Using Your Strategy to Guide Your Program . . . 24

    Self-Check 27

  2.2 Writing a Marketing Strategy and Plan 27
      2.2.1   Planning Rules and Tips 27
      2.2.2   Clarifying and Quantifying Your Objectives 30
      2.2.3   Preparing a Situation Analysis 31

	2.2.4	Writing Your Strategy	32
	2.2.5	Writing a Powerful Executive Summary	34
	Self-Check		35
2.3	Analyzing and Summarizing Your Marketing Program		35
	2.3.1	Analyzing Costs	36
	2.3.2	Exploring the Details	38
	2.3.3	Projecting Expenses and Revenues	39
	2.3.4	Creating Your Controls	41
	Self-Check		42
	Summary		42
	Key Terms		42
	Assess Your Understanding		44
	Summary Questions		44
	Review Questions		45
	Applying This Chapter		45
	You Try It		46

Part II Analyzing Marketing Opportunities 47

3.	**Knowing Consumers**		47
	Introduction		48
3.1	Consumer Buying Behavior		48
	3.1.1	Internal Influences on Consumer Buying Behavior	48
	3.1.2	External Influences on Consumer Buying Behavior	51
	Self-Check		54
3.2	Organizational Buying Behavior		54
	Self-Check		56
3.3	The Consumer Decision Process		56
	3.3.1	Stage 1: Need Identification	58
	3.3.2	Stage 2: Information Search and Processing	59
	3.3.3	Stage 3: Identification and Evaluation of Alternatives	61
	3.3.4	Stage 4: Product/Service/Outlet Selection	61
	3.3.5	Stage 5: The Purchase Decision	62
	3.3.6	Stage 6: Postpurchase Behavior	62
	Self-Check		63
3.4	The Organizational Buying Process		63
	Self-Check		66
	Summary		66

Key Terms 66

Assess Your Understanding 68

Summary Questions. 68

Review Questions. 69

Applying This Chapter. 69

You Try It 70

4.   **Segmenting and Targeting Markets** 71

Introduction. 72

4.1   Segmenting Markets. 72
       4.1.1   Succeeding with the Undifferentiated Market . . 73
       4.1.2   Differentiating Your Product in an
                Undifferentiated Market 73
       4.1.3   Strategizing with a Segmented Market. 74
       4.1.4   Methods of Segmenting Markets 76

       Self-Check 77

4.2   Segmentation Factors. 77
       4.2.1   Geographic Segments 77
       4.2.2   Demographic Segments. 78
       4.2.3   Usage Segments. 79
       4.2.4   Psychological Segments. 79

4.3   Segmenting Business 82
       4.3.1   Segmenting Business Customers 82
       4.3.2   Multi-Base Segmentation. 84

       Self-Check 85

4.4   Targeting Your Market 85
       4.4.1   Qualifying Customers in Segments 86
       4.4.2   Concentrating on One Segment. 87
       4.4.3   Adding a Segment to Expand Your Market 87
       4.4.4   Selecting a Target Market. 88
       4.4.5   Positioning Your Product or Service 89

       Self-Check 90

       Summary 90

       Key Terms 90

       Assess Your Understanding 92

       Summary Questions. 92

       Review Questions. 93

       Applying This Chapter. 93

       You Try It 94

5.   Marketing Research **95**

Introduction. 96

5.1   Primary Research 96
    5.1.1   Observation 96
    5.1.2   Survey Research Methods 97
    5.1.3   Experimental Methods 99
    5.1.4   Listening to Your Customers 100

    Self-Check 103

5.2   Secondary Research 103
    5.2.1   Government Databases 103
    5.2.2   Media Data 104
    5.2.3   Demographic Data 104
    5.2.4   Customer Profiles 105
    5.2.5   Competitive Comparisons. 105
    5.2.6   Customer Records. 106

    Self-Check 106

5.3   Analyzing Your Research Needs 106
    5.3.1   Researching to Find Better Ideas 107
    5.3.2   Researching to Make Better Decisions 107
    5.3.3   Researching to Understand Love and Hate . . . 107
    5.3.4   Planning Your Research. 110

    Self-Check 112

5.4   The Research Process 112
    5.4.1   Types of Research 112
    5.4.2   Activities Common to All Research 112

    Self-Check 113

    Summary 114

    Key Terms 114

    Assess Your Understanding 115

    Summary Questions. 115

    Review Questions. 116

    Applying This Chapter. 116

    You Try It. 117

Part III Product and Distribution 118

6.   Developing and Managing Products. **118**

Introduction. 119

6.1   Introducing a New Product 119
    6.1.1   The New Product Development Process 119
    6.1.2   Planning Through the Product Lifecycle 124

    Self-Check 125

6.2 Branding and Protecting Your Product 125
   6.2.1 Naming Your Product 125
   6.2.2 Designing and Managing Product Lines. 126
   6.2.3 Branding and Protecting Your Product's Name
         and Identity. 128

   Self-Check 129

6.3 Packaging and Labeling 129

   Self-Check 132

6.4 Product Mix Strategies 133
   6.4.1 Modifying a Product 133
   6.4.2 Positioning Your Product. 134

   Self-Check 135

6.5 Deleting a Product 135
   6.5.1 The Market is Saturated. 135
   6.5.2 A Series of Improvements Fails to Create
         Momentum 136
   6.5.3 Something is Wrong with Your Product. 137
   6.5.4 How to Delete or Replace a Product 138

   Self-Check 139

   Summary 139

   Key Terms 140

   Assess Your Understanding 142

   Summary Questions. 142

   Review Questions. 143

   Applying This Chapter. 143

   You Try It 144

7. **Marketing Channel Management** **145**

   Introduction. 146

7.1 Understanding Market Channels 146
   7.1.1 Channel Functions 146
   7.1.2 Types of Channel Members 147

   Self-Check 151

7.2 Channel Design 151
   7.2.1 Supply Chain Management 152
   7.2.2 Finding Distributors 152
   7.2.3 Getting Closer to the Customer. 153
   7.2.4 Channel Marketing Systems 155
   7.2.5 Channel Design Strategies 156

   Self-Check 157

7.3   Understanding Channel Dynamics. 158
       7.3.1   Roles. 158
       7.3.2   Communication 158
       7.3.3   Conflict. 159
       Self-Check 159
7.4   The Channel Management Process. 160
       7.4.1   Step 1: Analyze the Consumer. 160
       7.4.2   Step 2: Establish the Channel Objectives. 161
       7.4.3   Step 3: Specify Distribution Tasks 161
       7.4.4   Step 4: Evaluate and Select Intermediaries. . . . 162
       7.4.5   Step 5: Evaluating Channel Member
                Performance 164
       Self-Check 165
       Summary. 165
       Key Terms 166
       Assess Your Understanding 168
       Summary Questions. 168
       Review Questions. 169
       Applying This Chapter. 169
       You Try It. 170

8.   Retailing. 171
       Introduction. 172
8.1   Types of Retailers 172
       Self-Check 173
8.2   Merchandising Strategies 174
       8.2.1   General Merchandise Retailing 174
       8.2.2   Limited-Line Retailing. 175
       8.2.3   Scrambled Merchandising. 175
       8.2.4   Price and Quality Strategies. 176
       8.2.5   Pursuing Retail Sales 177
8.3   Creative Retailing. 177
       8.3.1   Creating Atmosphere. 178
       8.3.2   POP! Stimulating Sales at Point of Purchase . . 180
       8.3.3   Designing POP Displays 181
       8.3.4   Answering Questions about POP. 182
       Self-Check 183
8.4   Direct Marketing 183
       8.4.1   Using Databases to Keep Track of Customers . 184
       8.4.2   Using Direct-Response Ads and Direct Mail . . 185
       8.4.3   Responsible Telemarketing 187
       8.4.4   Boosting Sales From Direct Marketing. 189
       Self-Check 190

Summary 190

Key Terms 190

Assess Your Understanding 192

Summary Questions. 192

Review Questions. 193

Applying This Chapter 193

You Try It 194

9.   Pricing 195

      Introduction. 196

9.1   The Facts of Price. 196
      9.1.1   Exploring the Impact of Pricing on Sales 197
      9.1.2   Finding Profits without Changing Prices 198

      Self-Check 199

9.2   Factors to Consider When Setting a Price 200
      9.2.1   Step 1: Figure Out Who Sets Prices. 200
      9.2.2   Step 2: Examine Your Costs. 202
      9.2.3   Step 3: Evaluate Customer Perception of
               Price 203
      9.2.4   Step 4: Examine Secondary Influences on
               Price 203
      9.2.5   Step 5: Set Your Strategic Objectives 204

      Self-Check 206

9.3   General Pricing Approaches. 206
      9.3.1   Coupons and Other Special Offers 207
      9.3.2   Estimating Redemption Rates and Costs 208
      9.3.3   Customers' Price Perceptions. 210
      9.3.4   Pricing a New Product. 212

      Self-Check 212

9.4   Keeping It Legal. 213
      9.4.1   Price Fixing and Its Variants 213
      9.4.2   Bid Rigging 214
      9.4.3   Offenses against Competitors 214

      Self-Check 215

      Summary 215

      Key Terms 216

      Assess Your Understanding 218

      Summary Questions. 218

      Review Questions. 219

      Applying This Chapter 219

      You Try It 220

Part IV Advertising and Promotion. 221

10.   **Marketing Communications and Personal Selling**. 221
       Introduction. 222
       10.1 Developing a Recipe for Good Marketing Communication . . 222
             10.1.1 Starting with a Clear Message 222
             10.1.2 Creating Great Writing and Visuals 225
             Self-Check 227
       10.2 Strengthening Your Marketing Communications 227
             10.2.1 Giving Products Personality. 227
             10.2.2 Stopping Power: Catching the Customer's Eye . . 229
             10.2.3 Pull Power: Building Customer Traffic. 231
             Self-Check 232
       10.3 Sales and Service Essentials 232
             10.3.1 The Sales and Service Process 233
             10.3.2 Service Recovery 233
             10.3.3 Organizing Your Sales Force 236
             10.3.4 Finding and Compensating Your Reps. 236
             Self-Check 239
       10.4 Generating Sales Leads and Making the Sale 239
             10.4.1 Finding New Approaches through Your
                     Marketing 240
             10.4.2 What to Avoid. 240
             10.4.3 Developing Great Sales Presentations and
                     Consultations 242
             Self-Check 243
             Summary 243
             Key Terms 243
             Assess Your Understanding 245
             Summary Questions. 245
             Review Questions. 246
             Applying This Chapter. 246
             You Try It. 247

11.   **Advertising**. 248
       Introduction. 249
       11.1 Print Ads and Brochures 249
             11.1.1 Media Buying 249
             11.1.2 Is Your Ad Working?. 250
             11.1.3 Designing Effective Print Advertising. 251
             11.1.4 Keeping It Simple 254
             11.1.5 Designing Brochures That Do More. 256
             Self-Check 257

11.2 Billboards, Banners, and Signs 259
      11.2.1 Signing Your Company's Name 259
      11.2.2 Creating Billboards That Get Noticed 260
      Self-Check 262
11.3 Radio, Video, and Television 263
      11.3.1 On the Radio. 263
      11.3.2 The Emotional and Visual Appeal of TV 264
      11.3.3 Video Production Tips. 266
      11.3.4 Buying Ad Time 268
      Self-Check 270
      Summary. 270
      Key Terms 271
      Assess Your Understanding 273
      Summary Questions. 273
      Review Questions. 273
      Applying This Chapter. 274
      You Try It 275
12.   Publicity, Public Relations, and Sales Promotions 276
      Introduction. 277
12.1 The Role of Publicity 277
      12.1.1 Finding the Story 278
      12.1.2 Cultivating Media Relationships 279
      Self-Check 280
12.2 Tools for Getting Talked About 281
      12.2.1 Writing Press Releases. 281
      12.2.2 Creating Exciting Publicity 283
      12.2.3 Making the Most of Word of Mouth 284
      Self-Check 286
12.3 Sales Promotions 286
      12.3.1 Price Promotions and Coupons. 286
      12.3.2 Premiums: Used and Abused. 288
      12.3.3 Using the Quality Strategy. 290
      Self-Check 291
      Summary. 291
      Key Terms 292
      Assess Your Understanding 293
      Summary Questions. 293
      Review Questions. 293
      Applying This Chapter. 294
      You Try It 295

13.   **Internet Marketing** **296**

Introduction 297

13.1   The Digital Explosion 297
    13.1.1   Budgeting Your Web Marketing 298

13.2   Marketing Domains 299
    13.2.1   Business to Consumer 299
    13.2.2   Business to Business 299
    13.2.3   Consumer to Consumer 299
    13.2.4   Consumer to Business 300

    Self-Check 300

13.3   Designing an Effective Web Page 301
    13.3.1   Finding Resources to Help with Design 301
    13.3.2   Creating Engaging Content 302
    13.3.3   Chats and Webcasts: Adding Human Contact
          and Support 304
    13.3.4   Developing a Registration-Based Site 305

    Self-Check 305

13.4   Drawing Traffic to Your Site 306
    13.4.1   Selecting a Web Address 306
    13.4.2   Buying Visibility on Search Engines 307
    13.4.3   Keeping Track of Visitors 308
    13.4.4   Using Header and META Tags 309
    13.4.5   Interpreting Click Statistics 310

    Self-Check 310

13.5   Utilizing E-Mail, E-Zines, and Web Advertising 311
    13.5.1   Understanding E-Mail Etiquette 311
    13.5.2   E-Publishing 314
    13.5.3   Designing and Placing a Banner Ad 315

    Self-Check 316

    Summary 316

    Key Terms 316

    Assess Your Understanding 318

    Summary Questions 318

    Review Questions 319

    Applying This Chapter 319

    You Try It 320

Glossary **321**

Index **335**

ACKNOWLEDGMENTS

Taken together, the content, pedagogy, and assessment elements of *Marketing* offer the career-oriented student the most important aspects of the marketing field as well as ways to develop the skills and capabilities that current and future employers seek in the individuals they hire and promote. Instructors will appreciate its practical focus, conciseness, and real-world emphasis. We would like to thank the following reviewers for their feedback and suggestions during the text's development. Their advice on how to shape *Marketing* into a solid learning tool that meets both their needs and those of their busy students is deeply appreciated.

David Bland, Cape Fear Community College
Linda Coleman, Salem State College
Michael Drafke, College of Dupage
Michael Fowler, Brookdale Community College
Charlene Held, Onandaga Community College
Judith Hogan, Middlesex Community College
Sharon Hoover-Dice, Scott Community College
George Kelley, Erie Community College
Cindy Snell, Blackhawk Tech College
Joseph Turner, College of the Albemarle
Fran Ucci, College of Dupage

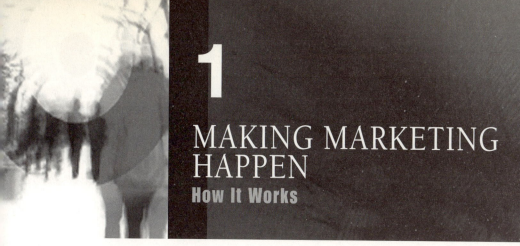

1

MAKING MARKETING HAPPEN

How It Works

Starting Point

Go to www.wiley/college/Hiam to assess your knowledge of the basics of marketing.
Determine where you need to concentrate your effort.

What You'll Learn in This Chapter

▲ Influence points for different types of businesses
▲ Effective ways to improve your marketing
▲ The five Ps of the marketing mix

After Studying This Chapter, You'll Be Able To

▲ Demonstrate ways of focusing your marketing
▲ Explain the significance of consistency in your marketing
▲ Employ an informational approach, an emotional approach, or a balanced mix in your marketing

Goals and Outcomes

▲ Assess the role of different marketing Ps in your marketing
▲ Evaluate how well focused a program is, based on criteria
▲ Predict whether a cross-selling effort is viable

INTRODUCTION

Successful marketing requires programs. Marketing is about knowing your customer and finding ways to make your product appealing. Your program needs to be focused, by finding your strengths and your influence points. You can improve your marketing program by being consistent across your activities and by continuing to innovate.

1.1 What Is Marketing?

Marketing is all around us. It ranges from a crudely lettered sign saying "Lemunade — 5 sents," to salespeople helping customers find the perfect gift, to multi-million-dollar advertisements during the Super Bowl. What makes for effective marketing? Money helps, but without creativity and organization, your marketing will be much less effective. You can waste a great deal of money on ineffective marketing efforts. Some products sell themselves, and others do better than they should because of stellar marketing. But even the best marketing will not sell a bad product, once people know it's bad. Marketing is primarily about understanding people and what makes them buy. It's getting inside the customer's head and trying to think as he or she thinks.

1.1.1 Getting to Know Your Customer

The first and most important principle of marketing is: Know your customer. When you understand how customers think and what they like, you can find appropriate and appealing ways to communicate with them about the product or service you want them to buy. You need to understand your customer in two ways: the informational, rational dimension of making a purchase decision, and the emotional dimension. Every purchase, whether of a soda, a software program, a consulting service, a book, or a manufacturing part, has both rational and emotional elements. So to truly know your customer, you must explore two questions:

1. **What do they think about your product?** Do they understand it? Do they think its features and benefits are superior to the competition and can meet their needs? Do they feel that your product is a good value given its benefits and costs?

2. **How do they feel about your product?** Does it make them feel good? Do they like its personality? Do they like how it makes them feel about themselves?

> ### FOR EXAMPLE
>
> #### Make 7-Up Yours!
>
> A teenager is wearing a T-shirt that says "Make 7" on the front, and on the back, "Up Yours!" The T-shirt represents a play on the slogan "Make 7-Up Yours." For those in the know, the "Make 7" from the front of the shirt can replace the insult on the back of the T-shirt. If you do not find this amusing, you are probably not in the 12- to 24-year-old demographic group that the Make 7-Up Yours! ad campaign targeted. It was used to sell the beverage to American teens — frequent soda drinkers — and it worked, especially with males.

Sometimes, one of these two dimensions dominates for the customer you want to sell to. In other instances they're equally important. Which will be true of your customers? To cover all your bases, you will need to take one of the three following approaches:

▲ **Informational approach:** The approach you use if your customers buy in a rational manner.

This is the case for many business-to-business marketers. It involves showing the product and talking about its benefits. Comparisons to worse alternatives are a great idea when using an informational approach. Use this approach when you think buyers are going to make a careful, thoughtful, informed purchase decision or when you have strong evidence in favor of their buying *your* product or service instead of others.

▲ **Emotional approach:** This approach pushes emotional instead of rational buttons.

For example, a marketer of virus-scanning software may try to scare computer users by asking them in a headline, "What would it cost you if a virus destroyed everything on your computer right now?" That emotional appeal can be much more powerful than a pile of statistics about the frequency and types of viruses on the Web. Use an emotional approach when your customers have strong feelings you can tap into and relate to your product or service, or when you think people are going to make an impulse decision.

▲ **Balanced mix approach:** This approach uses a combination of informational and emotional appeals.

> ## FOR EXAMPLE
>
> ### Marketing to Children
>
> Children are now being systematically pursued by marketers, and many people question whether this is ethical. Young children do not know the difference between advertising and other types of content. The use of cartoon characters to market adult products such as cigarettes and beer is particularly disturbing to many consumer groups and parents. Research shows that children notice and recognize these cartoon characters, even if they are too young to buy the product. Consumer groups are demanding that Congress restrict or better regulate advertising to children, and in response, some marketers have listened, whereas others continue to target children in irresponsible ways. In an intensely competitive marketplace, the results of this social experiment will be revealed in the children of the baby boomers.

It would work for selling antivirus software, and many other products, because it engages both the rational and emotional dimensions. For example, after a scare-tactic (emotional) headline asking what would happen if a virus destroyed everything on your computer, follow up with a few statistics such as, "One out of every ten computer users suffers a catastrophic virus attack each year." The facts reinforce the nervous feelings the headline evoked, helping move the prospect toward purchase.

Decide which of these three approaches to use, and use it consistently in all your communications. And when in doubt, use the balanced mix to hedge your bets.

The first and most revealing question asked in marketing is, "What is the best way to attract customers?" The answer differs for every successful business. Here are some possibilities:

▲ **Referrals:** Customers sell the product (see coverage of word of mouth in Section 12.2.3 for how to stimulate them).

▲ **Trade shows and professional association meetings:** Contacts sell the product (see Section 10.3).

▲ **Sales calls:** Salespeople sell the product (see Section 10.3).

▲ **TV, radio, or print ads:** Advertising sells the product (see Chapter 11).

▲ **Product demonstrations, trial coupons, or distribution of free samples:** Product sells itself (see Section 12.3).

▲ **Web sites and newsletters:** Internet information sells the product (see Chapter 13).

▲ **Placement and appearance of buildings/stores:** Location sells the product (see Chapter 7).

Every business has a different optimal formula for attracting customers. However, in every case, successful businesses report that one or two methods work best. Their programs are therefore dominated by one or two effective ways of attracting customers. They put one-third to two-thirds of their marketing resources into the top ways of attracting customers, and then use other marketing methods to support and leverage their most effective method. They do not spend any time or money on marketing activities that are inconsistent with their best method and that rob resources from it.

1.1.2 The Marketing Mix

You can think about your marketing creatively as a recipe with a few essential ingredients that have to be used for the recipe to work. But the amount and type of these ingredients can and will vary, making for an ever-changing mix.

The **marketing mix,** sometimes explained in terms of the "five Ps," describes where marketers focus their attention. Every marketer uses a different strategy or mix of Ps, depending upon the company's needs.

Here's one common version of the five Ps to consider:

▲ **Product.** What aspects of the product itself are important and have an influence on customer perception and purchase intentions? Include tangible features and intangibles like personality, look and feel, and also packaging.

Remember that first impressions are important for initial purchase, but that performance of the product over time is more important for repurchase and referrals. (And remember that by product, marketers mean whatever it is you offer your customers, whether it's a product or a service.)

▲ **Price.** What does it cost the customer to obtain and use your product? The list price is often an important element of the customer's perception of price, but it isn't the only one. Discounts and special offers are part of the list of price-based influence points, too.

Do not forget any extra costs the customer may have to incur, like the cost of switching from another product to yours. This can really affect the customer's perception of how attractive your product is. (If you can find ways to make it easier/cheaper to switch from the competitor's product to yours, you may be able to charge more for your product and still make more sales.)

▲ **Place.** When and where is your product available to customers?

Place is a big influence, because most of the time, customers are not actively shopping for your product. Nobody runs around all day every day looking for what you want to sell. When someone wants something, he or she is most strongly influenced by what is available. Getting the place and timing right is a big part of success in marketing and often very difficult.

▲ **Promotion.** What are the ways you choose to communicate to customers?

Do you advertise? Send mailings? Hand out brochures? What about the visibility of signs on buildings or vehicles? Do distributors or other marketing partners also communicate with your customer? If so, include their promotional materials and methods because they help shape the customer's perception too. And what about other routine elements of customer communication, like bills? They're a part of the impression your marketing communications make, too.

▲ **People.** Who are the human contacts you offer to customers and prospective customers? This can include salespeople, receptionists, service and support personnel, collections personnel, and sometimes shipping, billing, repair, or other personnel, too.

All these points of human contact are important parts of the marketing program, even though they may not all be working well to help keep your program focused and effective right now. Some other P words that are sometimes included or added to the mix are positioning, packaging, public relations, placement, and personnel.

Table 1-1 shows an example of how the five Ps look for three different products or services.

You can see from this chart that these three different products will have very different marketing strategies. How much of each P do you focus on? You cannot do everything, so you have to choose, based upon knowing your customer and knowing your product well. Marketing is an ever-evolving analysis of the five Ps and what mix to use. Your marketing needs to be responsive and flexible, or your company will lose sales to competitors.

Within each of the five Ps of marketing, one or two things will have the biggest impact and give you the most bang for your buck. Ask yourself which of the Ps need to be emphasized in your marketing program. Your marketing mix reflects your broader strategy (see Section 1.2). Make your best guess or do some research to find out what works best. You need to find efficient, effective ways to positively influence customer perception. You want to use elements of your marketing program to motivate customers to buy and use your product (or service or firm). Think about each of the five Ps and study competitors or successful marketers in different product categories and industries for some fresh ideas. Good marketing ideas do not have to come from within your own industry or category. The longer your list of possibilities, the more likely you are to create a strong successful marketing program.

Table 1-1: Understanding the Five Ps for Goods and Services

	Brand-Name Soft Drink	*Midpriced Legal Services*	*Pool Chemicals*
Product	Brand personality can be more important than taste	Perceived quality is very important	Similar formulas
Price	Not as important	Charging more may influence perception of quality	Customers will not pay more for the same thing
Place	Easy to find	Limited by geography and by state bar associations	Not sold in many places, a limited market of pool owners
Promotion	Highly important, huge ad budgets	Mostly word of mouth and referrals, advertising may cheapen image	Not much to differentiate from competition, limited advertising
People	Not as important because little contact with seller	Very important because high contact with seller, relationship-based	Can be important if other relationship can be leveraged, e.g. sell other pool supplies

Do not be tempted to make price the main focus of your marketing program. Many marketers emphasize discounts and low prices to attract customers. But price is a dangerous emphasis for any marketing program; you're buying customers instead of winning them. So unless you actually have a sustainable cost advantage (a rare thing in business), do not allow low prices or coupons and discounts to dominate your marketing program. Price reasonably, use discounts and price-off coupons sparingly, and look for other things to focus on in your marketing program.

SELF-CHECK

- Cite the first and most important principle of marketing.
- Describe three different approaches you can take.
- List some possibilities for attracting customers.
- Describe the **five Ps** of marketing.

1.2 Focusing Your Marketing Program

Your marketing program requires a **marketing strategy,** which is the big-picture idea driving your success. A **marketing program** is based on a marketing strategy, and shows all the coordinated activities that together make up the tactics. In other words, your program is the way you implement your strategy.

You'll have to carefully monitor the results for each part. This involves focusing your efforts, developing a marketing plan (the subject of Chapter 2), and continuously improving upon the program.

1.2.1 Finding Your Strengths

Every business, just like every person, has strengths and weaknesses. You must be able to clearly and succinctly define your special strength or advantage. You need to be able to finish this sentence: "My product (or service) is special because. . . ." Your answer to that question will help you develop your marketing program.

Use this strength-based marketing method to add an additional degree of focus to your marketing program. To succeed, you need to pinpoint what makes your firm or product special, and why customers are attracted to it. Then make sure your program amplifies and reflects your light and never loses sight of it.

FOR EXAMPLE

Providing Good Customer Service

If you're known for good customer service, make sure to train, recognize, and reward good service in your employees, and to emphasize good service in all communications with your customers and prospects. Some ways to do this would be to feature a photo of a friendly, helpful employee in your advertising, brochures, sales sheets, or Web page; collect and quote customer testimonials that praise your service; or offer a satisfaction guarantee of some sort.

1.2.2 Finding Your Influence Points

The late Peter Drucker, one of few justly famous management gurus, has defined marketing as the whole firm, taken from the customer's point of view. This definition is powerful, because it reminds you that your view from the inside is likely to be very different from the customer's view. Nobody cares what *you* see. The success of any business comes down to what customers do, and they can act only based on what *they* see. That is why marketing and advertising gurus often say, "Perception is everything." You must find ways to listen to your customers and to understand their perceptions of your firm and offerings.

From the customer's point of view, identify the components of your marketing program. (The components include everything and anything that the customer sees, hears, talks to, uses, or otherwise interacts with.)

▲ An **influence point** is each customer interaction, exposure, or contact.

Influence points are where good marketing can help build customer interest and loyalty. Table 1-2 gives you some questions to start with when developing a marketing program.

1.2.3 Finding Your Markets

A **market** is a group of potential buyers with needs and wants and the purchasing power to satisfy them. Who and where is your market, exactly? Can you make sales outside of the state, or the country? Is it all of the general public? Are they affluent or working class? Male or female? Any particular ethnic group or nationality? Finding a market for your product means either

▲ **Market expansion,** increasing the overall market for whatever it is you do.
▲ **Segmenting markets,** focusing your efforts to cover a narrow market by increasing **market share,** or your sales as a percentage of total sales for your product category in your market.

Developing a marketing plan and strategy (explained in Chapter 2) are written ways to begin accomplishing these objectives. As a marketer, you face a great many decisions and details. Marketing tends to be fragmented, so that marketing efforts spring up with every good idea or customer demand, rather like rabbits.

The strategies you select will determine how successful your marketing efforts will be. Even if a given company does not seem to have a strategy or plan because there's nothing written down, there still will be some ideas influencing its choices. However, its marketing will be uncoordinated and inefficient. In most organizations, hundreds of marketing rabbits are running around, each one in a slightly different direction from any other. The best way to make the strategy happen is to have a written plan.

Table 1-2: Focusing Your Marketing Program for Fun and Profit

Customer Focus

Define your customers clearly: Who are they? Where and when do they want to buy?
Are they new customers, existing customers, or a balanced mix of both?
Understand what emotional elements make them buy: What personality should
your brand have? How should customers feel about your product?
Understand what functional elements make them buy: What features do they want
and need? What information do they need to see in order to make their decision?

Product Attraction

What attracts customers to your product?
What are your special strengths that set you apart in the marketplace?
Do you reflect your strengths through all your marketing efforts?

Most Effective Methods

What is the most effective thing you can do to attract customers?
What is the most effective thing you can do to retain customers?
Which of the five Ps (product, price, place, promotion, people) are most impor-
tant in attracting and retaining customers?

Controlling Points of Contact

What are all the ways you can reach and influence customers?
Are you using the best of these right now?
Do you need to increase the focus and consistency of some of these points of
contact with customers?
What can you do to improve your control over all the elements that influence
customer opinion of your product?

Action Items

Draw up a list of things you can do based on this analysis to maximize the effectiveness of your marketing program.

SELF-CHECK

- Define a **marketing strategy,** and explain how it ties in to a marketing plan.
- What are influence points?
- Describe the difference between market expansion and segmenting markets.

1.3 Improving Your Marketing Program

When you make improvements to your marketing program, what kind of results can you expect? As a general rule, the percentage change in your program will, at best, correspond with the percentage change you see in sales.

For example, if you change only 5 percent of your program from one year to the next, you cannot expect to see more than a 5 percent increase in sales over whatever their natural base would be. **Base sales** are what you can reasonably count on if you maintain the status quo in your marketing.

If, for example, you have seen steady growth in sales of 3 percent per year (varying a bit with the economic cycle), then you may reasonably project sales growth of 4 percent next year, presuming everything else stays the same. But things rarely do stay the same, so you may want to look for any threats from new competitors, changing technology, shifting customer needs and desires, and so on, and be careful to adjust your natural base downward if you anticipate any such threats materializing next year.

Keep these points in mind when making improvements:

▲ **Start small.** Use new ideas and methods and do not overcommit to any single plan or investment. That way you can afford to fail, learn, and adjust.

▲ **Plan to fail, but try, try again.** Effective marketing formulas are developed through trial and error, as well as planning. Small failures are okay if you learn from them.

▲ **Be flexible.** Be cautiously optimistic, and plan for contingencies. You need room to be creative and innovative.

▲ **Do not expect to solve all the company's problems through marketing.** If you have a flawed product, the best thing you can do as a marketer is to present the evidence and encourage your company to improve the product.

1.3.1 Being Consistent

American Marine is a Singapore-based manufacturer of high-quality, attractive Grand Banks motor yachts. Its products are handsome, rugged, and seaworthy, and customers have an almost fanatical love of and loyalty to the product. (In other words, the product sells itself, if they can afford it.) This manufacturer showcases the product in its well-designed, full-color brochures and product sheets, with both attractive color photos of the boats and detailed specifications and floor plans. (This covers both the informational and emotional dimensions of the purchase decision.)

But Grand Banks yachts are sold through regional distributors, who occasionally fail to maintain the same high standards when they add their own cover letter or other printed materials to the manufacturer's marketing materials. Imagine you received a plain, low-quality brown envelope with a boring, black-ink cover letter lacking any picture or logo-type drawing of the product. Hidden beneath this unimpressive packaging and form letter were the truly impressive corporate brochures about the product. A used boat costs a half million dollars or more, and a new one can cost more than a million. To make a sale like that, you need to put some extra care and effort into ensuring that everything you show the prospect is sophisticated and impressive.

This happens all too often. Why? It's hard to control all the influence points in a marketing program. The Grand Banks mailing would have been much more effective if the entire package was done to the high standards set by the corporate marketing materials and the product itself. Both the envelope and cover letter ought to

▲ Demonstrate high-quality design and materials to represent the fine craftsmanship of the product.
▲ Show the product, because the product makes the sale in this case.

Little details can and do make all the difference in closing a sale. Does your marketing program display this kind of inconsistency, and does it also miss opportunities to get the message across fully and well? If so, you can increase your program's effectiveness by eliminating these pockets of inconsistency to prevent out-of-control marketing.

1.3.2 Keep Moving

Every time you put your marketing hat on, seek to make at least a small improvement in how marketing is done in your organization and for your customers. Marketing programs need to constantly evolve and improve.

Think big when it comes to marketing. You can always do something more to improve your effectiveness and maximize your results. Here, for example, are some general ways to maximize your marketing program:

▲ **Talk to some of your best customers.** Do they have any good ideas for you? (Ignore the ideas that are overly expensive, however. You cannot count on even a good customer to worry about your bottom line.)
▲ **Change your marketing territory.** Are you spread too thin to be visible and effective? If so, narrow your focus to your core region or customer type. But if you have expansion potential, try broadening your reach bit by bit to grow your territory.
▲ **Get more referrals.** Spend time talking to and helping out folks who can send customers your way. And make sure you thank anyone who sends you a lead. Positive reinforcement increases the behavior.

▲ **Make your marketing more attractive (professional, creative, polished, clear, well written, well produced).** Often, marketing programs can pull better simply by upgrading the look and feel of all the marketing communications and other components. (Did you know that the best-dressed consultants get paid two to five times as much as the average in their fields?)

▲ **Know what you want to be best at and invest in being the best.** Who needs you if you're ordinary or average? Success comes from being clearly, enticingly better at something than any other company or product. Even if it is only a small thing that makes you special, know what it is and make sure you keep polishing that brilliance. It is why you deserve the sale.

▲ **Try to cross sell additional products (or related services) to your customer base.** Increasing the average size of a purchase or order is a great way to improve the effectiveness of your marketing program. But keep the cross sell soft and natural. Do not sell junk that isn't clearly within your focus or to your customer's benefit.

Remember, marketing is a people business, so treat your customers well. Keeping your customers happy and satisfied is the key to a successful marketing effort. Here are some ways to do that:

▲ **Thank customers for their business.** A friendly "thank you" and a smile, a card or note, or a polite cover letter inserted into the invoice envelope — all are ways to tell them you appreciate their business, and people tend to go where they're appreciated.

▲ **Smile to attract and retain business.** Make sure your people have a positive, caring attitude about customers. If they do not, their negativity is certainly losing you business. Do not let people work against your marketing program. Spend time making sure they understand that they can control the success of the program, and help them through training and good management so that they can take a positive, helpful, and productive approach to all customer interactions.

▲ **Offer a memorable experience for your customer or client.** Make sure that doing business with you is a pleasant, memorable experience. Plan to do something that makes it memorable.

▲ **Debrief customers who complain or who desert you.** Why were they unhappy? Could you have done something simple to retain them? (But ignore the customers who do not match your target customer profile, because you cannot be all things to all people.)

FOR EXAMPLE

Telephone Slamming

After the long-distance telephone deregulation in the 1980s, AT&T and its new rivals MCI and Sprint were competing fiercely for customers. Some of them hired outside contractors to call customers and try to get them to switch companies. Unfortunately, some of the telemarketers resorted to slamming (changing customers' providers without their consent or knowledge), which angered customers and made them suspicious of special offers. The FCC passed new regulations. Bad will was generated toward phone companies that were not directly responsible for the slamming.

SELF-CHECK

- What is the general rule regarding expected results when making a change in your marketing program?
- List three tips to maximize the effectiveness of your marketing program.
- List four ways to keep customers happy.

SUMMARY

Know your customer and find a marketing mix that appeals to him or her. Your program needs to be focused, by finding your strengths and your influence points. Keep improving your marketing program by monitoring your results, innovating, being consistent, and treating your customers well.

KEY TERMS

Balanced mix approach	A marketing approach that uses a combination of informational and emotional appeals.
Base sales	What you can reasonably count on if you maintain the status quo in your marketing.
Emotional approach	A marketing approach that pushes emotional instead of rational buttons.
Five Ps or marketing mix	Where marketers focus their attention.

Influence point	Each customer interaction, exposure, or contact.
Informational approach	A marketing approach used if your customers buy in a rational manner.
Market	A group of potential buyers with needs and wants and the purchasing power to satisfy them.
Market expansion	Increasing the overall market for whatever it is you do.
Market share	Your sales as a percentage of total sales for your product category in your market.
Marketing program	Based on a marketing strategy, and shows all the coordinated activities that together make up the tactics.
Marketing strategy	The big-picture idea driving your success.
Segmenting markets	Targeting your efforts to cover a narrow market.

ASSESS YOUR UNDERSTANDING

Go to www.wiley.com/college/Hiam to evaluate your knowledge of the basics of marketing.
Measure your learning by comparing pretest and post-test results.

Summary Questions

1. An informational approach is most effective when it pushes emotional buttons. True or false?
2. Most companies put one-third to two-thirds of their marketing budgets into their most effective way of attracting customers. True or false?
3. You should always try to regain the customers you've lost. True or false?
4. Which of the following is a way to increase your markets?
   (a) Segmenting markets
   (b) Informational approaches
   (c) Market expansion
5. Your marketing program failed to increase sales. Which of the following reasons is the most unlikely?
   (a) The product is flawed.
   (b) You didn't commit all of your resources to it.
   (c) It's inconsistent with your other businesses.
6. You should devote your resources equally to each P of the marketing mix. True or false?
7. Which of these are influence points?
   (a) Your Web site
   (b) Your price
   (c) Customer-service representatives
8. If you change 10 percent of your program in the next year, you can reasonably expect sales to increase by 5 percent, all other things being equal. True or false?

Review Questions

1. List two products or services that are best sold with the use of a rational approach. Then list two that lend themselves to an emotional approach.
2. Why is it risky to choose price as your most important marketing "P"?

Applying This Chapter

1. Discuss the five Ps of marketing in relation to an exterminating service.
2. To increase profits, you've decided to cross sell to your customer base at the Cadillac dealership you manage. You are going to offer to sell PDAs to these customers, who you believe can easily afford them. You have one and you love it. What are the potential problems with this plan?
3. You have some extra funds, so you're putting together a marketing program for your computer consulting services. What are the questions you need to ask yourself before you go any further?
4. You're marketing a new educational toy. Think about the five Ps discussed in this chapter. Which two do you think will be most important to emphasize in the initial stages of your marketing, when launching this new product? Explain why you picked them.
5. Name four influence points for Wal-Mart.

Telephone Slamming
Reread the "Telephone Slamming" example in 1.3.2. What could long-distance companies have done to repair the relationships with the angry customers who'd been slammed? Why was it so important for them to put an end to this practice? What are the influence points for a telephone company?

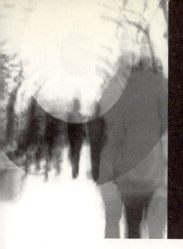

2

THE MARKETING PLAN
Linking Your Strategy and Program

Starting Point

Go to www.wiley.com/college/Hiam to assess your knowledge of the basic marketing plan
Determine where you need to concentrate your effort.

What You'll Learn in This Chapter

▲ Different marketing strategies
▲ The components of a marketing plan
▲ Common methods of forecasting sales

After Studying This Chapter, You'll Be Able To

▲ Use a marketing strategy to organize a marketing program
▲ Prepare a marketing-program budget
▲ Practice writing marketing objectives

Goals and Outcomes

▲ Write a marketing plan
▲ Distinguish between marketing objectives and marketing strategies
▲ Assess strategies for companies in different stages of growth
▲ Appraise how well your marketing program is working

INTRODUCTION

Marketing can get out of control or confused quickly without a plan. Your plan must link a *strategy,* based on the strengths of your position, to your marketing *program.* You will need to write your strategy and plan down once a year. This includes analyzing your costs, projecting expenses and revenues, and creating controls.

2.1 Developing a Marketing Strategy

A marketing plan starts with a strategy — a big-picture vision of what you are trying to do. A good strategy gives a special kind of high-level direction and purpose to all you do. By centering your program around a single, core strategy with an overarching goal, you can take your focus to an even higher level. With a core marketing strategy, your program begins to fall into place naturally.

Your marketing strategy may be a pure version of one of the following strategies, or it may be a variant or even a blend of more than one of them. You will probably modify this strategy over the life of your product or service, so be prepared to reevaluate your strategy periodically.

2.1.1 Growing with a Market-Expansion Strategy

A **market-expansion strategy** is the most common strategy in marketing. It has two variants:

▲ You can expand your market by finding new customers for your current products (often this means going into new geographic territory to do so), or

▲ You can try to sell new products to your existing customers and market.

If you choose to adopt a market-expansion strategy as your main focus, make sure a majority of your marketing activity is working toward this goal. For example, if you seek publicity, make sure most of it is about your new product or in your new market, not about the old. It may take all your resources to effectively expand your market, and the faster you get through the transition and achieve your growth goal, the better, because extra costs come about with the transition.

Risk increases if you experiment with new products or anything that you are not accustomed to making and marketing. So you should discount your first year's sales projections for a new market by some factor to reflect the degree of risk. A good general rule is to cut back the sales projection by 20 to 50 percent, depending upon your judgment of how new and risky the product is to you and your team. Risk also increases if you enter any new market — defined as new kinds of customers at any stage of your distribution channel. You should discount those sales projections by 20 to 50 percent if you are entering a new market, to reflect your lack of familiarity with the customers.

What if you are introducing a new product into a new market? *Start-up firms* often run both these risks at once, and must discount sales projections even further to reflect this risk. Sometimes a market-expansion strategy is so risky that you really should not count on any revenues in the first year. Better to be conservative and last long enough to figure out how to correctly handle the marketing than to overpromise and have the program die before it succeeds.

2.1.2 Specializing with a Market-Segmentation Strategy

A **market-segmentation strategy** is a specialization strategy in which you target and cater to (specialize in) just one narrow type or group of customer. (Chapter 4 deals with segmenting and targeting markets.)

If you are in the consulting business, you can specialize in for-profit businesses, or you can specialize in not-for-profits. You can even design and market your services to individuals — as, for example, a career-development consultant does. Each of these types of customer represents a subgroup, or segment, of the larger consulting industry. You can drill down even further to define smaller segments if you want. You can specialize in consulting to the health-care industry, or to manufacturers of boxes and packaging, or to start-up firms in the high-tech sector. Certain consultants use each of these strategies to narrow down their markets.

The advantage of a segmentation strategy is that it allows you to tailor your product and your entire marketing effort to a clearly defined group with uniform, specific characteristics. For example, the consulting firm that targets only the health-care industry knows that prospective clients can be found at a handful of health-care industry conferences and that they have certain common concerns around which consulting services can be focused. Many smaller consulting firms target a narrowly defined market segment in order to compete against larger, but less specialized, consulting firms.

A segmentation strategy may be effective if

▲ Your business can be made more profitable by specializing in a more narrowly defined segment than you do now.

▲ You face too many competitors in your broader market and you cannot seem to carve out a stable, profitable customer base of your own.

▲ It takes better advantage of things you are good at, part of the idea of focusing better, based on your unique qualities or strengths (see Section 1.2).

▲ You are running out of customers and market and need to expand by targeting a new segment.

An example of the last one would be if a consultant specializing in coaching executives in the health-care industry decided to start offering a similar service to not-for-profits. A different approach and marketing program may be needed, because the two industries are different in many ways and have only partial overlap (some hospitals are not-for-profits, and many not-for-profits are not hospitals). By specializing in two segments instead of just one, the consulting firm may be able to grow its total sales significantly.

2.1.3 Developing a Market-Share Strategy

Another common and powerful strategy is to increase your market share through your marketing activities, by taking some business from your competitors.

▲ **Market share:** This is your sales as a percentage of total sales for your product category in your market (or in your market segment if you use a segmentation strategy too). If you sell $2 million worth of shark teeth and the world market totals $20 million per year, then your share of the global shark-tooth market is 10 percent.

What unit should you measure sales in? Dollars, units, pesos, containers, or grams are fine, as long as you use the same unit throughout. You can calculate your share of the North American market for fine hardwoods in board feet sold, as long as both your sales and industry sales are measured in board feet sold, and dollar sales or tons aren't mixed into the equation by mistake.

What is your product category? This may be the most important strategic question you ever ask or answer. For example, if you sell specialty teas, are you competing with the mass-market brands like Lipton, or not? Should you count their sales in your market-share calculations and try to win sales from them? Ask customers whether they are choosing from among all the tea options, or just some of them.

▲ **Customer perception:** How the customer sees the category, and what matters when determining a **market-share strategy**.

So watch customers or ask them what their purchase options are (see Chapter 5 if you want to conduct a formal study). Get a feel for how they view their choices. Then include all the likely or close choices in your definition of the market. With specialty teas, you may find that a majority of consumers sometimes drink the cheaper mass-market brands, too. And you may also find that you must, as a wholesaler, fight for grocery shelf space and room on restaurant menus against the mass-market brands. So you probably do need to use total market sales as your base, not just specialty sales.

On the other hand, you do compete more closely against other specialty teas, so you may want to track this smaller market-share number also, and set a secondary goal for it. A wholesale tea importer's strategic goals may therefore look something like this:

▲ Increase dollar sales of our products to U.S. end consumers of tea from 13.5 percent to 15 percent.

▲ Protect our share of the specialty tea market by keeping it at 54 percent or higher.

▲ Differentiate ourselves even more from Lipton, Tetley, and other mass-market tea brands by emphasizing what makes our tea special, to avoid having to compete directly against much larger marketers.

2.1.4 Considering Other Core Strategies

Strategy, like everything in marketing, is limited only by your imagination and initiative. Here are some other examples of core strategies that have worked for companies:

▲ **Simplicity marketing.** This strategy positions a company as simpler, easier to understand, and easier to use or work with than the competition.

New gas pumps that allow you to swipe your own credit card are an example of a simplicity strategy. So-called *simplicity positioning* is a new opportunity, according to research firm Datamonitor. They predict that people are going to be increasingly attracted to simple brands that are easy to buy and use. In fact, their studies indicate that many customers are willing to pay a premium in order to avoid complexity and make purchase decisions simply and quickly. Look for technologies or processes that can make your customers' lives simpler and easier.

▲ **Quality strategies:** Most marketers grossly underrate quality. All else being anywhere near equal, a majority of customers choose the higher-quality option.

But be careful to find out what your customers think quality means. They may have a different view than you do. Integrate your quality-based marketing messages with a genuine commitment to quality in all aspects of your business. Remember, you cannot just say you are better than the competition; you have to deliver.

▲ **Reminder strategies:** A reminder strategy is good when you think people would buy your product if they thought of it — but may not without a reminder.

A lot of routine purchases benefit from this strategy (Got milk?). *Point-of-purchase* (POP) marketing is often an effective way to implement the reminder strategy.

> ## FOR EXAMPLE
>
> ### Swiss Army Knife
>
> Although its pocketknives are old standbys, Wenger Swiss Army Knife has a strong brand identity that allows it to maintain a large market share simply by reminding consumers of its product. Precise International uses this strategy to market its knives in jewelry and knife stores. Working with Phoenix Display and Packaging Corp., Precise creates a variety of countertop and floor display cases with giant models of the distinctive red pocketknife with its white cross logo. Often consumers walking by realize that a Swiss Army knife is the perfect gift, maybe even for themselves.

▲ **Point-of-purchase marketing:** Doing whatever advertising is necessary to sway the consumer your way at the time and place of their purchase.

For retail products, this often means a clever in-store display or sign to remind the consumer.

▲ **Positioning strategies:** A positioning strategy takes a psychological approach to marketing, by getting people to see your product in a favorable light.

The positioning goal you articulate for this kind of strategy is the position your product holds in the customer's mind. You can position your company against a competitor, emphasize a distinctive benefit such as a health claim, or affiliate yourself with something the customer values, such as environmental consciousness. Everything you do in your marketing program, from packaging to advertising and publicity, should work to convince customers of the points your positioning statement contains.

2.1.5 Using Your Strategy to Guide Your Program

Your strategy needs to be a hub around which all your marketing activities rotate. After you develop a marketing strategy, be sure to follow it. We recommend that you do some formal planning to figure out exactly how you will implement your strategy in all aspects of your marketing program.

Figure 2-1 shows how a strategy provides an organizing central point to a program of marketing activities. This example is for the gift shop at an art museum. The museum's strategic goal was to get museum visitors to come into the shop and make a substantial purchase. It developed a variety of tactics for its marketing program, each of which is clearly helpful in achieving the strategy.

Figure 2-1

A strategy wheel for a museum's gift shop.

Make sure you can draw a solid arrow from your chosen strategy to each of the activities on the rim. Try to explain in simple words how the activity helps implement your strategy and achieve your strategic goal. If the link to the big picture strategy isn't clear, modify or eliminate the activity. If you have more than one strategy, draw more than one wheel. But avoid having too many or your resources get spread so thin you cannot achieve any of your goals. Also, try to select strategies that have some synergy. The strategy wheels need to belong on the same wagon or they cannot move you forward.

The advertising life-cycle model says that products go through three stages, each requiring a different marketing strategy:

▲ **Pioneering strategy:** Used when the majority of prospects are unfamiliar with the product

▲ **Competitive strategy:** Used when the majority of prospects have tried at least one competitor's product

▲ **Retentive strategy:** Used when attracting new customers costs more than keeping old customers

By understanding these stages, you can choose the right strategy based on the current growth rate trend in your market. Your strategy will be revised over the life of your product category, so you need to adjust. Table 2-1 shows the strategic objectives of each of these stages.

Everything about your marketing program follows from these simple strategies. Look at where you are in your product's life cycle — that makes your strategic thinking fairly simple.

For instance, if you are marketing a radical new product that has just begun to experience accelerating sales, then you know you are moving from the introduction to the growth stage of the product life cycle. Table 2-1 indicates that a pioneering strategy should apply. You need to educate consumers about the new product, encourage them to try it, and make sure that the product is widely distributed. How should you price this pioneering product — high or low? Price should be low enough to keep from discouraging new customers, so the high end of the price range may be a mistake. On the other hand, no mandate exists to compete head-to-head on price (that would be more appropriate to the competitive strategy later on). So the best time to use low prices is probably in special offers to stimulate trial. In fact, perhaps free samples are appropriate now, especially if coupled with a moderately high list price.

And your advertising? It certainly needs to be informative, showing potential consumers how to benefit from the product. Similarly, you know you need to encourage distributors to stock and push the product, so special offers to the trade and a strong sales effort (through your own salespeople or through reps or distributors) should get a fair share of your marketing budget. All these conclusions are fairly obvious — if you stay focused on the strategic guidelines in the model. And that is the beauty of strategy — it makes the details of your tactics so much clearer and simpler.

Table 2-1: What to Do in Each Product Stage

Pioneering	Competitive	Retentive
Educate consumers	Build brand equity	Retain customers
Encourage trial usage	Position against competitors	Build relationships with customers
Build the distribution channel	Capture a leading market share	Improve quality
Segment market to better serve specific needs	Improve service	Upgrade product

SELF-CHECK

- • What types of marketing strategies are discussed here?
- • List the three strategies of the life-cycle model.
- • How does the strategy relate to the program?
- • Give some reasons for using a segmentation strategy.

2.2 Writing a Marketing Strategy and Plan

Writing a marketing plan is not as hard as you may think, and, most important, a good plan increases the odds of success. In fact, most successful businesses — small or large, new or old — write a careful marketing plan at least once a year.

2.2.1 Planning Rules and Tips

Marketing plans vary significantly in format and outline from company to company, but all have core components covering

- ▲ **Your current position** in terms of your product, customers, competition, and broader trends in your market.
- ▲ **For established businesses, what results you got in the previous period** in terms of sales, market share, and possibly also in terms of profits, customer satisfaction, or other measures of customer attitude and perception. You may want to include measures of customer retention, size and frequency of purchase, or other indicators of customer behavior, if you think them important to your new plan.
- ▲ **Your strategy** regarding the big picture that will help you get improved results.
- ▲ **The details of your program** including all of your company's specific activities, grouped by area or type, with explanations of how these activities fit the company's strategy and reflect the current situation.
- ▲ **The numbers** including sales projections and costs. Consider whether knowing these additional numbers would help your business: market share projections, sales to your biggest customers or distributors, costs and returns from any special offers you plan to use, sales projections and commissions by territory, or whatever helps you quantify your specific marketing activities.

▲ **Your learning plans** if you have a new business or new product, or if you are experimenting with a new or risky marketing activity, you want to set up a plan for how to test the waters or experiment on a small scale first. You need to determine what positive results you want to see before committing to a higher level. Wisdom is knowing what you do not know — and planning how to figure it out.

If you are a start-up, you should really consider a stepwise plan with a time line and alternatives or options in case of problems. The more unfamiliar the waters, the more flexibility and caution your plan needs. Make flexibility your first objective for the plan if you are writing a marketing plan for the first time. You want to avoid large advance purchases of media space or time, use short runs of marketing materials at the copy shop over cheaper offset printing of large inventories, and so on. Optimizing your plan for flexibility entails preserving your choice and avoiding commitment of resources. Spending in small increments allows you to change the plan as you go.

If your business has done this all before and your plan builds on years of experience, you can more safely favor *economies of scale* over flexibility. If you know a media investment is likely to produce leads or sales, go ahead and buy media in larger chunks to get good rates. And do not be as cautious about testing mailing lists with small-scale mailings of a few hundred pieces. A good in-house list supplemented by 20 percent or fewer newly purchased names probably warrants a major mailing without as much emphasis on advance testing. Adjust your plan to favor economies of scale if you feel confident that you can make sound judgments in advance. But always leave yourself at least a *little* wiggle room. Reality never reflects your plans and projections 100 percent of the time. Aim for an 80 percent match in marketing, and plan accordingly.

Total up your costs fully and carefully. Marketing programs end up like leaky boats very easily. Each activity seems worthy at the time, but too many of them fail to produce a positive return — ending up like holes in the bottom of your boat. Too many of those holes, and the water starts rising. We list here some of the common ways marketers lose money (so that you can try to avoid them):

▲ **Do not ignore the details.** You build good plans from details like customer-by-customer, item-by-item, or territory-by-territory sales projections. Generalizing about an entire market is hard. Your sales and cost projections are easier to get right if you break them down to their smallest natural units (like individual territory sales or customer orders), do estimates for each of these small units, and then add those estimates up to get your totals.

▲ **Do not imitate the competitors.** Even though everyone seems to market their products in a certain way, you do not have to imitate them. High-performing plans clearly point out what aspects of the marketing program are conventional and why — and these plans also include some original, innovative, or unique elements to help differentiate your company from — and outperform — the competition. Your business is unique, so make your plan reflect your special talents or advantages.

▲ **Do not feel confined by last period's budget and plan.** Repeat or improve the best-performing elements of the past plans, but cut back on any elements that didn't produce high returns. Every plan includes some activities and spending that aren't necessary and can be cut out (or reworked) when you do it all over again next year. Be ruthless with any underperforming elements of last year's plan!

▲ **Do not engage in unnecessary spending.** Always think it through and run the numbers before signing a contract or writing a check. Many of the people and businesses you deal with are salespeople themselves. Their goal is to get *you* to buy their ad space or time, to use their design or printing services, or spend money on fancy Web sites. They want your marketing money. They do not care as much as you do whether you get a good return. You have to keep them on a tight financial rein.

If your marketing activities are consistent and clearly of one kind, a single plan is fine. But what if you sell services (like consulting or repair) and products? You may find that you need to work up one plan for selling products (perhaps this plan aims at finding new customers) and another plan for convincing product buyers to also use your services. If your plan is complicated, break it down into simple subplans. Then total everything up to get the big picture: overall projections and budgets.

If you have 50 products in five different product categories, writing your plan becomes much easier if you come up with 50 sales projections for each product and five separate promotional plans for each category of product. (This method sounds harder but is really much simpler.) Some methods to break down your planning, making it easier and simpler to do, are

▲ **Analyze, plan, and budget sales activities by sales territory and region** (or by major customer if you are a business-to-business marketer with a handful of dominant companies as your clients).

▲ **Project revenues and promotions by individual product and by industry** (if you sell into more than one).

▲ **Plan your advertising and other promotions by product line or other broad product category,** as promotions often have a generalized effect on the products within the category.

▲ **Plan and budget publicity for your company as a whole.** Only budget and plan publicity for an individual product if you introduce it or modify it in some way that may attract media attention.

▲ **Plan and budget for brochures, Web sites, and other informational materials.** Be sure to remain focused in your subject choices: one brochure per topic. Multipurpose brochures or sites never work well. If a Web site sells cleaning products to building maintenance professionals, do not also plan for it to broker gardening and lawn-mowing services to suburban homeowners.

2.2.2 Clarifying and Quantifying Your Objectives

If your marketing strategy involves raising the quality of service and opening a new territory in order to grow your sales and market share, you need to think through how you'll do all that and set a percentage increase goal for sales and a new, higher goal for market share. These numbers become your **objectives,** or the quantified, measurable versions of your strategies.

They flow from your thinking about strategies and tactics, but put them up near the front of your plan to help others quickly understand what you are saying.

Some guidance for writing objectives:

▲ What objectives do you want your plan to help you accomplish? Will the plan increase sales by 25 percent, reposition a product to make it more appealing to upscale buyers, or introduce a direct-marketing function via the Internet? Maybe the plan will combine several products into a single family brand and build awareness of this brand through print and radio advertising, which will gain market share from several competitors and cut the costs of marketing by eliminating inefficiencies in coupon processing, media buying, and sales-force management. Address these sorts of topics in the objectives section of the plan. These points give the plan its focus.

▲ Write clear, compelling objectives and you will never get too confused about what to write in other sections — when in doubt, you can always look back at these objectives and remind yourself what you are trying to accomplish and why.

▲ Try to write this part of the plan early, but keep in mind that you will rewrite it often as you gather more information and do more thinking. Objectives are such a key foundation for the rest of the plan that you cannot ever stop thinking about them. However, they do not need to be long — a half page to two pages, at most.

Every plan should include (along with more unique or situation-specific variables) the objective of reinforcing the brand image at every point of contact or *influence point*, with prospective or current customers. An audit of all your communications at every point of human contact will reveal many places where you do not achieve this objective as fully or consistently as you can, so put this objective in every marketing plan and aspire to achieve it more fully every year.

2.2.3 Preparing a Situation Analysis

A **situation analysis** examines the context by looking at trends, customer preferences, competitor strengths and weaknesses, and anything else that may impact sales. The question your situation analysis must answer is, "What's happening?" The context is different for every marketing plan.

The answer to this question can take many forms, so there isn't an easy formula for preparing the situation analysis. You should analyze the most important market changes to your company — these changes can be the sources of problems or opportunities. (See Chapter 4 for formal research techniques and sources.)

Consider what important changes have occurred since you last examined the situation. Your goal is to see the changes more clearly than the competition does. Why? If your situation analysis is less accurate than the competition's, you'll lose market share to them. If your analysis is about the same as your competition's, then you may hold even. Only if your situation analysis is better than your competitor's can you gain market share on the competition.

What you want, at the very least, from your situation analysis is

▲ **Information parity:** When you know as much as your leading competitors know. If you do not do enough research and analysis, your competitors will have an information advantage. Therefore, you need to gain enough insight to put you on a level playing field with your competitors.

That includes knowing about any major plans they may have. Collect rumors about new products, new people, and so on. At a minimum, do a weekly search on a Web-based search engine for any news about them. What you would like to have is

▲ **Information advantage:** Insight into the market that your competitors do not have. Information advantage puts you on the uphill side of an uneven playing field.

That is a very good place from which to design and launch a marketing program or advertising campaign. Look for new fashions, new technologies, new ways to segment the market — anything that you can use to change the rules of the game even slightly in your favor.

Most marketing plans and planners do not think about their situation analysis this way. Do not waste time on the typical pro forma situation analysis, in which the marketer rounds up the usual suspects and parades dull information in front of them without gaining an advantage from it. That approach, although common, does nothing to make the plan a winner.

What kinds of information can you collect about your competitors? You can certainly gather and analyze examples of their marketing communications. You may have (or be able to gather) some customer opinions from surveys or informal chats. You can group the information you get from customers into useful lists, like figuring out the three most appealing and least appealing things about each competitor. You can also probably get some information about how they distribute and sell, where they are (and aren't) located or distributed, who their key decision makers are, who their biggest and/or most loyal customers are, and even how much they sell. Gather any available data on all-important competitors and organize the information into a table for easy analysis. Here is an example of a format for a generic Competitor Analysis Table. Make entries on the following rows in columns labeled for Competitor 1, Competitor 2, Competitor 3, and so on:

- ▲ **Company:** Describe how the market perceives it and its key product.
- ▲ **Key personnel:** Who are the managers, and how many employees do they have in total?
- ▲ **Financial:** Who owns it; how strong is its *cash position* (does it have spending power or is it struggling to pay its bills); what were its sales in the last 2 years?
- ▲ **Sales, distribution, and pricing:** Describe its primary sales channel, discount/pricing structure, and market-share estimate.
- ▲ **Product/service analysis:** What are the strengths and weaknesses of its product or service?
- ▲ **Scaled assessment of product/service:** Explore relevant subjects like market acceptance, quality of packaging, ads, and so on. Assign a score of between 1 and 5 (with 5 being the strongest) for each characteristic you evaluate. Then sum the scores for each competitor's row to see which seems strongest, overall.
- ▲ **Comparing yourself to competitor ratings:** If you rate yourself on these attributes, too, how do you compare? Are you stronger? If not, you can include increasing your competitive strength as one of your plan's strategic objectives.

2.2.4 Writing Your Strategy

Even if you aren't writing a marketing plan, you should take some time to write down your marketing strategy clearly and thoughtfully. Put it in summary form in a single sentence. (If you must, add some bullet points to explain it in more detail.) This is a good example of a direct, clear statement of strategy:

> *Our strategy is to maximize the quality of our security alarm products and services through good engineering and to grow our share of a competitive market by communicating our superior quality to high-end customers.*

Your strategy guides the direction and sets the tone of the marketing plan. However, many plans use the strategy section to get specific about the objectives by explaining how the company will accomplish them. This happens because the difference between objectives and strategies can be a pretty fine line.

▲ The **objective** states something your business hopes to accomplish in the next year.

▲ The **strategy** stresses the big-picture approach to accomplishing that objective, giving some good pointers as to what road you'll take.

Here are two more examples:

> *Solidify our leadership of the home PC market by increasing market share by two points.*

> *Introduce hot new products and promote our brand name with an emphasis on high-quality components, in order to increase our market share by two points.*

The first example is an objective, and the second is a strategy. Strategies are bigger in scope and need not be as quantifiable as objectives. You can combine this section with the objectives section and title it *Objectives and Strategies*. The objectives put your strategies into practice using the tactics (the marketing mix) of your marketing plan. (See Section 1.1.2 for a discussion of the marketing mix.) The plan explains how your strategies drive your objectives. Your strategy should make sense. Unlike a mathematical formula or a spreadsheet column, you do not have a simple method to check a marketing strategy to make sure that it really adds up. But you can subject a marketing strategy to common sense and make sure that it has no obvious flaws. Here are some to guard against:

▲ **Strategy ignores limitations in your resources.** If you are currently the 10th-largest competitor, do not write a plan to become the number-one largest by the end of the year simply based on designing all your ads and mailings to claim you are the best. Make sure that your strategy is reasonable. Would the average person agree that your strategy sounds attainable with a little hard work? Do you have enough resources to execute the strategy in the available time?

▲ **Strategy demands huge changes in customer behavior.** You can move people and businesses only so far with a marketing program. If you plan to get employers to give their employees every other Friday off so those employees can attend special workshops your firm sponsors, well, we hope you have a backup plan. Employers do not give employees a lot of extra time off, no matter how compelling your sales pitch or brochure may be. The same is true of consumer marketing. You simply cannot change strongly held public attitudes without awfully good new evidence.

> ### FOR EXAMPLE
>
> #### Saving the Grapefruit
>
> Grapefruit sales have fallen for the past 5 years. Consumers see the fruit, according to research from the Florida Department of Citrus, as an "old person's" breakfast item. People find dealing with the fruit a hassle. So how to make the grapefruit popular again? Grapefruit growers are trying to revive sales with a new ad campaign that positions grapefruit juice as a hip alternative beverage for health-conscious women in their 20s and 30s. But marketers have real difficulty dictating what *cool* is. They're placing ads in magazines that they think the hip women read. They're also introducing new alcoholic mixed drinks that use grapefruit juice — using venues like alternative film festivals to do so. Still, it's a risky strategy. "Coolness" is the most fickle and fleeting of brand images.

▲ **A competitor is already doing it.** This assumption is a surprisingly common error. To avoid it, include a summary of each competitor's strategy in the *Strategy* section of your plan. Add a note explaining how yours differs from each of theirs; you need a distinctive strategy to power your plan.

▲ **Strategy requires too much information you do not have.** Some brilliant strategies may be doomed because they require knowledge of too many things outside of your expertise. You can write a grand plan describing how you'll capture 10 percent of the computer-training market in the northeastern United States next year, but if you have no experience in computer training, you probably cannot execute it. Strategies that involve doing a lot of things you have little or no expertise in are really start-up strategies, not marketing strategies.

2.2.5 Writing a Powerful Executive Summary

An executive summary is a one-page plan. This wonderful document conveys essential information about your company's planned year of programs and activities in a couple hundred well-chosen words or less. If you ever get confused or disoriented in the rough-and-tumble play of sales and marketing, this clear, one-page summary can guide you back to the correct strategic path. It's also a powerful advertisement for your program, communicating the purpose and essential activities of your plan in a compelling manner.

Draft the executive summary early in the year as a guide to your thinking and planning. But revise it often, and write it last, because it needs to summarize the whole plan. Help yourself and others by giving an overview of what's the same and what's different in this plan, compared to the previous period's plan. Draft a short paragraph covering these two topics.

Summarize the main points of your plan and make clear whether the plan is

▲ **Efficiency oriented:** Your plan introduces a large number of specific improvements in how you market your product.

▲ **Effectiveness oriented:** Your plan identifies a major opportunity or problem and adopts a new strategy to respond to it.

Summarize the bottom-line results: what your projected revenues will be (by product or product line, unless you have too many to list on one page) and what the costs are. Also show how these figures differ from last year's figures. Keep the whole summary under one page in length if you possibly can.

If you have too many products to keep the summary under one page in length, you can list them by product line. But a better option is to do more than one plan. You probably haven't clearly thought out any plan that cannot be summarized in a page. Many businesses have marketing prepare a separate plan for each product.

SELF-CHECK

- Name the common components of a marketing plan.
- List the four ways that marketers often lose money.
- What do you want to get, ideally, from your situation analysis?
- Cite the difference between objectives and strategies.

2.3 Analyzing and Summarizing Your Marketing Program

A strong marketing program starts with an analysis of your **influence points** (explained in Section 1.2.2) or how your organization can influence customer purchases. The program ends with some decisions about how to use these influence points. Usually you can come up with tactics in all five of the marketing Ps: product, price, placement (or distribution), promotion, and people.

Prioritize by picking a few primary influence points — ones that will dominate your program for the coming planning period. This approach concentrates your resources, giving you more leverage at certain points of influence. Make the choice carefully; try to pick no more than three main activities to take the lead in your program. Use the other influence points in secondary roles to support your primary points. Now you begin to develop specific plans for each, as you decide how to use your various program components.

Say that you are considering using print ads in trade magazines to let retail store buyers know about your hot new line of products and the in-store display options you have for them. Now you need to get specific. You need to pick some magazines. Research prices and demographics. You also need to decide how many of what sort of ads you will run, and then price out this advertising program. (Section 11.1 discusses print advertising.)

Do the same analysis for each of the items on your list of program components. Work your way through the details until you have an initial cost figure for what you want to do with each component. Total these costs and see if the end result seems realistic. Is the total cost too big a share of your projected sales? Or (if you are in a larger business), is your estimate higher than the budget can go? If so, adjust and try again. After a while, you get a budget that looks acceptable on the bottom line and also makes sense from a practical perspective.

2.3.1 Analyzing Costs

A spreadsheet greatly helps this process. Just build formulas that add the costs to reach subtotals and a grand total, and then subtract the grand total from the projected sales figure to get a bottom line for your program. Figure 2-2 shows the format for a very simple spreadsheet that gives a quick and accurate marketing program overview for a small business. In this figure, you can see what a program looks like for a company that wholesales products to gift shops around the United States. This company uses personal selling, telemarketing, and print advertising as its primary program components. It also budgets some money in this period to finish developing and begin introducing a new line of products.

This company's secondary components do not use much of the marketing budget when compared to the primary components (which use 87 percent of the total budget). But the secondary components are important, too. A new Web page is expected to handle a majority of customer inquiries and act as a virtual catalog, permitting the company to cut way back on its catalog printing and mailing costs. Also, the company plans to introduce a new line of floor displays for use at point of purchase by selected retailers. Marketers expect this display unit, combined with improved see-through packaging, to increase turnover of the company's products in retail stores. If your marketing plan covers multiple groups of customers, you need to include multiple spreadsheets (such as the one in Figure 2-2) because each group of customers may need a different marketing program.

For example, the company whose wholesale marketing program you see in Figure 2-2 sells to gift stores. But they also do some business with stationery stores. Although the same salespeople call on both, each of these customers has different products and promotions. They buy from different catalogs. They do not use the same kinds of displays. They read different trade magazines. Consequently, the company has to develop a separate marketing program for each, allocating any overlapping expenses appropriately. (For example, if you make two-thirds of your sales calls to gift stores, then the sales-calls expense for the gift-store program should be two-thirds of the total sales budget.)

Figure 2-2

Overview of Program to Target Retail Store Buyers

Program Components	Direct Marketing Costs ($)
Primary influence points:	
- Sales calls	$450,700
- Telemarketing	276,000
- Ads in trade magazines	1,255,000
- New product line development	171,500
	Subtotal: $2,153,200
Secondary influence points:	
- Quantity discounts	$70,000
- Point-of-purchase displays	125,000
- New web page with online catalog	12,600
- Printed catalog	52,000
- Publicity	18,700
- Booth at annual trade show	22,250
- Redesign packaging	9,275
	Subtotal: $309,825
Projected sales from this program	$23,250,000
Minus total program costs	-2,463,025
Net sales from this marketing	**$20,786,975**

A program budget, prepared on a spreadsheet.

2.3.2 Exploring the Details

In this part of your plan, you need to explain the details of how you plan to use each component in your marketing program. Devote a section to each component, which means that this part of your plan may be quite lengthy. The more you get on paper, the easier it will be to implement the plan later — and to rewrite the plan next year.

This portion includes specific components of a marketing program, from product positioning to Web pages (covered in Chapter 13) to pricing (covered in Chapter 9).

At a minimum, this part of the plan should have sections covering the **five Ps** — the **product, pricing, placement** (or distribution), **promotion** (how you communicate with and persuade customers), and **people** (salespeople, customer service staff, distributors, and so on). But more likely, you'll want to break these categories down into more specific areas. You can be as detailed as you like.

Do not bother elaborating in your marketing plan on program components that you cannot alter. Sometimes, the person writing the marketing plan cannot change pricing policy, order up a new product line, or dictate a shift in distribution strategy. Explore your boundaries and even try to stretch them, but you need to admit they exist or your plan cannot be practical. If you can only control promotion, then this section of the plan should concentrate on the ways that you'll promote the product. Acknowledge in writing any issues or challenges you have to cope with, given that you cannot change other factors. Now write a plan that does everything you can reasonably do given your constraints. (A section called *Constraints* ought to go into the Situation Analysis if your company has such constraints.)

The main purpose of the management section of the plan is simply to make sure that enough warm bodies are in the right places at the right times to get the work done. The management section summarizes the main activities that you, your employees, or your employer must perform in order to implement your marketing program. The section then assigns these activities to individuals, justifying the assignments by considering issues such as an individual's capabilities, capacities, and how the company will supervise and control that individual.

Sometimes this section gets more sophisticated by addressing management issues, like how to make the sales force more productive or whether to decentralize the marketing function. If you have salespeople or distributors, develop plans for organizing, motivating, tracking, and controlling them. Also develop a plan for them to use in generating, allocating, and tracking sales leads. Start these subsections by describing the current approach, and do a strengths/weaknesses analysis of that approach, using input from the salespeople, reps, or distributors in question. End by describing any incremental changes/improvements you can think to make.

But make sure that you've run your ideas by the people in question *first* and gotten their input. Do not surprise your salespeople, sales reps, or distributors with new systems or methods. If you do, they'll probably resist the changes, and sales will slow down. People execute sales plans well only if they understand and believe in those plans.

2.3.3 Projecting Expenses and Revenues

You'll need to:

- ▲ Estimate future sales, in units and dollars, for each product in your plan.
- ▲ Justify these estimates and, if they're hard to justify, create worst-case versions, too.
- ▲ Draw a time line showing when your program incurs costs and performs program activities. (Doing so helps with the preceding section and also gets you prepared for the task of designing a monthly marketing budget.)
- ▲ Write a monthly marketing budget that lists all the estimated costs of your programs for each month of the coming year and breaks down sales by product or territory and by month.

For a start-up or small business, we highly recommend doing all your projections on a *cash basis*. In other words, put the payment for your year's supply of brochures in the month in which the printer wants the money, instead of allocating that cost across 12 months. Also factor in the wait time for collecting your sales revenues. If collections take 30 days, show money coming in during December from November's sales, and do not count any December sales for this year's plan. A cash basis may upset accountants, who like to do things on an accrual basis, but cash-based accounting keeps small businesses alive. You want a positive cash balance (or at least to break even) on the bottom line during every month of your plan. If your cash-based projection shows a loss some months, fiddle with the plan to eliminate that loss (or arrange to borrow money to cover the gap). Sometimes a careful cash-flow analysis of a plan leads to changes in underlying marketing strategy.

FOR EXAMPLE

How a New Strategy Improved Cash Flow

One business-to-business marketer adopted as its primary marketing objective the goal of getting more customers to pay with credit cards instead of on invoices. The company's business customers cooperated, and average collection time shortened from 45 days to under 10, greatly improving the cash flow and thus the spending power and profitability of the business.

Several helpful techniques are available for projecting sales, such as **buildup forecasts, indicator forecasts,** and **time-period forecasts.** Choose the most appropriate technique for your business. If you are feeling nervous, just use the technique that gives you the most conservative projection. Here's a common way to play it safe: Use several of the following techniques and average their results.

▲ **Buildup forecasts:** These predictions go from the specific to the general, or from the bottom up.

If you have sales reps or salespeople, have each one project the next period's sales for her territories and justify her projections based on what changes in the situation she anticipates. Then aggregate all the sales force's forecasts to obtain an overall figure. If you have few enough customers that you can project per-customer purchases, build up your forecast this way. You may want to work from reasonable estimates of the amount of sales you can expect from each store carrying your products or from each thousand catalogs mailed. Whatever the basic building blocks of your program, start with an estimate for each element and then add these estimates up.

▲ **Time-period forecasts:** Work by week or month, estimating the size of sales in each time period, and then add these estimates for the entire year. This approach helps when your program or the market isn't constant across the entire year.

Ski resorts use this method because they get certain types of revenues only at certain times of the year. And marketers who plan to introduce new products during the year or to use heavy advertising in one or two pulses (concentrated time periods) also use this method because their sales go up significantly during those periods. Entrepreneurs, small businesses, and any others on a tight cash-flow leash need to use this method because you get a good idea of what cash will be flowing in by week or month. An annual sales figure doesn't tell you enough about when the money comes in to know whether you'll be short of cash in specific periods during the year.

▲ **Indicator forecasts:** This method links your forecast to economic indicators that ought to vary with sales.

For example, if you are in the construction business, you find that past sales for your industry correlate with GDP (gross domestic product, or national output) growth. So you can adjust your sales forecast up or down depending upon whether experts expect the economy to grow rapidly or slowly in the next year.

▲ **Multiple-scenario forecasts:** You base these forecasts on what-if stories. They start with a straight-line forecast in which you assume that your sales will grow by the same percentage next year as they did last year. Then you make up what-if stories and project their impact on your plan to create a variety of alternative projections.

For each scenario, think about how customer demand may change and how your marketing program would need to change. Then make an appropriate sales projection. For example, if a competitor introduced a technological breakthrough, you may guess that your sales would fall 25 percent short of your straight-line projection. The trouble with multiple scenario analysis is that . . . well, it gives you multiple scenarios. Your boss (if you have one) wants a single sales projection, a one-liner at the top of your marketing budget. One way to turn all those options into one number or series of numbers is to just pick the option that seems most likely to you. That's not very satisfying if you aren't at all sure which, if any, will come true. So another method involves taking all the scenarios that seem even remotely possible, assigning each a probability of occurring in the next year, multiplying each by its probability, and then averaging them all to get a single number.

2.3.4 Creating Your Controls

This section is the last and shortest of your plan — but in many ways, it's the most important. This section allows you and others to track performance. Identify some performance benchmarks and state them clearly in the plan. For example:

▲ All sales territories should be using the new catalogs and sales scripts by June 1.

▲ Revenues should grow to $75,000 per month by the end of the first quarter if the promotional campaign works according to plan.

These statements give you easy ways to monitor performance as you implement the marketing plan. Without them, nobody has control over the plan; nobody can tell whether or how well the plan is working. With these statements, you can identify unexpected results or delays quickly — in time for appropriate responses if you have designed these controls properly.

A survey by the research firm, The Aelera Corporation, concluded that only 61 percent of marketing programs are effective. That's just a little more than half. Those odds aren't very good, so use plenty of controls and track your marketing activities on a weekly basis, if you can. Look for deviations from the plan and take action early to correct or improve the plan. Good controls allow you to make it into that minority of marketers who can look back at the end of the year and actually rate their plan a success.

SELF-CHECK

- What is the purpose of the management section?
- Which total is subtracted from projected sales to get the bottom line?
- What information is included in the monthly budget section of your plan?
- Name the available techniques discussed for projecting sales.
- Which part of your plan helps you to track performance?

SUMMARY

For your marketing plan to work, you need to develop the appropriate strategy and connect it to the activities of your marketing program. Write it down annually. Include your objectives, your situation analysis, costs and sales projections, and controls.

KEY TERMS

Buildup forecasts	These predictions go from the specific to the general, or from the bottom up.
Competitive strategy	Used when the majority of prospects have tried at least one competitor's product.
Customer perception	How the customer sees the category, and what matters when determining a market-share strategy.
Indicator forecasts	This forecasting method links your forecast to economic indicators that ought to vary with sales.
Information advantage	Insight into the market that your competitors do not have.
Information parity	When you know as much as your leading competitors know.
Market-expansion strategy	The most common marketing strategy, with two variants: You can expand your market by finding new customers for your current products or you can try to sell new products to your existing customers and market.
Market-segmentation strategy	A specialization strategy in which you target and cater to (specialize in) just one narrow type or group of customers.

Market share	Your sales as a percentage of total sales for your product category in your market (or in your market segment if you use a segmentation strategy too).
Market-share strategy	A strategy that relies on market share as your competitive advantage.
Multiple-scenario forecasts	You base these forecasts on what-if stories. They start with a straight-line forecast in which you assume that your sales will grow by the same percentage next year as they did last year. Then you make up what-if stories and project their impact on your plan to create a variety of alternative projections.
Objectives	The quantified, measurable versions of your strategies.
Pioneering strategy	Used when the majority of prospects are unfamiliar with the product.
Point-of-purchase marketing	Doing whatever advertising is necessary to sway the consumer your way at the time and place of their purchase.
Positioning strategy	A positioning strategy takes a psychological approach to marketing, by getting people to see your product in a favorable light.
Quality strategy	Using quality as your competitive advantage when marketing.
Reminder strategy	A reminder strategy is good when you think people would buy your product if they thought of it — but may not without a reminder.
Retentive strategy	Used when attracting new customers costs more than keeping old customers.
Simplicity marketing	This strategy positions a company as simpler, easier to understand, and easier to use or work with than the competition.
Situation analysis	Examines the context, looking at trends, customer preferences, competitor strengths and weaknesses, and anything else that may impact sales.
Strategy	A big-picture vision of what you are trying to do.
Time-period forecasts	Work by week or month, estimating the size of sales in each time period, and then add these estimates for the entire year. This approach helps when your program or the market isn't constant across the entire year.

ASSESS YOUR UNDERSTANDING

Go to www.wiley.com/college/Hiam to evaluate your knowledge of the basic marketing plan.
Measure your learning by comparing pretest and post-test results.

Summary Questions

1. A situation analysis is used to project sales. True or false?
2. One variant of the market-expansion strategy is selling new products to your existing customers. What is the other?
    (a) Selling new products to new customers
    (b) Finding new customers for current products
    (c) Adding a segment to your market
3. If you correlate your forecast to the GDP, you are using what kind of technique?
4. Which one is not a core component of your marketing plan?
    (a) Sales projections and costs
    (b) Learning plans
    (c) Historical data from the first year of business
    (d) Marketing strategy
5. Market expansion is the most common marketing strategy. True or false?
6. Which is an important strategic question?
    (a) What's your product category?
    (b) What are your competitors' sales figures for last year?
    (c) How much does television advertising cost in your market?
7. A learning plan can help you test the waters for your new product. True or false?
8. A point-of-purchase display is an example of simplicity marketing. True or false?
9. How long should your executive summary be?
    (a) one paragraph
    (b) under one page
    (c) five pages maximum
10. The monthly marketing budget includes estimates of future sales. True or false?

Review Questions

1. What are two strategic ways of expanding your markets?
2. What are the three stages of the advertising life-cycle model?
3. What is a situation analysis used for?

Applying This Chapter

1. When putting together a marketing plan, how can you avoid the common error of copying a competitor's strategy?
2. You are a regional provider of banking services in the Southwest, and you are growing rapidly by acquiring smaller banks that do not necessarily share your vision. Write a possible marketing strategy for your bank that will unify your marketing plan. How would you make yourself distinctive? Would you focus on getting more business from existing customers, or finding more customers?
3. Write two possible marketing objectives for the marketing plan described in the previous question.
4. What core marketing strategies would be good bets for a bedding manufacturer that's launching a special line of mattresses that it claims help you sleep better? What sort of life-cycle strategies apply?
5. If you were developing the marketing plan for a small landscaping company located in New England, which type of sales projection would you strongly consider using and why?

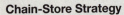

Chain-Store Strategy

You are working for the marketing department of a new regional chain of hardware stores. The store wants to position itself as a high-end provider of premium products, with very well trained personnel who provide excellent customer service. Its marketing strategy is:

Grow the home-improvement market by 2 percent and attain 20 percent of the current market by convincing affluent, busy professionals that home repair and renovation is easier and less time-consuming than they think. Critique this strategy.

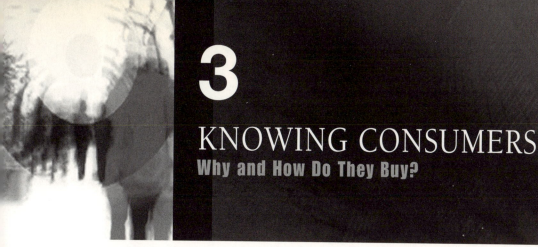

3

KNOWING CONSUMERS
Why and How Do They Buy?

Starting Point

Go to www.wiley.com/college/Hiam to assess your knowledge of consumers.
Determine where you need to concentrate your effort.

What You'll Learn in This Chapter

▲ Internal and external sources of influence on buying
▲ Reference groups, socialization agents, and opinion leaders
▲ The consumer and organizational buying decision process

After Studying This Chapter, You'll Be Able To

▲ Discriminate between consumer and organizational purchasing patterns
▲ Order the consumer and organizational decision processes
▲ Analyze opportunities for influencing buying decisions

Goals and Outcomes

▲ Assess the usefulness of various buying factors
▲ Predict buying patterns based upon consumer life cycle
▲ Estimate marketing effectiveness in various buying situations

INTRODUCTION

Consumers are a mystery to many marketers, and marketers have been studying their buying decision process for decades. Consumer buying behavior can be influenced by many external and internal factors, including demographics, lifestyle, and reference groups. Organizational buying behavior is more standardized and predictable, with eight typical stages.

3.1 Consumer Buying Behavior

Buying behavior is the subject of market research, as discussed in Chapter 5. That chapter explains how and why to conduct market research; this chapter explains what information about the consumer you are looking for when you research. Before doing any market research, you will need to analyze and understand who is making the buying decision and what influences their decisions. If you are selling automobiles, you need to consider who is buying your cars and market accordingly.

Is it an individual buying a new car for him- or herself? Or is your customer another business that needs a fleet of cars for use by its salespeople? In the second situation, you are likely to have a group of people making the decision rather than one person.

What factors influence these very different decisions? To try to understand consumers better, marketers have looked at both external and internal influences on their buying decisions. Before you can segment and target markets, described in Chapter 4, or do market research, as explained in Chapter 5, you need to understand buying behavior and what influences it.

Internal influences include

▲ Lifestyle
▲ Attitudes

External influences include

▲ Whether it's a novel or routine purchase
▲ Involvement with the decision
▲ Demographics
▲ Market offerings

3.1.1 Internal Influences on Consumer Buying Behavior

No two people make a decision in exactly the same way. The reasons people actually buy what they buy are hard to pin down and full of surprises. Studying the buying behavior of the consumer, who can be quite fickle and unpredictable, is an ongoing process. Marketers thought they had older people figured out, but then along came the baby-boomer generation, which is defying marketing stereotypes.

Learning can take place firsthand through experience, or secondhand through hearing about someone else's experience. Let's say you are thinking about buying a bottle of Zinfandel wine. You ask the salesclerk what it tastes like, and she tells you it tastes like a strong ginger ale. If you don't like ginger ale, you are not going to buy the wine! You've learned you do not like Zinfandel, although you've never tasted it.

Most of our learning is secondhand. You hear about fun places to visit from your friends, or you read about them in books or see them on television or the Internet. Advertising itself represents this kind of learning. You are learning about new products and their attributes all the time through advertising, although you may not even be in the market for that product or service for some time.

One of the most important kinds of learning to advertisers is **socialization,** the process by which people acquire knowledge, skills, and habits that they work on over a lifetime.

▲ **Consumer socialization:** How people learn about products and services by taking part in social interactions with other people.
▲ **Socialization agent:** A person who influences you.

Teenagers will buy the clothing brands that their friends wear. Spokespersons for companies, such as Bill Cosby for Jell-O, can influence entire target groups to purchase. The agent, therefore, can be anyone from a parent or friend to a celebrity or a salesperson you meet in a store.

FOR EXAMPLE

Baby Boomers Won't Fade Away

The American generation born between 1946 and 1964 is one of the largest and most influential. Now that they're aging, marketers are reevaluating whether to stop pursuing them, says *BusinessWeek* magazine (October 24, 2005). Traditionally marketers saw older people as undesirable in terms of their willingness to switch brands and try new things. But Baby Boomers are acting differently from previous generations. The "aging boomer" group has enormous purchasing power and is challenging conventional marketing wisdom about people over the age of 50. They frequently start second careers or second families, and are continuing to work and to work out later in life. Lifestyle assumptions about older people may not be valid anymore. Marketers, as usual, must pay attention.

A motive is the inner drive or pressure to take action to satisfy a need. So, to be motivated is to have a goal. That goal is what marketers want to know so they can do their jobs. The difficulty, however, of defining motives and of dealing with motivation in consumer research means it has limited application.

For motivation to be useful, marketers must understand how motives are influenced by specific situations. Marketers of target groups with strong self-esteem needs, for example, have used psychologist A. H. Maslow's theory of individual motivation, which places all human needs in a hierarchy from basic survival to self-actualization. But motivation, along with personality, is difficult to measure, and is still a tough nut to crack for marketers.

Marketers have used **lifestyle** traits, or a set of attitudes, interests, and opinions of the potential customer, as a useful alternative to motivation and personality. You will find more discussion of this in Chapter 4.

If you like to hunt, if you think dressing well is important, if you have traditional values, these are all part of your lifestyle and explain why you purchase the things you do. Lifestyle provides a lot of information about target groups by combining demographics with psychological characteristics. It has useful applications.

Consumers' shopping orientations, for instance, predict buying behavior. Some people dislike shopping and prefer to get the decision over with as quickly as possible, often on-line, whereas others see shopping as entertainment.

Attitudes, a component of lifestyle, predict buying behavior best in high-involvement situations.

Marketers find comparing attitudes very useful. Consider these two opposing possibilities:

▲ If you have a strong attitude about wearing stylish clothes, you may restrict your purchases to a particular set of brands.
▲ If you do not care about style but are focused on price, you will shop more indiscriminately. The brand will not matter.

As a marketer, learning consumer attitudes about your product can help you to try to influence them positively. If you can change your potential buyer's attitude toward small cars, for example, you can help him to also feel more positive about buying your fuel-efficient vehicle, and even change his actions. (He may buy your car instead of a gas-guzzling truck when he needs a new car.)

Marketers have two choices about attitudes and buying behavior: They can try to influence attitudes, or they can change the product itself to match consumers' attitudes. Changing the product may be easier in some cases than others, but if you cannot change the product, you can sometimes modify the attitude. The stronger a person's loyalty to a brand, for example, the harder it is to change that attitude.

3.1.2 External Influences on Consumer Buying Behavior

External factors are equally as important as internal factors in consumer buying behavior. (See Figure 3-1.)

If you are buying something inexpensive that you buy all the time, such as bread, the buying process is typically quick and routine. You are not going to spend hours in the bread section scrutinizing each loaf of bread. If you are buying a home, however, your decision will be very complex, involving many hours of visiting homes and prioritizing what's important to you: location, size, schools, architectural style, new construction or renovation, and so on.

Whether a consumer's decision is simple or complex in a given buying situation depends on

▲ **Whether the decision is novel or routine.** How often do you have to make this decision? Is it a habit, like buying gasoline? It's probably not very important to you if it's repetitive.

▲ **How involved you are with the decision. A high-involvement decision** is very important to you. It's tied up with your ego and self-image, and has either financial, social, or psychological risk. (What if your friends do not like it? What if you regret it later?)

When you've bought a similar product many times in the past, the decision making is likely to be simple, regardless of whether it is a high- or low-involvement decision. It may have started as a high-involvement decision, but then you were satisfied with your purchase and you are now loyal to a particular brand. Then your decision becomes a simple, low-involvement one, influenced by habit and not by ego. Low-involvement decisions involve little risk, and thus you do not worry about them very much.

What else in your situation influences your decision? Demographics and market offerings do.

▲ **Demographics:** Statistics — such as age, gender, or income — that give information about a population.

More on demographics is discussed in Section 5.2.3. Variables about your customers can have significant influence on your consumer behavior. For example, K-Mart appeals to different people than Williams-Sonoma. People at different ages, incomes, or with different educations make their decisions in various ways. Some demographic factors considered important are

▲ Age

▲ Gender

▲ Income
▲ Education
▲ Marital status
▲ Mobility

The more extensive the product and brand choices available to the consumer, the more complex the purchase decision process is likely to be. **Market offerings** are the selection of goods and services available for purchase in the marketplace. Consumers have more choices today, but they can be overwhelmed with the information needed to make their decision.

If you want to buy a DVD player, you have many brands to choose from — Sony, Samsung, Panasonic, Mitsubishi, Toshiba, and Sanyo, to name several. Each manufacturer sells several models that have different features such as slow motion, stop action, and single or multiple event selection. Which features are important to you? The decision can quickly become complicated.

In other cases, your need can be met by only one product that may be available in only one place or a few places. Suppose you are a student on a campus in a small town many miles from any stores. Your campus and town has only one bookstore. You need a textbook for class, so you must buy it from the college bookstore. You either buy the book (or maybe try to find it on the Internet for less) or you go without. This is not an ideal situation from the consumer's perspective, but it does simplify the buying decision!

Social factors also influence consumers in what they buy. Most of us live in communities and families, and we are affected by what others buy and what they think of us. Many times the influence is subtle and we are unaware of the importance of social, external factors driving what we choose to purchase. Four factors deserve mention here:

▲ **Culture:** Traditional American culture values hard work, thrift, achievement, security, and the like. Marketing strategies reinforcing traditional values show a particular product or service as part of this cultural heritage. Cultural customs such as buying cards for holidays and birthdays are promoted by greeting-card manufacturers, among others. American culture can also be divided into various subcultures, such as African Americans, Latinos (who can be Mexicans, South Americans, Puerto Ricans, and so on), Asian Americans (Chinese, Korean, Japanese, and so on), and Italian Americans.

▲ **Social class:** Determined by such factors as occupation, wealth, income, education, power, and prestige, social class influences consumer behavior a great deal. The best-known classification system includes upper-upper, lower-upper, upper-middle, lower-middle, upper-lower, and lower-lower.

Lower-middle and upper-lower classes make up the mass market. People in similar classes tend to have similar attitudes, live in similar neighborhoods, dress alike, and shop at the same kinds of stores. Marketers who target the upper classes must meet the expectations of this group in terms of quality, service, and atmosphere.

▲ **Reference groups:** A reference group is an informal or formal group of people with whom you identify. Churches, clubs, schools, notable individuals, co-workers, and friends can all be consumer reference groups. Also, many marketers have discovered recently that television and movies can influence who consumers aspire to live like. People may not want to "keep up with the Joneses" (their neighbors) as much today as they want to keep up with their television reference groups, such as *Friends*. Within these groups are often **opinion leaders** or **decision influencers,** or, people in reference groups who are seen as having greater expertise or knowledge than the rest. These people set the trends for the group, so are eagerly sought out by marketers. (See Section 12.2.3 for more on decision influencers and word of mouth.)

Figure 3-1

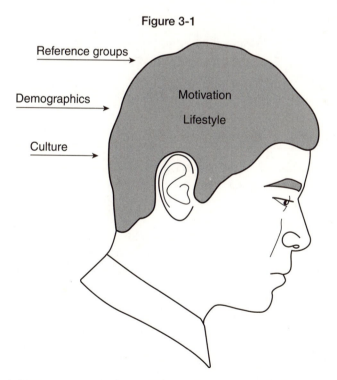

Influences on the buying decision can be internal or external.

▲ **Family:** An important reference group for consumers is the family, impacting his or her attitudes and behaviors. Interactions between husband and wife and the number and ages of children in a family can significantly change buying behavior. Marketers seek to discover the decision maker for the purchase being made. That's the person who dominates the decision — sometimes the husband, sometimes the wife, sometimes even the child. With large purchases, it's often a joint decision. The family life cycle is also important when marketing to families. Whether people are married or have children at home greatly influences their lifestyles, and therefore their buying behaviors. People go through various stages in the life cycle (not everybody goes through every stage, though) in a predictable order, and marketers can market accordingly.

SELF-CHECK

- Define **demographics** and **market offerings**.
- Compare the influences of life cycle, motivation, and attitudes.
- List four external factors driving a purchase decision.
- What's the difference between a socialization agent and an opinion leader?

3.2 Organizational Buying Behavior

The buying behavior of organizations differs from consumer buying behavior. Those who sell goods and services to consumers who are themselves in need of goods and services to run their own businesses are engaged in **organizational marketing**.

Producers, resellers, and government make up vast marketing organizations that buy a large variety of products, including equipment, raw material, labor, and other services. Some organizations sell only to other companies and never come into contact with consumers at all. Much more research has been conducted on consumer markets than on organizational markets, but we can identify some key similarities and differences.

Businesses have their own unique business philosophies or missions that guide their actions in resolving conflicts, handling uncertainty and risk, searching for solutions, and adapting to change.

FOR EXAMPLE

Who Plays It Safe?

In general, companies in declining industries will be far more conservative in their purchasing than those in new industries who are expanding their markets. A purchaser for a coal company relies on a conservative purchase strategy in an attempt to maintain the status quo. This company cannot afford to take risks. A company that is growing and expanding, however, will be able to tolerate the risk of a purchasing error.

Most businesses differ in their buying from individual consumers in the following ways:

▲ **Many individuals are involved in the buying decision.**

▲ **The organizational buyer is motivated by both rational and emotional factors.** They have to follow the quantitative criteria established for most organizational decisions, yet the decision makers are also people, subject to many of the same emotional factors that affect personal purchases.

▲ **Business buying often involves a range of complex technical dimensions.** A purchasing agent for Volvo Automobiles, for example, must consider many technical factors, such as the electronic system, the acoustics of the interior, and the shape of the dashboard, before ordering a radio to go into the new model.

▲ **The organizational decision process typically takes a long time.** This creates a significant lag time between the marketer's initial contact with the customer and the actual purchasing decision. Because many new factors can enter the picture during this time, the marketer needs to monitor and adjust to these changes.

▲ **Businesses cannot be grouped precisely, because each organization has its own way of functioning and a personality.** Ben and Jerry's personality, for example, is different from General Motors' personality.

Having multiple people involved in the purchasing decision has important implications. Often companies have rules and policies about buying that individuals do not have. So to predict organizational buying behavior requires knowing

▲ Who is involved in the decision
▲ What criteria each member is using to evaluate their suppliers

▲ What rules the organization has about buying

▲ What influence each member has on the decision

▲ What the buying situation is

The type of buying situation is important because it affects how the decision is made and can represent an opportunity for the marketer to influence the actual buying decision. The best marketing opportunities arise when companies are buying things for the first time.

The three types of organizational buying situations are

▲ **The straight rebuy:** The simplest situation, where the company reorders a good or service without any modifications. The transaction tends to be routine and may be handled totally by the purchasing department.

▲ **The modified rebuy:** This is a little more complicated, because the buyer is seeking to modify product specifications, prices, or something else. A negotiation takes place, and several participants may take part in the buying decision.

▲ **A new task:** When buying a product for the first time, the company provides a good opportunity for the marketer to provide input to influence the decision. The number of participants and the amount of information sought increases with the cost and risks of the transaction.

SELF-CHECK

- Define **organizational marketing**.
- List the three types of organizational buying situations.
- How does organizational buying differ from consumer buying?

3.3 The Consumer Decision Process

How do consumers and businesses approach the actual decision of what to buy? What are the stages of the buying process? Each transaction needs a buyer and a seller, and the seller is usually guided by certain company policies and objectives that do not change much over time. The seller needs to make a certain profit margin to survive. The buyer, in contrast to the seller, does not make his or her part of the deal quite so clear. That's why marketers study the decision process.

Two key questions marketers ask about buyer behavior, which help them decide on target markets and on what to sell, are

▲ How do potential buyers go about making purchase decisions?
▲ What factors influence their decision process and in what way?

Marketers view consumer purchasing as a type of problem solving. The consumer has a problem — a want or need, and purchases something to fulfill that need. Problems can be seen in terms of two types of needs:

▲ **Physical:** The need for food and shelter, for example.
▲ **Psychological:** The need to be accepted and liked by others, for example.

Marketers distinguish between wants and needs by considering the want to be more specific than the need. You may need a watch, but you want a Rolex watch.

▲ **Need:** A basic deficiency that is outside the marketer's control. You may need clothes, but you want to buy the Polo label.

Marketers seek to fulfill and create wants, not needs.

▲ **Wants** are what marketers try to influence by trying to get the consumer to choose their product or service instead of someone else's.

Figure 3-2 shows the process a consumer goes through in making a purchase decision. For a first-time purchase or for a high-priced, long-lasting, infrequently purchased item (a complex decision), the tendency is for the consumer to go through all six stages. Otherwise, at any stage the consumer may decide to opt out.

For a routine purchase of many products, the purchasing behavior means the need is satisfied in a habitual manner by repurchasing the same brand. They like the product so they keep buying it, skipping over the second and third stages — information search and processing, and identification and evaluation of alternatives.

This simple decision making occurs unless something changes. If, for example, the price, product, or availability of the purchased item changes, the buyer may reenter the full decision process and consider alternative brands. That's the marketer's chance to gain a customer.

Figure 3-2

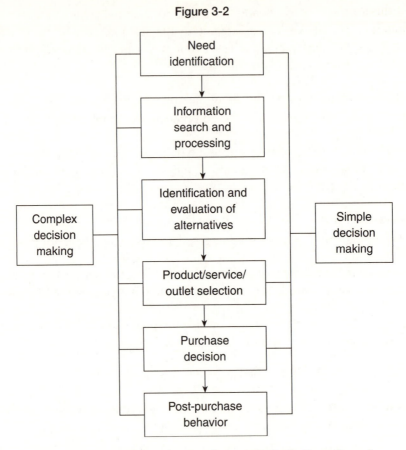

The consumer decision process. Consumers typically go through six possible stages in the decision process.

3.3.1 Stage 1: Need Identification

This first stage occurs when two conditions have been met:

▲ There's a big gap between what we have and what we want.
▲ The problem is seen as important.

So, if you want a new Cadillac and you own a 5-year-old Chevrolet, you may meet the first condition, but it may not be important compared to the other problems in your life, such as your need to fix the furnace this winter. But another person may have a car that is 2 years old and running great, but still considers it extremely important to purchase a car this year. Both conditions have to be resolved for the consumer to move to Stage 2.

At this stage, you may also have a problem, but not know how to fix it. If your problem is running out of toothpaste, you know that buying more is the solution. But what if your problem is more complicated, such as being dissatisfied with your professional appearance? You may not know how to go about fixing the problem until you are able to define the problem more specifically.

So where do marketers come in? They can help in the following ways:

▲ **Marketers find out what problems consumers face and develop solutions as part of their marketing mixes.** This involves measuring the extent of the problems.

▲ **Marketers help consumers recognize their problems.** For instance, public service announcements warn about smoking, or owners keep their stores open later.

▲ **Marketers help shape the definition of a need or problem.** Let's say a person needs a new coat. Will he define this problem as needing an inexpensive covering, needing a way to stay warm in cold temperatures, needing something that will last a long time, or needing something to express personal style? A salesperson or an ad can help him answer this question.

3.3.2 Stage 2: Information Search and Processing

To make a complicated buying decision, people need help. They need information to help identify and evaluate alternative products, services, and outlets that will meet their needs. Where does it come from?

▲ Family
▲ Friends
▲ Personal observation
▲ Publications such as *Consumer Reports*
▲ Salespeople
▲ Mass media

Marketers go to work providing information to consumers to both assist them, and to influence them to choose particular products.

Sometimes the consumer already has enough information. Maybe they've bought something like it before. Bad experiences and lack of satisfaction can destroy repeat purchases. But if you've bought tires that you liked before, you will probably go back to the same dealer and buy the same brand.

Information search can reveal new needs. As you research tires, you may realize that you really need a new car, not just tires. Then you will start a new search for information.

FOR EXAMPLE

Neuromarketing Probes the Consumer's Brain

A controversial new marketing approach, based on neuroscience, attempts to use electroencephalography (EEG) technology to understand people's brain waves while they are making purchasing decisions. *Business 2.0* magazine reports that companies such as Bridgestone, Hewlett-Packard, and others who refused to be publicly identified are using a British firm, Neuroco, to help understand consumers better with "neuromarketing." Subjects have their brain waves monitored while watching advertising or while shopping to see how colors, logos, and product features affect their brain activity. The technology, however, is limited to measuring attentiveness and attraction — researchers admit it cannot tell you whether somebody will actually buy. And consumer groups are already complaining to Congress about the "creepy" Orwellian intrusiveness of the research.

This process can be tiring and time consuming. People do it, however, because of the perceived benefits in saving money, getting a better selection, and reducing risks. The popularity of the Internet for shopping indicates the importance people place on getting information.

What do people do with the information they get while they're searching? How do they spot pertinent information, understand it, and recall what they've seen? This is the subject of information processing for marketers, and has been studied extensively. Some marketers are even trying to get inside customers' heads, turning to neuroscience for answers about subconscious processes.

Mostly marketers try to figure out how customers are reacting by observation and by interviewing, but it is hard to get good information on things hidden from view. The following is a widely accepted marketing theory of how people process information in five steps:

1. **Exposure:** There's a source of stimulation, such as a television advertisement, going to the supermarket, or getting direct mail at your house. Marketers must start the process.

2. **Attention:** Without attention, exposure doesn't do much. At any moment, people are being bombarded with all kinds of stimuli, but they can only process some of it. Marketers can provide relevant cues that will get the person's attention at this point.

3. **Perception:** You may process something you see, but what meaning do you attach to it? You may classify it as not relevant to your needs, and ignore it.

4. **Retention:** Heavy repetition and putting a message to music are two things marketers do to enhance retention. If you do not retain the message, you won't act on it later.

5. **Retrieval and application:** When you remember an ad you heard on the radio while you are in the supermarket, you are retrieving the information. If you consider buying the product using that information, you are applying the information to your decision.

What if you see an ad for cars, but you don't drive? You won't pay any attention. If you are in the market for a car, you will pay attention — but what if you want a sedan and the ad is for pickup trucks? The marketer has lost you at the perception stage. But if you do find the ad meaningful — say, you do drive a pickup but want to replace it—you are likely to retain the message. Retention is even more likely if you hear the ad repeatedly, and you remember that brand when you are reading about cars on the Internet and go to that company's Web site for more information on their trucks.

If you are really thinking about the information you receive, you are doing elaborate or central processing. But if you are barely paying attention, as when passengers ignore the flight attendant's speech, you are processing peripherally. Marketers want people to process the information actively, not passively.

3.3.3 Stage 3: Identification and Evaluation of Alternatives

After you've collected and processed information about a product or service, you will probably realize there are other options available to you. Depending on your finances and your psychological needs, you will evaluate these other options and make your choice.

How you evaluate will depend upon your priorities. Is price very important to you, or is quality or convenience? The search is heavily influenced by:

▲ Time and money cost.

▲ How much information you already have.

▲ The amount of perceived risk if a wrong selection is made.

▲ Your predisposition toward particular choices as influenced by your comfort level with the selection process. If you hate choosing, you will try to minimize your options quickly. If you enjoy it, you will keep collecting alternatives and processing information.

3.3.4 Stage 4: Product/Service/Outlet Selection

What if you decide which brand you want, then go to a convenient store, only to find that it's out of stock? At this point, you have to do more evaluating. You have to decide whether you will wait until the product comes in, accept a substitute, or go to another store. Sometimes you will pick the store first, and decide on the product after you get there.

3.3.5 Stage 5: The Purchase Decision

Finally, you are ready to buy. Anything marketers can do to simplify your purchase will be welcome. In their advertising they may suggest the best size for a particular use, or the right wine to drink with a particular food. Sometimes several decisions can be combined and marketed as one purchase. For example, package travel tours help you decide which airline to fly and which hotel room to buy simultaneously.

Marketers need to know answers to many questions about shopping behavior at this stage to be effective:

▲ How much effort is the consumer willing to spend shopping for the product? Will he spend his weekends driving to car dealerships, or will he do most of his research on-line?

▲ What factors influence when the consumer will actually purchase? Can you get someone to buy quickly by offering a coupon or other discount, or a product sample?

▲ Are there any conditions that would prohibit or delay purchase? If you do not have clear labels with price and product information, for instance, the consumer may leave the store in frustration.

3.3.6 Stage 6: Postpurchase Behavior

Why do marketers care about what happens after the purchase is made? They care because customer satisfaction can influence repeat sales and also influence what the customer tells others about the product or the brand.

Keeping the customer happy is what marketing is all about. Yet consumers typically experience some **postpurchase anxiety,** or buyer's remorse, after all but the most routine and inexpensive purchases. You may realize after purchasing something that you went against the recommendation of your good friend, and that creates dissonance in your mind. You trust her judgment. Or maybe some disturbing information came later, after the purchase. How do you resolve this *cognitive dissonance?*

Marketers take steps to reduce postpurchase dissonance by:

▲ Creating advertising that stresses the positive attributes of the product or confirms its popularity.

▲ Providing personalized reinforcement with big-ticket items such as cars and major appliances by sending cards or making follow-up personal calls.

SELF-CHECK

- Explain the difference between a need and a want, in marketing terms.
- What are the six stages of the consumer buying process?
- What do marketers do during need identification to help consumers?
- What two things do marketers do to reduce postpurchase dissonance?

3.4 The Organizational Buying Process

Organizations buy in a more formal way than consumers do, but many of the stages parallel those of the consumer decision process. Figure 3-3 shows the eight stages.

Most of the information an industrial buyer receives is from his or her direct contacts such as sales representatives or information packets. Information is provided to buyers at trade shows, but it's unlikely that they would use this information as the sole basis for a buying decision.

The complete process, described below, occurs only for a new task. For a rebuy or modified rebuy, not all stages are necessary.

1. **Problem recognition.** The process begins when someone in the organization recognizes a problem or need that can be met by acquiring a good or service. It can be stimulated from an outside source, such as a presentation by a salesperson, an ad, or information picked up at a trade show, or internally.

2. **General need description.** After they realize a need exists, the buyers must describe it. Working with engineers, users, purchasing agents, and others, the buyer identifies and prioritizes important product characteristics. Table 3-1 lists many sources of information used by industrial buyers. Trade advertising helps smaller or isolated customers. Public relations departments get stories placed in trade journals that industrial buyers read.

3. **Product specification.** Usually it is engineers who are responsible for putting together technical specifications for products. They'll design several alternatives, depending upon the priorities of the buyer.

4. **Supplier search.** The buyer now knows what he or she wants, in detail, so he or she begins looking for someone selling it. The appropriate vendor is found either in trade directories, through computer searches, or by phoning other companies for recommendations. Marketers can influence this stage

by contacting possible opinion leaders and getting support for their products or by contacting the buyer directly. Personal selling can seal the deal.

5. **Proposal solicitation.** Qualified suppliers are invited to submit proposals.
Some will send only a catalog or sales representative. Developing proposals
requires extensive research and skilled writing and presentation. Some proposals are even as detailed as complete marketing strategies in the consumer
sector.

Figure 3-3

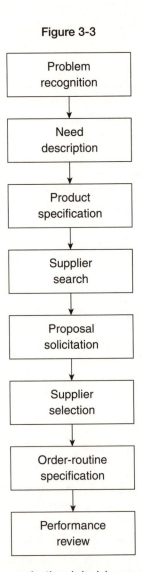

The organizational decision process.
Eight stages typically make up the
business buying decision.

6. **Supplier selection.** At this stage, buyers screen the various proposals and choose a supplier. Evaluating the vendor is critical — some purchasing managers feel the vendor is more important than the actual proposal. Important characteristics in a vendor are delivery capability, consistent quality, and fair price, depending on the buying situation.

7. **Order-routine specification.** The buyer writes the final order with the chosen supplier, listing the technical specifications, the quantity needed, the warranty, and so on.

8. **Performance review.** At the end of the process, the buyer reviews the supplier's performance, either formally or informally.

Table 3-1: Industrial Buyer Information Sources

Source	Description
Salespeople	Salespeople representing manufacturers or distributors
Technical sources	Engineers working either for the buyer or outside
Co-workers of buyer	Peer-group references, such as other purchasing agents
Purchasing agents from other companies	Peer-group references from outside
Trade associations	Groups of businesses formed to jointly address mutual problems
Advertising in trade journals	Commercial messages placed by suppliers
Articles in trade journals	Messages not under the control of buyer or seller
Vendor files	Information developed and maintained by buyer's company
Trade registers	Buyer guides providing listings of suppliers and other marketing information
Product literature	Specific product and vendor information supplied by seller

SELF-CHECK

- What are the eight stages of the organizational buying process?
- Are all the stages needed for a modified rebuy?
- What are the characteristics frequently looked for when choosing a supplier?

SUMMARY

External and internal factors, including demographic, lifestyle, and reference group, shape consumer buying behavior. Marketers try to predict consumer and organizational purchase patterns based on different buying factors. Organizational buying behavior has eight stages, which occur during a new buying task, but not for rebuys and modified rebuys.

KEY TERMS

Attitudes	A component of lifestyle.
Consumer socialization	How people learn about products and services by taking part in social interactions with other people.
Demographics	Statistics — such as age, gender, or income — that give information about a population.
High-involvement decision	A decision that is very important to you. It's tied up with your ego and self-image, and has financial, social, or psychological risk.
Lifestyle	A set of attitudes, interests, and opinions of the potential customer.
Low-involvement decision	A routine purchase — the opposite of a high-involvement decision.
Market offerings	The selection of goods and services available for purchase in the marketplace.
Need	A basic deficiency that is outside the marketer's control. You may need clothes, but you want to buy the Polo label.
Opinion leader	A person who is part of a reference group and sets the trends for buying behavior for the group.

Organizational marketing   Selling goods and services to consumers who are themselves in need of goods and services to run their own businesses.

Reference groups   An informal or formal group of people with whom you identify.

Socialization agent   A person who influences you.

Want   What marketers try to influence by trying to get the consumer to choose their product or service instead of someone else's.

ASSESS YOUR UNDERSTANDING

Go to www.wiley.com/college/Hiam to evaluate your knowledge of consumers. *Measure your learning by comparing pre-test and post-test results.*

Summary Questions

1. What is a high-involvement decision?
2. When a consumer buys something that is a routine purchase, this is called a straight rebuy. True or false?
3. Which factor do marketers find most useful when studying consumer buying decisions?
   (a) Lifestyle
   (b) Needs and desires
   (c) Motivation
   (d) Personality
4. Organizational buyer behavior differs from consumer behavior. Which statement is **not** true for organizations?
   (a) Behavior is motivated by both rational and emotional factors.
   (b) Lag time exists between contact and actual decision.
   (c) Organizations can be grouped into precise categories.
5. Supplier selection is the last stage of the industrial buyer decision process. True or false?
6. One of the most important kinds of learning to advertisers is
   (a) Rational factors
   (b) Personality
   (c) Socialization
7. A decision influencer is a person with whom you identify. True or false?
8. Organizational buying decisions generally take longer than consumer buying decisions. True or false?
9. The business buying decision requires that buyers go through all of the stages. True or false?

Review Questions

1. Explain why consumer socialization matters to marketers.
2. Why are opinion leaders important for marketers to identify?
3. How is organizational purchasing different from consumer buying? List three differences.

Applying This Chapter

1. Explain why marketers use a consumer's lifestyle to understand buying behavior more than they use a consumer's motivation and personality.
2. Show the steps of a consumer buying decision. Under what circumstances are Stages 2 and 3 skipped over?
3. Explain how marketers help to shape the buying decision for new cars. Name one thing they might do at each decision stage to influence the consumer to buy their products.
4. What assumption about people in their 50s and older are marketers now questioning, because of the Baby Boomers? What do you think is the likely future strategy from marketers?

Marketing Knowledge

You have put together some instructional videos that you think would be great for use in the classroom, although you have never been a teacher or worked in a school. Your goal is to become a leading vendor for educational videos, so you attend some educational conferences, hoping to interest teachers and schools in your products. What are some of the questions you need answered in order to successfully market your products? What do you need to know about your market?

Buying Decisions

What are some products that you think can be successfully marketed to a married couple who have no children? How do you imagine that couple to be different from an empty-nester couple in terms of its buying decisions?

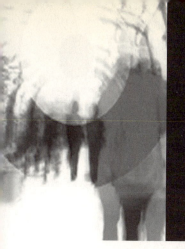

4

SEGMENTING AND TARGETING MARKETS
Finding Your Audience

Starting Point

Go to www.wiley.com/college/Hiam to assess your knowledge of the basics of targeting an audience.
Determine where you need to concentrate your effort.

What You'll Learn in This Chapter

▲ The advantages of segmenting markets
▲ Different strategies and segmentation types
▲ Various bases for segmentation

After Studying This Chapter, You'll Be Able To

▲ Differentiate between consumer and business segmenting
▲ Compare a concentration strategy to an undifferentiated strategy
▲ Discriminate between key segmentation factors and those that aren't as significant

Goals and Outcomes

▲ Judge whether a segment is a viable market
▲ Select appropriate segments to target, based on criteria
▲ Model a five-step process to target a market

INTRODUCTION

Segmenting and targeting markets is a common marketing strategy. Markets are segmented according to different bases. Business is also segmented into markets, but the bases are different from consumer segmentation. After you've segmented your market, you can use your marketing to target that segment.

4.1 Segmenting Markets

A **market-segmentation strategy** is a specialization strategy in which you target and cater to (specialize in) just one narrow type or group of customer. Segmenting and targeting markets concentrates your resources efficiently, so you can market your product narrowly.

Of the three strategic approaches to the market listed here,

▲ Undifferentiated
▲ Segmented
▲ Combination

the segmentation strategy is the primary marketing approach used today. Why? In today's global markets, it's very difficult to treat the market as a vast, homogeneous group. In this chapter we'll look at which types of products are marketed using which types of strategies.

First we'll clarify what we mean by **market**. A market is a group of potential buyers with needs and wants and the purchasing power to satisfy them.

If you focus on the market as people, you need those people to meet certain criteria to be a viable market that you can sell to:

▲ They must have a true need and/or want for the product, service, or idea.
▲ The person/organization must be able to pay for the product in a way the marketer accepts.
▲ They must be willing to buy the product.
▲ They must have the authority to buy the product.
▲ The total number of people/organizations meeting the previous criteria must be large enough to be profitable for the marketer.

If you study the list above, you can see that failing to meet even one of them means you won't have a market. In the pharmaceutical industry, for instance, some serious diseases remain sadly uncured because a large enough group of people haven't contracted them. The cost of research to develop these drugs would not be justified by the size of the market. Although the first four criteria may be met, a small potential customer base means no viable market exists.

4.1.1 Succeeding with the Undifferentiated Market

For certain types of widely consumed items such as gasoline, milk, and bread, it makes sense to approach the market as undifferentiated. An **undifferentiated market** is one in which nearly everyone consumes these products, and they are perceived as almost identical. Walk through any supermarket and you will see hundreds of food products that are perceived as nearly identical by the consumer and treated as such by the producer — especially knock-off or generic items.

Assuming that the mass market is your market can be risky because the general marketing approach you will take with your product or service may wind up appealing to no one, and you will waste resources, rather than gain sales. This strategy applies if:

▲ You have a very large market share.

▲ Your product has universal appeal.

▲ You stay alert to and respond to constant changes in the mass market in values, attitudes, and beliefs.

▲ Cultural differences in your market do not weaken your appeal too much with different groups.

4.1.2. Differentiating Your Product in an Undifferentiated Market

How do you compete in the mass market if all the product offerings are basically the same and many companies are in fierce competition? You engage in **product differentiation,** or the attempt to distinguish your product in some tangible or intangible way from that of all the others in the eyes of customers.

Examples of tangible differences might be product features, performance, endurance, location, or support services. Chrysler once differentiated its product by offering a 7-year/70,000-mile warranty on new models. Offering products at a lower price or at several different prices can be an important distinguishing characteristic, as demonstrated by Timex watches. If you are Pepsi, you try to convince customers you taste better than Coke. If you are the number two company in your market, you try to convince people that you try harder or that you represent a real improvement over number one.

What if your product, is, alas, the same as your competitor's product? Smart marketers know how to create the image of difference by showing intangible benefits such as:

▲ How much fun you can have with the product

▲ How much status you will gain by having it

▲ How much more masculine or feminine you'll feel by using it

---

FOR EXAMPLE

Gateway Learns a Lesson about Differentiation

Personal computer maker Gateway, with its immediately recognizable black and white Holstein cow logo and packaging, has a successful mail-order and Internet business, and may have seemed a natural for a retail presence. But when it ventured into retail with 322 "Country Stores," consumers yawned. According to *Business 2.0* magazine (October 2005), Gateway closed its stores in 2004 after realizing that, unlike Apple Computer, its offerings weren't different enough to draw customers to a dedicated store. The shops were designed to educate customers, but Gateway learned the average personal computer user didn't need to try before he or she would buy. Now Gateway's back to selling directly and through electronics retailers, where consumers can comparison shop with Dell and other similar offerings.

What are the risks of using product differentiation? Done poorly, you can cause more harm than good to your brand's image. The following are some caveats:

▲ Do not lose sight of your most important features when differentiating on secondary features. If your bread has unique nutritional qualities, that's great, but do not forget to retain the core "freshness" feature in your advertising.

▲ Do not highlight features that are too different from the norm. It may not be effective.

▲ Do not differentiate on features that are unimportant to the customer or too difficult to understand. If the consumer has to work too hard to understand the technical aspect of your product, rather than what that technical aspect can actually do for them, drop it.

4.1.3 Strategizing with a Segmented Market

You cannot always be all things to all people, so segmentation happens. If you are in the consulting business, you can specialize in for-profit businesses, or you can specialize in not-for-profits. You can even design and market your services to individuals — as, for example, a career-development consultant does. Each of these types of customers represents a subgroup, or segment, of the larger consulting industry.

You can drill down even further to define smaller segments if you want. You can specialize in consulting to the health-care industry, or to manufacturers of boxes and packaging, or to start-up firms in the high-tech sector. Certain consultants use each of these strategies to narrow down their markets.

The advantage of a segmentation strategy is that it allows you to tailor your product and your entire marketing effort to a clearly defined group with uniform, specific characteristics. For example, the consulting firm that targets only the health-care industry knows that prospective clients can be found at a handful of health-care industry conferences and that they have certain common concerns around which consulting services can be focused. Many smaller consulting firms target a narrowly defined market segment in order to compete against larger, but less specialized, consulting firms. See Figure 4-1 for a comparison of a large consulting company's strategy with a small consultancy.

You may think segmenting your market will make you lose out on lots of potential customers who have bulging wallets, ready to buy your product. Yet reasons to segment your market exist that make it a much better strategy for many small and large businesses:

▲ Use the segmentation strategy if you think your business can be more profitable by specializing in a more narrowly defined segment than you do now. This works well when you face too many competitors in your broader market and you cannot seem to carve out a stable, profitable customer base of your own.

▲ Also segment your market if it will enable you to take better advantage of things you are good at. It goes along well with the idea of focusing better, based on your unique qualities or strengths. (See Section 1.2.1.)

Figure 4-1

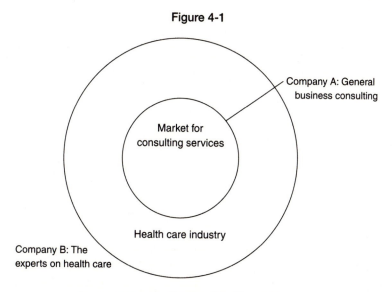

Large versus small consulting firm strategies.

This figure illustrates the example from earlier in the chapter. A small consultancy is represented by a segment within a circle that is labeled "Market for consulting services." The segment is maybe one fourth of the circle and is labeled "Health care industry." The larger consultancy is represented by the entire circle. The companies are named Company A: General business consulting and Company B: The experts on health care.

A larger consulting firm may go for the entire market, and a smaller firm may choose to specialize in one segment — health care consulting.

4.1.4 Methods of Segmenting Markets

Segmentation is a process that does not stop once you do it. Markets are very dynamic and products change, so segments are always changing also. When you analyze your potential segments, you need to consider these objectives:

▲ To reduce risk in deciding where, when, how, and to whom a product service or brand will be marketed

▲ To increase marketing efficiency by directing your effort toward the specific segment in a manner that matches that segment's characteristics

The way you segment your market will depend upon whether you are targeting businesses or consumers, or whether you are looking at their characteristics or at their purchase situations. Table 4-1 shows the possible bases for market segmentation, including consumer and business markets.

Table 4-1: Bases for Segmenting Consumer and Business Markets

Primary Dimension Market	Consumer	Business Market
Characteristics	Geography, age, sex, race, income, life cycle, personality, lifestyle	Industry, location, size, technology, profitability, legal, buying situation
Purchase situation	Purpose, benefits, purchase approach, choice criteria, brand loyalty, importance	Volume, frequency, application, choice criteria, purchasing procedure, importance

SELF-CHECK

- Define **market segmentation strategy, market, undifferentiated market, and product differentiation.**
- List the criteria for a viable market.
- Give an advantage of using a segmentation strategy.

4.2 Segmentation Factors

If you are selling to consumers, you'll want to take into account everything about your prospects that may make them want to buy your product or service — from their personality and lifestyle, to which brands they are loyal to and to how they make their purchase choices. We'll consider the following factors that might make up a potential market segment:

- ▲ Geography
- ▲ Demographics
- ▲ Usage
- ▲ Psychological factors

The importance of demographic features to marketing research is also discussed in Section 5.2, and demographics in relation to knowing consumers in Section 3.1 . Here we'll talk about all four, in turn.

4.2.1 Geographic Segments

Markets according to location are easily identified and form one of the oldest bases for segmentation. The problem is that regional differences may not hold true for everyone in the United States. People are increasingly geographically mobile, so the stereotypical Texan, for example, is hard to find in Houston, where one third of the population has immigrated from other states. Ethnic origins and income may overshadow geographic factors.

Domestic and foreign segments are the broadest type of geographic segment. Also, conditions such as weather; topography; and physical factors such as rivers, mountains, or oceans affect the purchase of many products. So does high humidity, flooding, snow, or cold.

Population density can create its own segment. High-density places such as California, New York, and Hong Kong need products such as security systems, fast-food restaurants, and public transportation.

The advantages of segmenting by geography are convenience and efficiency. Products, salespeople, and distribution networks can all be organized around a central location.

4.2.2 Demographic Segments

The youth market buys toys, records, snack foods, and video games, and also influences their parents' purchases. Senior citizens buy items such as low-cost housing, cruises, hobbies, and health care. Gender has been of use for some products, but is now changing as sex roles are changing. Women who work outside the home may get the car serviced or do other traditionally male tasks. Marketers have to be careful about assuming who makes what purchases in the home these days.

Marketers study the family life cycle to determine purchasing needs of families, based upon their stage of life. A young couple with one young child will have far different purchasing needs than a couple in their late 50s with no children at home. Newly married couples consume different products than families and singles.

Income is important because it dictates who can or cannot afford a particular product. For example, someone earning minimum wage cannot easily purchase a $30,000 sports car. Especially as the price of an item rises, income becomes more important as a segmentation tool. It also predicts buyer behavior such as coupon usage.

Some other demographic bases for segmenting markets:

▲ **Education:** Affects product preferences and characteristics demanded.
▲ **Occupation:** Physical laborers may want entirely different products than teachers, although their incomes may be similar.
▲ **Geographic mobility:** People who move often, such as military or corporate executives, have to change their shopping habits and may be less loyal to brands than others.
▲ **Race and national origin:** Market research has identified differences in preferences of blacks and Hispanics, for example, for food, transportation, and entertainment.
▲ **Religion:** Christians, Jews, and Muslims have different patterns.

Demographics can be misused. If you try to construct a typical "profile" of product users, you may be missing many people. The typical consumer of Mexican food is under 35 years old, has a college education, earns more than $10,000 a year, resides in the West, and lives in a suburban fringe of a moderate-sized urban community. Yet how useful is this profile? Consider that it also describes a lot of other consumers as well, and leaves out many Mexican food lovers who are older, live in cities, and reside in the South and the East.

4.2.3 Usage Segments

Frequent users, people who consume something heavily, are another popular target for marketers. The actual reasons that people buy something often is of great use and interest to marketers, not just the fact that they're frequent users. Marketers further segment people according to their buying habits like this:

▲ **Purchase occasion:** Why somebody goes on an airline trip or makes a long-distance call.

▲ **User status:** New car buyers, for example, need a great deal of supportive information. Regular users are different from one-time users, and nonusers are different from ex-users of a product.

▲ **Brand loyalty:** The brand-loyal consumer is the marketer's ideal target, although marketers are unsure how to measure brand loyalty.

▲ **Stage of readiness:** Customers can be segmented as either unaware, aware, informed, interested, desirous, or intending to buy. Different strategies will apply, although how to measure this dimension, like brand loyalty, is also uncertain.

4.2.4 Psychological Segments

You try to appeal to consumers' psychological needs and desires in your marketing, and groups of people with common needs form effective psychological segments. More on psychological influences is found in Section 3.1.1. Marketers seek to segment consumers, psychologically speaking, in several ways.

▲ **Attitudes:** Predispositions to behave in certain ways in response to a given stimulus.

Attitudes of prospective buyers toward certain products influence whether they buy or not. Marketers also look at personality, but research has not shown much promise in this area. Yet there are certain trends that advertisers can count on: Extroverts dress conspicuously, for example, and the newly rich spend disproportionately more on housing and cars.

▲ **Motives:** A buying motive, or reason for behavior, triggers purchasing activity.

Marketers would like to get right down to this level in segmenting the market, because it seems to be what market segmentation is really getting at. In other words, demographics, personality, and attitudes all seem to create buying motives. Both positive motives such as convenience and negative motives such as fear of injury seem to directly influence purchasing behavior. If marketers could get to motives, a difficult thing to pin down, they could segment effectively.

▲ **Lifestyle:** A pattern of attitudes, interests, and opinions held by a person.

Lifestyle studies focus on how people spend their money, their work and leisure patterns, their major interests, social and political opinions, and opinions about themselves and social institutions. This is a very popular way of segmenting because it's easy to measure.

Several research firms specialize entirely in this area. SRI International has developed a system, VALS 2, that is often used by marketers. It segments consumers into eight psychological stances, based on 43 questions, and works with businesses to help them use its system to segment their markets. The groups are arranged vertically by their financial situations and horizontally by their self-orientations. See Figure 4-2.

FOR EXAMPLE

The Good Driver

Do you consider yourself a good driver? Insurance companies such as Allstate Insurance have their own ideas about what makes a good driver, based on lifestyle criteria. Why? They want to target this person to offer him or her lower insurance rates. This is an example of lifestyle segmenting. If companies such as Allstate can figure out which drivers are the least likely to have car accidents, they can save money on claims. That's the reason these companies have been able to isolate and to offer this customer, "the good driver," a break on premiums.

Figure 4-2

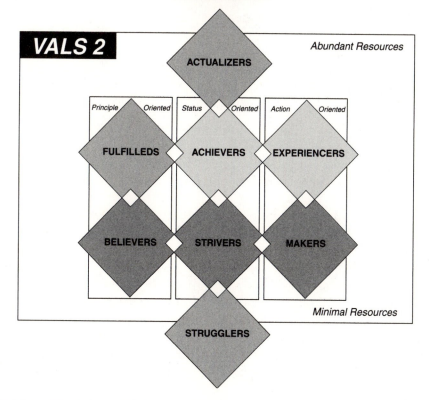

Lifestyle segmentation. VALS 2 is a commonly used consumer segmentation technique.

4.3 Segmenting Businesses

Of course, your business may not sell to consumers at all, but to other businesses. Segmentation also works for business-to-business marketers. Business buyers differ from consumers in a few ways:

▲ Most view their function from a rational (problem-solving) approach.
▲ Business buyers try to develop formal procedures or routines to simplify their buying.
▲ They have multiple purchase influences.
▲ Business buyers are buying to maintain the correct assortment of goods in inventory.
▲ The purchasing executive is responsible for disposing of waste and scrap.

These types of businesses, also known as industrial firms, must know how to segment in different industries.

4.3.1 Segmenting Business Customers

Some ways of segmenting business customers are

▲ Type of customer
▲ Standard Industrial Classification
▲ End uses
▲ Common buying factors
▲ Buyer size and geography

Customers, the group you are selling to, and industrial products, or what you are selling, can all be put into different groups. Customers will be either:

▲ **Original equipment manufacturers (OEMs),** such as Caterpillar in the road equipment industry
▲ **End users,** such as farmers who use farm machinery produced by John Deere and OEMs

Both OEMs and end users need machinery and equipment (computers, trucks, bulldozers). Materials (chemicals, metals, herbicides) are consumed in end-user products and thus are sold only to OEMs and end users. **Aftermarket customers** are those who purchase spare parts for a piece of machinery. Components and subassemblies (switches, pistons, machine tool parts) are sold to build and repair machinery and equipment and are sold to all three types.

North American Industry Classification System, or NAICS, codes are published by the United States government and classify business firms by the main product or service that they provide. Firms are classified in 20 broad sectors of the economy. The major groups of industries can be identified by the first two numbers of the NAICS code. For instance, number 52 classifies the finance and insurance sector.

Several publications help the business marketer find which manufacturers produce which products. Examples are:

▲ *Dun's Market Identifiers*
▲ *Metalworking Directory*
▲ *Thomas Register of American Manufacturers*
▲ *Survey of Industrial Purchasing Power*

Another way to segment business markets is by how the products are used by the end user. Typically, a cost-benefit analysis is done for each end-use application. So you would ask what benefits the customer wants from this product.

For example, an electric motor manufacturer learned that customers operated motors at different speeds. After making field visits to learn more about the situation, he divided the market into slow-speed and high-speed segments. For the slow-speed segment, he marketed a competitively priced product with a maintenance advantage, whereas in the high-speed market, superiority was emphasized.

Another approach is to identify groups of customers who consider the same buying factors important. This can be difficult, because people's priorities change all the time. In general, five buying factors are common:

▲ Service
▲ Delivery
▲ Price
▲ Product performance
▲ Product quality

Buyer size and geography are possible buying factors when the previously discussed ones have been ruled out. You can base your segments on geographic boundaries or by the size of accounts the business has with you. Sales managers have done this for years, but only recently have organizations learned how to develop different pricing strategies for customers that are both close and far away, and of different sizes.

4.3.2 Multibase Segmentation

Large organizations with large markets may not be able to make do with just one base for segmenting their markets. Gender, age, and income, for instance, provide valuable insights into who uses what products. But these factors may not be precise enough to segment an entire market.

Multibase segmentation strategies were created to further narrow down markets. The housing market is one example of multibase segmentation. The types of housing are so varied that within these types the housing market can be further segmented by family size, income, and age. (See Figure 4-3.)

American Log Home, for instance, offers a wide variety of packages and options to its customers based on their needs, incomes, skills, family size, and usage. These packages range from one-room shelters designed mostly for hunters to a 4,000-square-foot unit complete with a hot tub, chandeliers, and three decks. Customers who are do-it-yourselfers can choose to finish part of the interior or part of the exterior. Those who have the resources and do not want to do the work can pay to have the entire structure finished by American Log Home.

The benefit of multibase segmentation is an increased ability to target markets, but the drawback is that to succeed at such complex segmentation requires offering a great many options to customers.

Figure 4-3

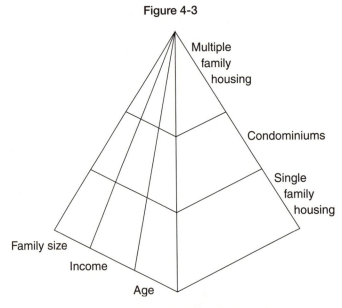

Multibase segmentation in the housing industry.

The housing industry offers choices to different types of families, within segments for types of housing.

4.4 Targeting Your Market

Segmenting is the primary marketing approach used by the majority of producers. Once a process by which one or more target markets, or segments, are chosen from the rest, and you have learned about the market and decided on the approach you want to take toward it, you will want to think about targeting markets. **Targeting markets** is a process by which one or more target markets, or segments, are chosen from the rest.

Figure 4-4 shows the general steps in this process.

Product differentiation and market segmentation make up the most common modern marketing strategies. Even makers of soft drinks — generally considered a mass-market product — are segmenting their markets now by introducing diet, caffeine-free, and diet caffeine-free versions of their basic product.

Figure 4-4

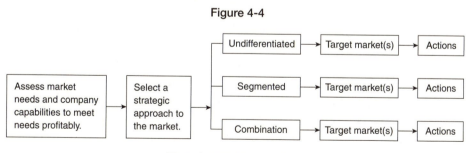

Steps in targeting markets.

Although it is relatively easy to identify segments of consumers, most firms do not have the capabilities or the need to effectively market to every segment that can be identified. The process has two steps:

1. Identifying and classifying people into homogenous groupings, or segments
2. Determining which of the segments are viable target markets

Strangely enough, the first step may, in practice, consist of identifying only one person. This is because the process requires the marketer to reduce the market to its smallest components, then to find common dimensions that will allow those components to be part of larger, profitable segments.

For example, when you think about going out on your own and marketing your services, you may have only one person or potential customer in mind who can be considered to represent your ideal target customer. Then you think about who else fits that mold — who else is like your existing, actual customer, and can you get enough of them for you to make a go of your business? Maybe there are thousands of people in your geographic area who are similar to your customer, let's say a profitable small business owner who is computer savvy, but strapped for time.

So, now you've targeted your market, beginning with identifying a single person. Then you want to tailor your marketing activities with this target market in mind. That's after you do step two, determining which segments are viable target markets.

4.4.1 Qualifying Customers in Segments

Once you've segmented your markets, you want to think about whether the customers you've identified as part of those segments are really viable customers. Will they actually buy?

You have to judge whether they are real prospects who are likely to buy or people who may fit into a segment because they have similar characteristics, but are not likely to be converted into purchasers of your product or service.

Not all market segments are created equal. Here are five criteria traditionally used to gauge the worth of a market segment:

1. **Clarity of identification:** Can you actually identify who is in a segment? Gender is obviously a simple classification to identify, but what about psychological characteristics? Obtaining data can be a challenge.
2. **Actual or potential need:** You need to be able to measure the intensity of the need for something. For example, a 40-story building has a clear need for elevators. The need must exist in a large enough quantity to justify a separate segmentation strategy.
3. **Effective demand:** For this to exist, there must be a need and the purchasing power to satisfy the need. Ability to buy means the customer must have

income, savings, or credit. The possession of a valid credit card meets the criteria for most products.

4. **Economic accessibility:** The people in a segment must be reachable and profitable. For instance, they could be concentrated geographically, shop at the same stores, or read the same magazines. Many important segments, those based on motivational characteristics in particular, cannot be reached economically. The affluent elderly are such a segment.

5. **Positive response:** A segment must react uniquely to marketing efforts. You need a reason to market differently to your segments. Otherwise why would you go to all the trouble of designing a separate marketing program for each of them?

4.4.2 Concentrating on One Segment

A **concentration strategy** targets only one segment of the market. For this strategy, you will only develop one marketing mix. Rolex, for instance, only concentrates on the luxury segment of the watch market. Other companies go after the mass market.

An organization that adopts a concentration strategy gains an advantage by being able to analyze the needs and wants of only one segment and then focusing all its efforts on that segment. This gives you a differential advantage over other companies that market to this segment but do not concentrate all their efforts on it.

The drawback is that if demand in that particular segment declines, you have to readjust your marketing quickly or you will lose your customer base. You have, as the saying goes, all your eggs in one basket.

4.4.3 Adding a Segment to Expand Your Market

If you are running out of customers and market and need to expand (see the "Growing with a Market-Expansion Strategy" in Section 2.1.1), one way to do it is to decide to target a new segment. **Multisegment strategy** is targeting a new, unreached segment of your market.

For example, the consultant specializing in coaching executives in the health-care industry could decide to start offering a similar service to not-for-profits. See Figure 4-5.

A different approach and marketing program will be needed, because the two industries are different in many ways and have only partial overlap (some hospitals are not-for-profits, but many not-for-profits are not hospitals). By specializing in two segments instead of just one, the consulting firm may be able to grow its total sales significantly.

Figure 4-5

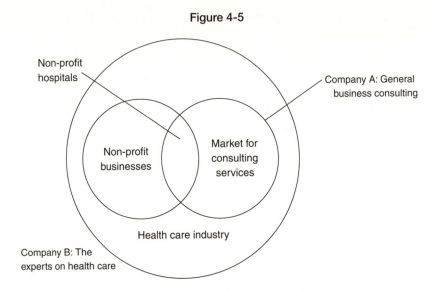

Adding another segment to your market.

Therefore, following this approach will likely have two outcomes:

▲ An increase in total sales, which you want, because of the extra customers you are attracting
▲ An increase in marketing costs, which you do not want, but is necessary to maintain distinct marketing programs

Targeting a new segment allows you to expand your business but requires new marketing activities.

4.4.4 Selecting a Target Market

Why bother going through the whole process of segmenting your market? The answer is to target your market or markets. If you do not use this information to select a target market, the segmentation process is worthless.

Selecting a target market has five steps:

1. Identify relevant personal or organizational and purchase situation variables other than the core product variable. For a type of camera, the core product variable would be fool-proof photographs, and other relevant variables might be age, income, family composition, occasion for use, and photographic experience.
2. Collect and analyze other related data about potential segments, for instance, characteristics of beginner camera users, price perceptions of potential users, size of group, trends, and minimum product features.

3. Apply criteria of a good segment.

4. Pick one or more segments as target markets. In this example, you might choose the following: beginning photographers, frustrated with necessary adjustments for 35 mm cameras, income of $35,000 or more, have a family, between 25 and 45 years old, male.

5. Develop appropriate action programs to reach target segment or segments. Some actions you might take for this group are as follows: price at $350; distribute through discount stores, camera stores, and department stores; promote through television and magazine ads.

4.4.5 Positioning Your Product or Service

If you have created a new model and make of car, you have to give a great deal of thought and consideration to how you will position the car with your advertising and marketing. **Positioning** is designing the company's offering and image to occupy a distinctive place in the target market's mind.

That's part of Step 5 from the previous section. (More on positioning as a marketing strategy can be found in Section 2.1.4 .)

The competition in the auto industry is fierce and you need to think about who is the most likely prospect to buy your car. Is it families with young children? Or is it young single males? You'll market a car with extensive safety features differently than a sports car with a gas-guzzling engine.

A strong positioning effort begins with the use of two things:

▲ Product differentiation

▲ Market segmentation

FOR EXAMPLE

Rolling Rock Finds Its Niche

On each bottle of Rolling Rock beer, a bold but simple "33" stands out. Plain white on the green glass, the number sits squarely below a block of type. Since 1939, when the brew from Latrobe, Pennsylvania, debuted, that "33" has been capturing consumers' imaginations. Fans steadily wrote to ask what it meant. Yet Rolling Rock had a blue-collar image and faltering sales until 1987 when Labatt's USA acquired Latrobe Brewing, repositioning it as a superpremium brand and using the "33" to link its long history, distinctive packaging, and special aura. Sales rose and the beer's primary audience is now a 21- to 35-year-old, white-collar male earning $40,000 or more. By targeting a segment that wanted a superpremium, unique brand, Rolling Rock has been successful.

These two elements define, as we said earlier, contemporary marketing strategies. Your advertising and marketing program in general will take its cues from the decisions you make about how to differentiate your product from its competition and how to segment your market.

SELF-CHECK

- Define **targeting, market concentration strategy, multisegment strategy, and positioning**.
- What are five criteria for gauging the viability of a marketing segment?
- List the five steps for selecting a target market.
- Which kind of strategy focuses all your efforts on one segment?

SUMMARY

Segmenting markets creates opportunities to target your audience efficiently. Businesses use different segmentation factors than consumer marketers do. Consumer markets can be segmented by internal or external bases. Different segments require different marketing programs. Qualifying customers in segments is necessary before targeting those segments.

KEY TERMS

Aftermarket customer	Those who purchase spare parts for a piece of machinery.
Attitudes	Predispositions to behave in certain ways in response to a given stimulus.
Concentration strategy	Targeting only one segment of the market.
End user	Those who purchase products produced by OEMs.
Lifestyle	A pattern of attitudes, interests, and opinions held by a person.
Market	A group of potential buyers with needs and wants and the purchasing power to satisfy them.
Market-expansion strategy	Gaining new customers.
Market-segmentation strategy	Breaking up your market into different segments.

Motives	A reason for behavior that triggers purchasing activity.
Multibase segmentation	Segmenting your market, using more than one basis.
Multisegment strategy	Targeting a new, unreached segment of your market.
NAICS codes	North American Industry Classification System codes, published by the United States government, to classify business firms by the main product or service that they provide.
OEM	Original equipment manufacturer.
Positioning	Designing the company's offering and image to occupy a distinctive place in the target market's mind.
Product differentiation	The attempt to distinguish your product in some tangible or intangible way from that of all the others in the eyes of customers.
Targeting markets	A process by which one or more target markets, or segments, are chosen from the rest.
Undifferentiated market	One in which nearly everyone consumes products that are perceived as almost identical.

ASSESS YOUR UNDERSTANDING

Go to www.wiley.com/college/Hiam to evaluate your knowledge of the basics of targeting an audience.
Measure your learning by comparing pre-test and post-test results.

Summary Questions

1. Which of the following is needed for selling to the undifferentiated market?
   (a) Universal appeal
   (b) Five percent of the market
   (c) Market research about each segment
2. It's possible to differentiate your product if it's the same as your competitor's. True or false?
3. Name the four major bases for consumer segmentation.
   (a) Demographics, lifestyle, usage, and personality
   (b) Demographics, life cycle, usage, and psychological factors
   (c) Geography, income, lifestyle, and personality
   (d) Demographics, geography, usage, and psychological factors
4. Usage segments look at demographic factors of the market. True or false?
5. Which of these is **not** a step in selecting your target market?
   (a) Apply criteria of a good segment.
   (b) Differentiate your product.
   (c) Collect and analyze data.
6. Using the NAICS codes helps manufacturers find customers and markets. True or false?
7. Common buying factors include
   (a) Price, quality, and income
   (b) Price, delivery, and service
   (c) Quality, performance, and account size
   (d) Price, quality, and account size
8. People with similar motivations can comprise a viable market segment. True or false?
9. Rolex watches are marketed with the use of a concentration strategy. True or false?
10. When you are using a multisegment strategy, you can keep your costs down by using the same approach and program. True or false?

Review Questions

1. Name four circumstances in which selling to the undifferentiated market may not be such a good idea.
2. VALS 2 was created in order to segment which factor of the consumer market?
3. What are the five criteria of a good market segment?
4. What is the essential pitfall of a concentration strategy?

Applying This Chapter

1. You are considering the common buying factors of your customers in order to segment them into target markets. What questions would you need answered about your market for cleaning services? (Assume you are selling to other businesses, not households.)
2. Describe a likely target group for each of the following products — high-performance tires, frozen waffles, exercise equipment, lumber.
3. You have invented a hiking boot that not only looks fashionable, but has a few high-performance features that you believe serious hikers are seeking. How do you target your market for this product? What is the core product variable for the boot?

YOU TRY IT

Segmentation Strategies

In the For Example section about Rolling Rock in this chapter, what are the potential problems with the segmentation strategy employed by Labatt's USA's advertising agency? Discuss other possible bases for segmentation that Rolling Rock could have used.

Sharpening Your Marketing

You've just acquired the patent for a new type of knife, one that stays razor sharp without ever needing sharpening. Unfortunately, at least one obstacle stands in the way of your success. This great invention requires the use of a mineral in its production process that's extremely rare and, thus, expensive. How would you market this product and why? Does it meet the criteria for having a viable market?

5

MARKETING RESEARCH
Learning about Your Markets

Starting Point

Go to www.wiley.com/college/Hiam to assess your knowledge of the basics of marketing research.
Determine where you need to concentrate your effort.

What You'll Learn in This Chapter

▲ Effective ways to conduct market research
▲ Primary and secondary research methods
▲ The difference between quantitative and qualitative methods

After Studying This Chapter, You'll Be Able To

▲ Identify your research questions
▲ Analyze the best way to obtain information
▲ Listen to your customers to solve their problems
▲ Determine whether market research is necessary

Goals and Outcomes

▲ Compare research methods
▲ Assess the significance of customer data
▲ Specify your information needs before doing research

INTRODUCTION

In this chapter, you will find out how to gain an understanding of your customers and competitors, and in the process, better understand your own product. Analyzing your research needs leads to better decision making. Market research can help you clarify your strategy, make more accurate sales projections, and better focus your marketing program. Simple market-research techniques need not be costly for the average marketer.

5.1 Primary Research

A little research can go a long way toward improving the effectiveness of your marketing, yet 1 percent of companies do 90 percent of the market research. Big businesses hire research firms to do extensive customer surveys and to run discussion groups with customers. This traditional approach is expensive, but you can also learn much about your market with some relatively simple and efficient ways of learning about customers and competitors. As a marketer, you need to ask questions and seek useful answers, something you can do on any budget.

Primary research gathers data from people in answers to questions. In general, this type of research gathers data by observing people to see how they behave or by asking them for verbal or written answers to questions. Research methods can be either:

▲ **Quantitative**: Data are generated through sampling — by telephone, face-to-face, or through the mail. Statistical analysis is used to come up with the numbers, charts, and graphs of your research. Data can be gathered through survey research or experimental methods. Quantitative research gives you a broad look at whatever you are researching. It's good for answering, "What's happening?"

▲ **Qualitative**: Data are gathered through personal interviews, observations, or **focus groups** (potential or actual customers who discuss your product while a trained moderator guides their conversation). Open-ended questions are usually the main emphasis of qualitative methods, and qualitative methods are excellent for getting a deep look at your data and discovering things you may not have expected. It helps in answering, "Why is it happening?"

5.1.1 Observation

Years ago, managers from the Boston Aquarium wanted to find out which attractions were most popular. They hired a researcher to develop a survey, but the researcher told them not to bother. Instead, he suggested they examine the floors for wear and for tracks on wet days. The evidence pointed clearly to certain attractions as most popular. The floors in front of those attractions had the most wear. And damp paths led to the attractions that visitors preferred to go to first.

Observation is the most underrated of all research methods. Yet consumers are all around you — shopping for, buying, and using products. Observing consumers is not hard. And even **business-to-business marketers** (who sell to other businesses instead of end consumers) can find plenty of evidence about their customers at a glance. The number and direction of a company's trucks on various roads can tell you where their business is heaviest and lightest, for example. Despite all the opportunities to observe, most marketers are guilty of Sherlock Holmes's accusation that "You have not observed, and yet you have seen."

Find a way to observe one of your customers as she uses one of your products. Learn to observe, not just watch. Bring along a pad and pencil, and take care to notice the little things. What does the customer do, in what order, and how long does she spend doing it? What does she say, if anything? Does she look happy? Frustrated? Uninterested? Does anything go wrong? Does anything go right — is she surprised with how well the product performs? Take detailed notes and then think about them. You will gain at least one insight into how to improve your product.

5.1.2 Survey Research Methods

The first — and most important — step in any research effort is to ask a penetrating question. **Survey research** is the bread and butter of the marketing research industry, and for a good reason. You can often gain something of value just by asking people what they think. The survey methods do have their shortcomings. Customers do not always know what they think or how they behave. And even when they do, getting them to tell you can be quite costly. Nonetheless, every marketer finds good uses for survey research.

If your product makes customers happy, those customers come back. If not, adios. And because recruiting new customers costs anywhere from 4 to 20 times as much as retaining old ones (depending on your industry), you cannot afford to lose customers, which means you cannot afford to dissatisfy them. So every marketer needs to measure and set goals for customer satisfaction.

If you work for one of the two-thirds majority of businesses that don't increase their customers' satisfaction each year, you need to get cracking. And the best whip to crack is a customer-satisfaction measure that portrays your company or product in a realistic light (you can measure with survey questions or with the rate of customer complaints; the best measures combine multiple sources of data into an overall index). After this measure gets reported to everyone on a regular basis, your company has to look hard at customer satisfaction. Watch out for two problems:

▲ **Exaggerating customer satisfaction to conceal problems:** In bigger companies, sometimes people pressure customers to give them good ratings because they're afraid of getting in trouble. For example, if you buy a new car, you may get a call from the dealer a few days later, asking you to rate the dealer's service highly when a research firm calls you the next day. This is like evaluating the comfort of a mattress by spreading a soft comforter over it and then seeing if it looks level. The best measures put some weight on the mattress. The more stress you induce, the more meaningful the response!

▲ **Overly general questions or ratings:** Any measure based on a survey that asks customers to "rate your overall satisfaction with our company on a 1-to-10 scale" isn't much use. What does an average score of 8.76 mean? Sure, that's pretty high. But are customers satisfied? You didn't really ask them. And even worse, you did not ask them if they're more satisfied with you than they used to be. Or, perhaps they are less satisfied with competitors than with you. Try a series of more specific questions, such as, "Was it convenient and easy to do business with us?"

Customer satisfaction changes with each new interaction between customer and product. Keeping up with customer opinion is a never-ending race, and you need to measure where you stand relative to those shifting customer expectations and competitor performances.

Your customer satisfaction has to be high, relative to both customer expectations and competitors' ratings, before that customer satisfaction has much of an effect on customer retention rates. Make sure that you ask tough questions to find out whether you are below or above customers' current standards. You can ask customers revealing questions, such as these:

1. Which company (or product) is the best right now? (Give a long list with instructions to circle one, and give a write-in blank labeled *Other* as the final choice.)
2. Rate [your product] compared to its competitors:

Far worse			*Same*			*Far better*
1	2	3	4	5	6	7

3. Rate [your product] compared to your expectations for it:

Far worse			*Same*			*Far better*
1	2	3	4	5	6	7

You can get helpful customer responses by breaking down customer satisfaction into its contributing elements. (Focus groups can help you put together a list of contributing elements.) For example, you can ask the following questions about an overnight letter carrier:

1. Rate Flash Deliveries compared to its competitors on speed of delivery.

Far worse			Same			Far better
1	2	3	4	5	6	7

2. Rate Flash Deliveries compared to its competitors on reliability.

Far worse			Same			Far better
1	2	3	4	5	6	7

3. Rate Flash Deliveries compared to its competitors on ease of use.

Far worse			Same			Far better
1	2	3	4	5	6	7

4. Rate Flash Deliveries compared to its competitors on friendliness.

Far worse			Same			Far better
1	2	3	4	5	6	7

5.1.3 Experimental Methods

Experimental research designs are used to show what happens when you change one variable in your marketing equation. Certain procedural rules must be followed, including using random selection of test subjects and statistical evaluation of data.

Experimental research is finding information about a basic problem through the use of a small-scale simulated program designed to test a specific research hypothesis.

For example, what if we want to test the question that families of similar size and economic characteristics living in three different cities purchase different amounts of three different formulas of Dr. Pepper. Here are the steps we would take:

1. We would establish the research hypothesis: "For a given time period, the average amount of purchases of A, B, and C (different formulas) in three different cities are the same."

2. A sample of families in each city would be selected and randomly assigned to either A, B, or C groups.

3. A survey would be conducted to determine the number of ounces of each formula purchased by each family.

4. Statistical analysis would determine the results. If statistically significant differences were found between the purchases, it could be concluded that taste does influence the amount of this drink purchased by families with the same social and economic characteristics (the answer to our research hypothesis).

These methods are reliable when done correctly; however, they can be costly to carry out. You may find easier ways to get the data you need.

5.1.4 Listening to Your Customers

When doing research, you can too easily lose sight of the end-of-process goal — customer satisfaction. Sure, you may need to find out about many other issues in order to design your marketing program or diagnose a problem. But nothing you find out matters unless it boils down to increased customer satisfaction in the long run. Whatever else you decide to research, keep one eye on customer satisfaction. It's the bottom line of any marketing program!

You do not have to spend a quarter of a million dollars researching ideas for a new ad campaign (or anything else). Instead, focus on ways of gaining insight or checking your assumptions using free and inexpensive research methods. If you want to spend tens of thousands of dollars on research, go ahead. Some quick primary research options are as follows:

▲ **Compare yourself to your competitors.** When you compare your marketing approach to your competitors', you easily find out what customers like best. List at least five points of difference between your business and its major competitors based on an analysis of marketing practices. Now ask 10 of your best customers to review this list and tell you what they prefer — your way or one of the alternatives. Ask why. You may find that your customers vote in favor of doing something differently than the way you do it now.

▲ **Entertain customers.** Invite good customers to a lunch or dinner, or hold a Customer Appreciation event. In a relaxed setting they'll be happy to chat and share their views. Use these occasions to ask them for suggestions and reactions. Bounce a new product idea off of them or find out what features they'd most like to see improved. Your customers can provide an expert panel for your informal focus group, and you just have to provide the food!

▲ **Use e-mail.** If you market to businesses, you probably have e-mail addresses for many of your customers. Try e-mailing 20 or more of them for a quick opinion on a question. Result? Instant survey!

▲ **Watch them use your product.** Be nosy. Find ways to observe people as they shop for and consume your product or service. What do they do? What do they like? What, if anything, goes wrong? You can gain insight into what your consumers care about, how they feel, and what they like by observing them in action. If you are in a retail business, be a *secret shopper* by going in and acting like an ordinary customer to see how you are treated and get a feel for what you do and do not like.

▲ **Establish a trend report.** E-mail salespeople, distributors, customer service staff, repair staff, or friendly customers once a month, asking them for a quick list of any important trends they see in the market. You flatter people by letting them know that you value their opinion, and e-mail makes giving that opinion simple. A trend report gives you a quick indication of a change in buying patterns, a new competitive move or threat, and so on.

▲ **Research your best qualities.** Your positive uniqueness is determined by your strengths. Find the simplest way to ask 10 good customers this simple but powerful question: "What is the best thing about our [fill in the name of your product or service], from your perspective?" (Or try the more detailed survey in this chapter.) After you know what you do best, you can focus on telling that story whenever you communicate with your market in any way. Concentrate your efforts on the things customers like most about you. Investing in your strengths (versus your competitors' strengths or your weaknesses) works best.

▲ **Survey your customers.** You can gather input from your customers easily because they interact with your employees or firm. Put a stamped postcard in shipments, statements, product packages, or other communications with your customers. Include three or fewer simple, nonbiased survey questions, such as, "Are you satisfied with this purchase? no = 1 2 3 4 5 = yes." Also leave a few lines for comments. You generally get low response rates with any such effort, but that's okay. If someone has something to tell you, they let you hear about it. And even a 5 percent response gives you a steady stream of input you wouldn't otherwise have.

▲ **Test your marketing.** Whether you are looking at a letter, broadcast fax, catalog, Web page, tear sheet, press release, or ad, try asking a few customers, distributors, or others with knowledge of your business if they like it. If they're only lukewarm about it, then you know you need to edit or improve it before spending the money to publish and distribute it. Customer reviewers can tell you quickly whether you have real attention-getting wow power in any marketing communication. An even simpler (and very effective) technique? Make a list of possible headlines for an ad on a piece of paper and ask potential customers (or anyone in the industry whom you can talk into helping) to select the one they like best. You may be surprised by the results.

▲ **Interview defectors.** Company records of past customers can be a gold mine. Figure out which types of customers defect, when, and why. If you cannot pinpoint why a customer abandoned you, try to contact the lost customer and ask him directly. Tracking them down may prove difficult, but your lost customers hold the key to a valuable piece of information: What you do wrong that can drive customers away. Talk to enough, and you see a pattern emerge. Probably three-fourths of them left you for the same reason. When your research reveals the most common reason for customers to defect, do something about it.

▲ **Ask kids.** Because kids lead the trends in modern society, why not ask them what those trends are? Your children, or any kids on hand that you can get to think about your market for a few minutes, probably have a more contemporary view than you. Ask simple questions like "What will the next big thing be in [name your product or service here]?" Or try this great question: "What's cool and what's not cool this year?" They may be aware of something you had not thought of.

FOR EXAMPLE

Your Customers May Surprise You

Whiskas cat food marketers developed an innovative series of TV ads that do not portray pet cats like children or as silly clowns. The ads portray cats as the semiwild animals they are, stalking prey, sneaking around, and generally being catlike. Where did this idea come from? Cat owners! When they talk, the wildness and independence of cats often comes up. Cats are like little lions. Cat owners feel that felines haven't "sold out" the way dogs have. Such comments gave the marketers of Whiskas the insight that overly cute, personified portrayals of cats do not jive with the cat-lover's image of his cat. The Whiskas ads reflect this important insight, which Whiskas marketers got by taking time to observe and listen to cat owners with an open mind and a fresh ear. If you haven't spent some time trying to understand your customers lately, then maybe you should. You are never too busy to listen to your customers.

SELF-CHECK

- Define **primary research, focus groups, observation,** and **survey research.**
- List ways to do primary research.
- What's the difference between quantitative and qualitative research?
- Name two common problems with survey research.
- Name two requirements for experimental research.
- What's the most important step in any research?

5.2 Secondary Research

Sometimes you do not need to do primary research at all. **Secondary research** involves data that have already been collected and published by someone else. All you have to do is put it together and draw your own conclusions from it. The world is overflowing with data, and some of it can be just what you need to get started on researching your market. So before you buy a report or hire a research firm, dig around for some free (or at least inexpensive) stuff.

Often, the best source of free or almost-free data is your national government. Many governments collect copious data on economic activity, population size, and trends within their borders. In the United States, the Census Bureau is the best general source of data on how many of what sorts of people and households live where. The Department of Commerce has endless data on what sorts of businesses do how much of what, where. Of course, you generally get what you pay for when it comes to free data. For example, you can get detailed census data from the government at a modest price, but it's more work. If money is less important than time, many private vendors will analyze and update the census data for you and sell you customized reports.

Sometimes free data are old or lacking in detail, and you need to decide whether it's good enough for your purposes. If you do not need 100 percent accuracy — if, let's say, you are just looking for general indications of market size — old data are just as useful. Also, the free stuff can get you started by narrowing down your focus and helping you form some good hypothetical answers to test later.

5.2.1 Government Databases

If you want to use the Web to explore useful data compiled and posted by various agencies of the U.S. government, go to www.census.gov, the main gateway into U.S. census data on households and businesses. You should also know www.census.gov/epcd/www/econ97.html, the current address for U.S. data from the economic census (which goes out to 5 million businesses every 5 years) and the Survey of Business Owners.

On the Web and by telephone, you can compile specific names and addresses of several dozen prospective companies if you are a business-to-business marketer. To develop the market, you can check company Web sites. You can also network to find people to call for details.

Also, you can search for articles about the companies in the local media. Before you even set up an appointment, you can gather a great deal of free information to help you know who to call, who to ask for, and what to talk about. You can usually focus a sales effort with the use of such free and (relatively) easy secondary research.

5.2.2 Media Data

Ask a magazine, newspaper, Web server, or radio station you buy advertising from for information about its customer base. This can help you make sure you reach an appropriate audience, and also give you some exposure numbers that are useful to calculate the effectiveness of your advertising.

You can buy placement of key-term listings on search engines. Along with the good exposure they provide, these search engines also make available a detailed report of how people accessing these search engines used the key-term listings.

You can (for free) find out from Google that in the past week, 2,045 people searched for the term *"leadership style,"* and that your listing ranked seventh, on average, in the results those searchers got — meaning it appeared as the seventh listing on their page. Of these 2,045 people doing a search for the term, you can discover how many of them clicked through to your site. You can determine how many clicks turn into an immediate order.

What if you want more orders? After you know your click-through rate, if you can double that rate, doubling the number of prospects coming to your site from Google, you can work on the numbers of people who order. Increasing your bid per click (or the amount you pay Google; see Section 13.3.2) slightly will get you a placement in the top three or four spots. When clicks go up, so do sales. You get the data for this research and planning entirely free.

5.2.3 Demographic Data

Demographics are statistics about a population. Trends in the ethnic makeup of your market, its average age, or its educational levels provide very good clues as to how your marketing ought to change. Consider the following example of the importance of demographics.

> ## FOR EXAMPLE
>
> ### What Does Aging Do for Marketers?
>
> The populations of the United States, Canada, most European countries, and Japan are aging. What does that mean to marketers? Older Americans share a common set of values and attitudes that makes targeting them with marketing messages easier. They have common needs — for example, they need easier-to-read packaging and easier-to-use controls. And they have a great deal of disposable income because elders hold the majority of the wealth in most societies. As the population ages, this already attractive marketing segment grows faster than others. You can find this sort of opportunity easily when you study demographic data. Yet many marketers ignore these inexpensive sources of data and thus overlook important changes in their markets.

5.2.4 Customer Profiles

Photograph people you characterize as your typical customers. Post these pictures on a bulletin board and add any facts or information you can collect about those customers, too. This board becomes your customer database.

Whenever you aren't sure what to do about any marketing decision, you can sit down in front of the bulletin board and use it to help you tune into your customers and what they do and do not like.

For example, make sure the art and wording you use in a letter or ad is appropriate to the customer on your board. Will they like it, or is the style wrong for them?

5.2.5 Competitive Comparisons

Take marketing materials (brochures, ads, Web pages, and so on) from competitors and analyze them, using a *claims table*. A **claims table** is a way to compare yourself to your competitors, through the eyes of your customers.

Open up a spreadsheet (or draw a blank table on paper) and label the columns of this new table, one for each competitor. Label each row with a feature, benefit, or claim. Enter key phrases or words from an ad in the appropriate cell. Include the most prominent or emphasized claims per competitor (put one to three claims per competitor).

When filled in, this table shows you, at a glance, what territory each competitor stakes out and how it does the staking. Compare your own claims with those of competitors. Are you impressive by comparison, or do a more dominant and impressive competitor's claims overshadow you? Do your claims stand out as unique, or are you a me-too marketer without clear points of difference?

The claims table helps you see yourself as customers do — through the lens of your marketing materials and in comparison to your competitors. Using this table often delivers uncomfortable moments of truth that force you to rethink and improve your marketing approach. (But be careful to base your claims on genuine strengths, not just advertising fluff.)

5.2.6 Customer Records

Most marketers fail to "mine" their own databases for all the useful information they may contain. A good way to tap into these free data is to study your own customers with the goal of identifying three common traits that make them different or special.

A computer store went through their records and realized that their customers are

▲ More likely to be self-employed or entrepreneurs than the average person

▲ More sophisticated users of computers than most people

▲ Big spenders who care more about quality and service than the absolute cheapest price

The store in the last example revised its marketing goal to find more people who share these three qualities. What qualities do your customers have that make them special and that would make a good profile for you to use in pursuing more customers like them?

SELF-CHECK

- Define **secondary research, demographics,** and **claims table.**
- Name three types of secondary research.

5.3 Analyzing Your Research Needs

Large companies do so much research, in part to protect the marketer's reputation if the marketing campaign subsequently fails. More than half of all marketing research spending really just builds the case for pursuing strategies the marketers planned to do anyway. That's a bad reason to waste time and money doing endless surveys and focus groups.

What are good reasons to do research? Basically, if you can get a better idea or make a better decision after conducting marketing research, then research is worth it. Also, research can help you explore your identity to improve your positioning in the market.

5.3.1 Researching to Find Better Ideas

Information can stimulate the imagination, suggest fresh strategies, or help you recognize great business opportunities. So always keep one ear open for interesting, surprising, or inspiring facts. Do not spend much money on this kind of research.

You never really know if you are going to get any useful information from this research — most of it just goes in one ear and out the other without suggesting anything new and clever. But subscribe to a diverse range of publications and make a point of talking to people of all sorts, both in your industry and beyond it, to keep you in the flow of new ideas and facts. Also, ask other people for their ideas.

Every marketer should carry an idea notebook in their pocket or purse and make a point of collecting a few contributions from people every day. This habit gets you asking salespeople, employees, customers, and strangers on the subway for their ideas and suggestions. You never know when a suggestion may prove valuable. Lee Iacocca kept an idea notebook in his early days as a marketing guy in the auto industry — and out of those jottings came the idea for the Ford Mustang!

5.3.2 Researching to Make Better Decisions

Do you have any situations that you want more information about before making a decision? Then take a moment to define the situation clearly and list the options you think are feasible.

Choosing the winning ad design, making a more accurate sales projection, or figuring out what new services your customers want — these situations provide examples of important decisions that research can help you make. Table 5-1 shows what your notes may look like.

5.3.3 Researching to Understand Love and Hate

The reactions to your product or service determine your success and your product's fate. If you collect a rating of all the descriptive features of your product from customers, many of those ratings will prove quite ordinary.

A bank branch offers checking, savings, and money-market accounts. So what? Every bank does. But a few of the features of that bank may be notably exceptional — for better or for worse. If the teller windows often have long lines at lunch when people rush out to do their banking, that notable negative stands out in customers' minds. They remember those lines and tell others about them. Long lines at lunch may lead customers to switch banks, and may drive away other potential customers through bad word of mouth.

Table 5-1: Analyzing the Information Needs of a Decision

Decision	Information Needs	Possible Sources	Findings
Choose between print ads in industry magazines and e-mail advertisements to purchased lists.	How many actual prospects can print ads reach?	Magazines' ad salespeople can tell us.	Three leading magazines in our industry reach 90 percent of good customers, but half of these are not in our geographic region. May not be worth it?
	What are the comparable costs per prospect reached through these different methods?	Just need to get the budget numbers and number of people reached and divide available money by number of people.	E-mail is a third the price in our market.
	Can we find out what the average response rates are for both magazine ads and e-mailings?	Nobody is willing to tell us, or they don't know. May try calling a friend in a big ad agency; they may have done a study or something.	Friend says response rates vary wildly, and she thinks the most important thing is how relevant the customer finds the ad, not the medium used.
	Have any of our competitors switched from print to e-mail successfully?	Can probably get distributors to tell us this. Will call several and quiz them.	No, but some companies in similar industries have done this successfully.

Conclusions?
Seems like we'll spend less and be more targeted if we design special e-mails and send them only to prospects in our region. Don't buy magazine ad space for now; we can experiment with e-mail, instead. But we need to make sure the ads we send are relevant and seem important, or people just delete them without reading them.

> ### FOR EXAMPLE
>
> #### To Scoot or Not to Scoot
>
> Have you heard about the high-tech Segway Human Scooter? In its first year or two, the press covered its wonderful abilities and sales grew. Then it dropped out of the headlines for a while, only to reemerge when manufacturers announced a recall. The problem? When its batteries run low, it can become unstable, leading to nasty spills (President Bush fell off one — how's that for bad publicity?).

Similarly, on the positive side of the ledger, if that bank branch has very friendly tellers and a beautifully decorated lobby with free gourmet coffee on a side table for its customers, this notable warmth and friendliness sticks in customers' minds, building loyalty and encouraging them to recruit new customers through word of mouth.

If you gather customer ratings, you can draw a graph of all the features of your product, rated from negative through neutral to positive. You find most features cluster in the middle of the resulting bell curve, failing to differentiate you from the competition. A few features stick out on the left as notably negative — and you have to fix those features fast! Other features, hopefully, stand out on the right as notably positive. You need to nurture and expand upon these features, and do not forget to boast shamelessly about them in all your marketing communications.

You can do some research in-house to understand the special abilities that make your company shine by asking customers to rank you on a laundry list of descriptors for your business/product/service. The scale ranges from 1 to 10 (to get a good spread), with the following labels:

1	2	3	4	5	6	7	8	9	10
Very bad		Bad		Average			Good		Very good

For example, the list of items to rate in a bank may include checking accounts (average), savings accounts (average), speed of service (bad), and friendliness of tellers (very good), along with many other things you'd need to put on the list in order to describe the bank, in detail. Getting customers to fill in a survey sheet is important enough that you may want to offer them a reward for doing so. You can waive the fees on their checking account for the rest of the year if they mail in a completed form. Or (if you do not mind honest feedback) you can ask them to fill in a rating form while standing in that long line!

One end of this scale represents the features customers think you do brilliantly. The other end represents the features you need to do some work on. If you want to get fancy, you can also ask some customers to rate the importance of each item on the list to them, personally.

If you are lucky, your brilliant areas are important to them and your bad areas aren't. But most likely, you need to clean up those worst-on-the-list features to make them average, at least (so they do not become what every customer remembers and talks about). And you definitely need to focus on leveraging the high-rated items. Talk them up in marketing and invest even more in them to maximize their attractiveness.

5.3.4 Planning Your Research

Research should start with a careful analysis of the decisions you must make. For example, say you are in charge of a 2-year-old software product that small businesses use to develop their marketing plans. As the product manager, what key decisions should you be making? The following are the most likely:

▲ Should we launch an upgrade or keep selling the current version?
▲ Is our current marketing program sufficiently effective, or should we redesign it?
▲ Is the product positioned properly, or do we need to change its image?

So before you do any research, you need to think hard about those decisions. Specifically, you need to

▲ Decide what realistic options you have for each decision.
▲ Assess your level of uncertainty and risk for each decision.

Then, for any uncertain or risky decisions, you need to pose questions whose answers should help you reduce the risk and uncertainty of the decision. And now, with these questions in hand, you are ready to begin your research! When you work through this thinking process, you often find that you do not actually need research.

For example, maybe your boss has already decided to invest in an upgrade of the software product you manage, so researching the decision has no point. Wrong or right, you cannot realistically change that decision.

But some questions make it through the screening process and turn out to be good candidates for research. For these research points, you need to pose a series of questions that have the potential to reduce your decision-making uncertainty or to reveal new and exciting options for you as a decision maker.

For example, you may ask, "Is the product positioned properly, or do we need to change its image?" To find out whether repositioning your product makes sense, you may ask how people currently perceive the product's quality and performance, how they view the product compared to the leading competitors, and what the product's personality is. If you know the answers to all these questions, you are far better able to make a good decision.

That's why you must start by defining your marketing decisions very carefully. Until you know what decisions you must make, marketing research has little point. See Figure 5-1 for a flowchart of the research process.

Figure 5-1

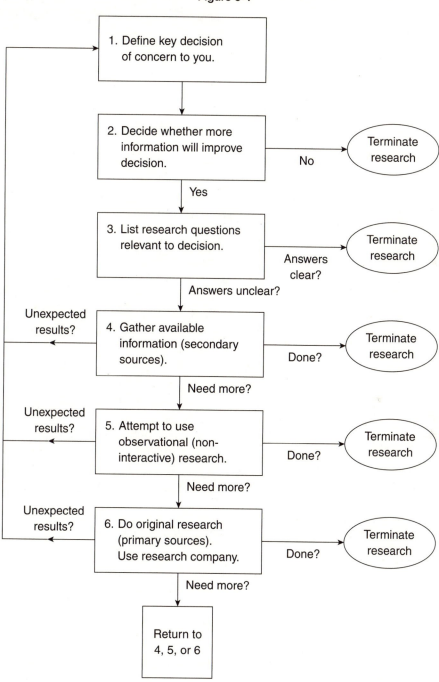

Follow this marketing research process to avoid common errors.

5.4 The Research Process

The research process is highly specialized, and has become very sophisticated since its inception in the 1930s. Even if you do not conduct any research yourself, marketing managers need to be conversant with the basics of the research process and its techniques so that they can work with and interpret research findings of outside firms.

5.4.1 Types of Research

Most marketing research is directed toward specialized areas of management. The types of research can be broken down this way:

▲ Research on markets — trends, market share, market potentials, market characteristics, completion, and other market intelligence

▲ Research on sales — sales analysis, sales forecasting, quota-setting, sales territory design, distribution costs, and inventories

▲ Research on products — new products, product features, brand image, concept tests, product tests, and market tests

▲ Research on advertising and promotion — promotion concepts, copy research, media research, merchandising, packaging, and advertising effectiveness measurement

▲ Research on corporate growth and development — economic and technological forecasting, corporate planning, corporate image, profitability measurement, mergers and acquisitions studies, and facilities locations

5.4.2 Activities Common to All Research

There is no single set of steps in market research procedure that is accepted by all. Each marketing problem requires its own unique procedure. But it is generally agreed that four major activities need to be part of a thorough research effort (see Figure 5-1):

FOR EXAMPLE

How Sweet It Is

Juicy Fruit gum was losing customers in the teen market, which is manufacturer Wm. Wrigley Jr. Company's target gum market. Market research provided some clues. After finding teens who chewed five sticks or more of Juicy Fruit a week, it asked them to find pictures that reminded them of the gum and write a short story about it. The focus group taught Wrigley that its gum was popular because it was sweet. Wrigley's ad agency confirmed that heavy gum chewers rated Juicy Fruit primarily as "sweet." This provided a new direction for the company's marketing strategy. Four commercials were developed with the slogan, "Gotta have sweet." Sales of Juicy Fruit rose 5 percent, and market share spiked.

▲ **Making a preliminary investigation.** This involves determining the purpose and scope of your research, and doing an informal assessment of the marketing environment. The problem must be stated correctly for it to be solved, and this is often the biggest stumbling block to good research. The assessment requires creating a set of research questions.

▲ **Creating the research design.** The research design needs to have an approach, whether experimental, survey research, or historical (finding secondary sources of data from which you can project into the future).

▲ **Conducting the investigation.** If staff cannot do this time-consuming part of the process, then sometimes outsiders are hired and trained to actually conduct the research, with close supervision and control.

▲ **Processing the data and reporting results.** The findings should be presented in a written report. Many marketing research projects are never translated into management action. Sometimes this is because the research did not enable the researcher to answer the research question, and other times this is because suggestions were not included in the report for implementing the findings. Make sure the report includes such a section.

SELF-CHECK

- What are the four major marketing activities needed in the research process?
- List five types of market research.

SUMMARY

Analyze your research needs before doing any market research. A variety of secondary and primary methods are available. Research can help define strategy, improve sales projections, and identify needed marketing activities.

KEY TERMS

Claims table	A way to compare yourself to your competitors, through the eyes of your customers.
Demographics	Statistics about a population.
Experimental research	Finding information about a basic problem through the use of a small-scale simulated program designed to test a specific research hypothesis.
Focus groups	Potential or actual customers who discuss your product while a trained moderator guides their conversation.
Observation	Gathering data by watching people.
Primary research	Gathering data by observing people to see how they behave or by asking them for verbal or written answers to questions.
Qualitative research	Research that involves qualitative analysis, to answer the question "Why?"
Quantitative research	Research that involves quantitative analysis, to answer the question "What happened?"
Secondary research	Data that have already been collected and published by someone else.
Survey research	Asking people what they think.

ASSESS YOUR UNDERSTANDING

Go to www.wiley.com/college/Hiam to evaluate your knowledge of the basics of marketing research.
Measure your learning by comparing pre-test and post-test results.

Summary Questions

1. A claims table is used to size up your marketing in the eyes of your customers. True or false?
2. All primary research methods are more difficult than secondary research methods. True or false?
3. Which of the following would be analyzed qualitatively?
   (a) Surveys
   (b) Focus groups
   (c) Telephone interviews
   (d) Demographic data
4. All marketing decisions should be based upon research. True or false?
5. Which is more expensive — retaining old customers or gaining new ones?
6. The first step of the marketing research process is
   (a) Gather information.
   (b) Conduct a preliminary investigation.
   (c) List the relevant questions.
7. Government databases are a form of primary research. True or false?
8. Media data is useful for telling you how your key term listings are doing. True or false?
9. Experimental research requires that you select your research subjects randomly. True or false?
10. All good research designs utilize the same four activities. True or false?

Review Questions

1. Explain how demographics can be useful to market researchers. Give an example that's not in the chapter.
2. Once you've defined a key decision your company needs to make, what other question do you need to ask before beginning any marketing research?
3. What are two possible pitfalls to avoid when conducting market research?

Applying This Chapter

1. Which would be the least helpful thing to ask your customers and why: "Please rate our product on a scale from 1 to 10," "What do you like best about our product?," "Would you use our product again and why?," or "Please compare our product to our competitor's product"?
2. If your customer surveys were indicating that people were increasingly dissatisfied with your product, but you didn't know why, how would you find out? Would this be a quantitative or qualitative method? Would you use primary or secondary research?
3. How could you get primary research easily on the following: a grocery store, a political candidate, and a brand of shoes marketed to teenagers?
4. What are good reasons to do market research? List three.

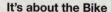

It's about the Bike

Why did the Segway get so much publicity and attention? What two things made headlines? What do the marketers of the Segway need to do next?

Dialing up Your Market

You are the number two cell-phone company in your market. A national ad campaign has not proven effective in gaining your company market share, although you lead other markets in other parts of the country. Before conducting any market research, name an important research question you'd ask about your market.

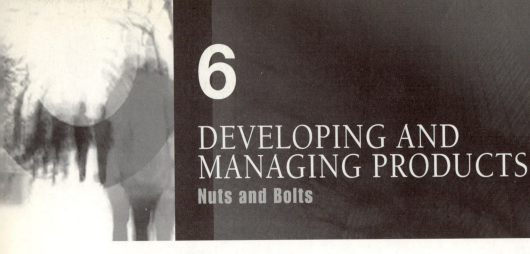

6

DEVELOPING AND MANAGING PRODUCTS
Nuts and Bolts

Starting Point

Go to www.wiley.com/college/Hiam to assess your knowledge of the basics of product management and development.
Determine where you need to concentrate your effort.

What You'll Learn in This Chapter

▲ Ways for devising new products and modifying old ones
▲ The impact of product packaging and labeling upon sales
▲ When to delete a product
▲ Legal protections for products

After Studying This Chapter, You'll Be Able To

▲ Choose ideas that are legally permissible
▲ Assess when a product is a good fit in its product line
▲ Demonstrate how to increase breadth and depth in your product lines

Goals and Outcomes

▲ Evaluate a package's effectiveness, based on criteria
▲ Judge when deleting a product is necessary
▲ Propose a strategy for deleting a product that has outgrown its usefulness

INTRODUCTION

The market is constantly changing, so a marketer's work of managing products is never done. Developing and branding new products, protecting them against competition and trademark infringement, and just avoiding stale marketing are all important. This chapter will explain how to develop and package exciting new products, how to brand and protect them, and what product-mix strategies will help your products compete successfully. We'll also explain how to discontinue a product, when necessary.

6.1 Introducing a New Product

You should introduce new products as often as you can afford to develop them. Innovations give you a major source of competitive advantage. A competitor's major new product introduction probably changes the face of your market — and upsets your sales projections and profit margins — at least once every few years. So you cannot afford to ignore new product development.

Ways to come up with ideas for new products are discussed in this section, as well as the steps in developing them.

6.1.1 The New Product Development Process

Where do you get the idea for a hot new product? One product strategy or multiple strategies? One market or more? How you answer this determines whether you need to have one product line and one strategy or multiple lines and strategies. Many businesses sell into multiple markets. PepsiCo sells in the beverage and snack markets. Small companies do this, too: A local cleaning service may have both homeowners and businesses as customers, and the marketing (and specifically the product offering) needs to be different for each.

Given sometimes high failure rates, you need to make sure your new product beats the odds. New products do better when customers see something strikingly new about them.

In your supermarket, notice the number of packages proclaiming something new. Without the word splashed across them, you may never have been able to tell they were new. Same with services: Take a look at the brochures and posters in your bank, for example, and see whether the "new" services are just repackaged old services with fancy new names and pricing.

Try to introduce something that's not only new, but that looks new and different to the market. Give it a radical distinction, a clear point of difference. Innovations that consumers recognize more quickly and easily provide the marketer with a greater return. Here we will look at the steps in developing new products, using Figure 6-1 for reference.

Figure 6-1

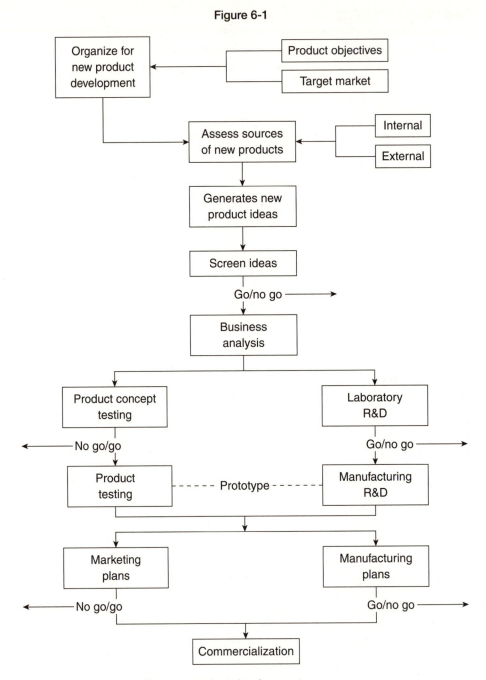

The new product development process.

Step 1: Generating New Ideas. Generating ideas is a creative task that requires a specific way of thinking. It is not difficult to come up with new ideas, but good new ideas are another story. Ideas can come from internal or external sources.

Some ways to find new product ideas:

▲ **Picking customers' brains:** Customers are the best source, but they do not know it. Ask a customer to describe a brilliant new product you should provide for him or her, and you get a blank stare or worse. Yet frustrations with the existing products and all sorts of dissatisfactions, needs, and wants lurk in the back of every customer's mind. Collecting the customers' words helps you gain insight into how they think — so talk to them and take notes that use quotes or tape-record their comments. Get them talking, and let them wander a bit, so that you have a chance to encounter the unexpected. Also watch customers as they buy and use your product. Observation may reveal wasted time and effort, inefficiencies, or other problems that the customer takes for granted — problems that the customer may happily say good-bye to if you point them out and remove them. Methods have been developed to systematically discover new opportunities. For example, **category appraisal** is trying to find new opportunities within an existing category by finding out what makes the category "tick." See the For Example section that follows.

▲ **Foreign markets:** Old products in one market may be new products in another. You may be able to turn your dead products from the United States or Europe into winners in other countries, if you can partner with local distributors.

▲ **Licensing:** A private inventor may have a great new product concept and a patent, but may lack the marketing muscle and capital to introduce the product. You can provide that missing muscle and pay the inventor 5 or 10 percent of your net revenues as a reward for inspiration. Many companies generate inventions that fall outside of their marketing focus. These companies are often willing to license to someone specializing in the target market.

▲ **Competitors:** We're not talking about stealing. You must respect the legal rights that protect other people's expressions of their ideas. Although a competitor may be upset to see you knocking off or improving upon its latest idea, nothing can stop you as long as your source was public (not secret) and you aren't violating a patent, trademark, or copyright. Do not violate **trade secrecy laws** — ask your lawyer before planning any questionable research. See Section 6.2.3 for more on legal protections.

▲ **Basic research:** Many companies, such as DuPont, have several scientists who are assigned the task of developing new product ideas and related technology.

▲ **Manufacturing and sales:** People who work in these departments often have ideas about improving existing products or adding new ones. Do not overlook your own human capital.

Step 2: Screening Product Development Ideas. This part is critical. New ideas that do not meet the organization's objectives should be rejected. If a poor product idea is allowed to pass the screening state, it wastes effort and money in subsequent stages until it is later abandoned. Even more serious is the possibility of screening out a worthwhile idea.

These are the two most common techniques for screening new product ideas:

▲ **Use a simple checklist.** For instance, rate new product ideas on a scale from excellent to poor.

▲ **Refine the checklist technique.** Assign weights to each criteria and rate each product on a point scale measuring product compatibility.

Step 3: Business Analysis. After the initial screen very few viable proposals will be left. Before developing prototypes, however, you need to analyze, using additional information, the costs (including social costs) and profits to be made. This involves estimating demand for the product, from sales as well as for the sales or licensing of technology developed for the product.

Step 4: Technical and Marketing Development. Technical development involves constructing a prototype model of the product that can be subjected to further research. The marketing department first tests the **product concept,** a synthesis or description of a product idea that reflects the core element of the proposed product. First the product's intended consumers give the product a concept test, a question such as, "How about something that would do this?" After the prototype is developed, various kinds of consumer tests are conducted, depending upon the type of product.

Step 5: Manufacturing Planning. In this stage, the manufacturing department is asked to come up with plans to produce the product efficiently. This requires appraising the existing production plant and the necessary tooling required to achieve the most economical production. Fancy designs and materials might be hard, if not impossible, to accommodate on existing production equipment, and new machinery can be expensive. Other issues include funding, facilities, and personnel.

> **FOR EXAMPLE**
>
> **Have Some Chocolate with Your Chocolate**
>
> To study the preferred properties of candy for consumers who buy candy in supermarkets, convenience stores, and movie theaters, a category appraisal was done. A database of in-depth sensory profiles of a wide range of candy types and "liking scores" of each of these was created. Researchers shopped for 25 to 30 types of candy, and rated their texture, flavor, size, and appearance. A questionnaire asked about hardness, chewiness, crispness, flavor intensity, degree of fruit flavor, sweetness, color, and so on. The point was to discover not what the favorite products were, but which attributes were most important. Brand was uninfluential and taste was the dominant factor. The study found the ideal product was chocolate-filled chocolates with chocolate dipping sauce.

Step 6: Marketing Planning. The product planner prepares a complete marketing plan. It starts with a statement of objectives and ends with the fusion of product, distribution, promotion, and pricing into an integrated program of marketing action.

Step 7: Test Marketing. This is the final step before commercialization. The objective is to test all the variables in the marketing plan, including elements of the product. Test marketing represents an actual launching of the total marketing program, but is done only on a small-scale basis. Test marketing answers:

▲ Overall workability of the marketing plan
▲ Alternative allocations of the budget
▲ Whether a new product is inspiring users to switch from previous brands and holding their interest

  Done properly, a market test is an accurate simulation of the national market and serves to reduce risk. Even after test results are in, adjustments to the product are still made. At this point the product may be deleted and never see the light of day.

Step 8: Commercialization. At this stage the product is ready to be launched. It has survived the development process and is on its way to commercial success. Its life-cycle marketing plan will guide its progress. Product life cycle is the subject of the next section.

6.1.2 Planning Through the Product Life Cycle

A company has to be good at both developing new products and managing them in the face of changing tastes, technologies, and competition. Every product goes through a life cycle with predictable sales and profits, as illustrated in Figure 6-2.

The **product life-cycle concept (PLC)** is a framework for planning the management of products. Managers must be adept at finding new products to replace those that are in the declining stage of the product life cycle and in managing their transition from one stage to the next. The five stages of the PLC and their components are as follows:

1. **Product development:** The period during which new product ideas are generated, operationalized, and tested prior to commercialization. (See Section 6.1.1.)

2. **Introduction:** The period during which a new product is introduced. Initial distribution is obtained as well as promotion.

3. **Growth:** The period during which the product is accepted by consumers and the trade. Initial distribution is expanded, promotion is increased, repeat orders from initial buyers are obtained, and word-of-mouth advertising leads to more and more new users.

4. **Maturity:** The period during which competition becomes serious. Toward the end of this period, competitors' products cut deeply into the company's market position.

5. **Decline:** The product becomes obsolete and its competitive disadvantage results in declining sales and eventual deletion. (See Section 6.5.)

Figure 6-2

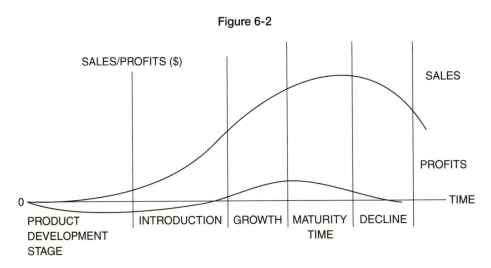

The product life cycle.

Of course, the PLC cannot predict all factors, and no two companies may follow the same exact pattern or produce the same results. For example, differences in the competitive situation during each of these stages may require different marketing approaches.

SELF-CHECK

- Define **product concept, product lifestyle concept, category appraisal,** and **commercialization.**
- Name five sources of new product ideas.
- List the five stages of the PLC.

6.2 Branding and Protecting Your Product

Should you launch your product under an existing brand identity or give it a new one? Should you attempt to add value (and raise the price) by creating a positive brand identity, or should you save your marketing dollars and just get the product out to point of purchase? You have to make all these tough decisions, but guidelines do exist.

6.2.1 Naming Your Product

Naming a new product isn't simple, but you can use a number of effective methods. You can choose a word, or combination of words, that tells people about the exact character of your product.

This approach is kind of like giving a new puppy a name. You want to get a feel for its personality first and then give it a name that fits. A standoffish poodle can be Fifi, but that name doesn't fit a playful mutt!

You can also name your product by making up a brand-new word that has no prior meaning. This approach gives you something you can more easily protect in a court of law. But it isn't necessarily effective at communicating the character of your product. You have to invest considerable time and money in creating a meaning for the new name in consumers' minds. A better way is to use **morphemes,** or meaningful components for a made-up name.

NameLab Inc. (a leading developer of such names) defines morphemes as the semantic kernels of words. For example, NameLab started with the word *accurate* (from the Latin word *accuratus*) and extracted a morpheme from it to use as a new car brand: Acura. They also developed Compaq, Autozone, Lumina, and Zapmail in the same manner. Each is a new word to the language, but each communicates something about the product because of meanings consumers associate with that word's components. This technique is known as *constructional linguistics*.

6.2.2 Designing and Managing Product Lines

Products can be goods, services, ideas, or even people — such as political candidates or stars. You usually identify product lines by an umbrella brand name with individual brand identities falling under that umbrella. A product line is any logical grouping of products offered to customers. The Macintosh computer line includes many different products, but they all bear the same Macintosh brand name (a trademarked asset of Apple Computers), and the company has made each product distinct enough that together they give the customer a wide range of choices. You can think of product lines like this one as families of products — and, like families, their relationship needs to be close and clear. Consider two key issues when designing product lines:

▲ **Depth:** How many alternatives should you give the customer within any single category? Options of the same product increase depth because they give a customer more options. Depth gives you an advantage because it increases the likelihood of a good fit between an interested customer and your product. Increase depth when you are losing customers because you do not have a product for them. Increasing your depth of choice reduces the chance of disappointing a prospective customer.

▲ **Breadth:** This option allows you to generate new sales. Adding anything that the customer views as a separate choice, not a variant of the same choice, adds breadth to the product line. Increase breadth whenever you can think of a new product that seems to fit in the line, so that customers can see the new product's obvious relationship to the line. Do not mix unrelated products — that's not a product line, because it does not have a clear, logical identity to customers.

FOR EXAMPLE

A Mustang by Any Other Name . . .

The Ford Mustang, an extremely successful brand name, takes its name strategically from the horse. Marketers presented the car as simply having the personality of the small, hardy horse of the American plains from which the car took its name. And those marketers hoped that the driver saw himself as a modern-day cowboy, akin to the real cowboys who broke and used the mustangs for their work. This strategy has a powerful effect because it uses existing terms whose meanings marketers apply to their product.

FOR EXAMPLE

T-Shirts for All

Make a single T-shirt design in a range of sizes and colors. Then you have a deep product line. If you sell one popular T-shirt design, you can increase breadth by offering more T-shirt designs in your product line. A broad line of T-shirts includes dozens and dozens of different designs. A broad and deep product line offers each of those designs in many sizes and on many different colors and forms of T-shirts. Keep stretching a successful line as much as you can. Doing so means you sell new products to old customers. Of course, the line may also reach new customers, which is great. But you can sell to your old customers more easily, so offering them new products makes sense.

The secret to good product management is the motto, "Don't leave well enough alone." Know when to change your product line. But if you keep growing your lines, you can obviously bump into some practical limits after a while. How do you know when the pendulum is going to swing the other way — when it is time to do some spring-cleaning?

You should decrease your depth or breadth (or both) if your distribution channels cannot display the full product line to customers. Often, distribution becomes a bottleneck, imposing practical limits on how big a product line you can bring to the customer's attention.

The Kellogg Brush Company, for instance, made many hundreds of different items, yet the grocery and hardware stores selling their products never displayed more than a couple dozen items. Obviously, their product line was far broader and deeper than their end customers ever realized. They cut the product line back to the top 20 or 30 items purchased by retailers and tried to make those items better and less expensive. Another option would have been to develop a direct, catalog-based distribution channel in order to bring these choices to customers.

You should also cut back your product line if customers do not understand it. Procter & Gamble chopped its product offerings roughly in half for this very reason. Surveys showed that all the variety confused their customers: Customers didn't have a clear idea of what the company offered or why. Too many choices frustrate customers and lead to confusion between products. Brand identities start to overlap, and you make customer decisions harder rather than easier.

Always calibrate your product line to your distribution channels and your customers. Do not overwhelm or underwhelm. Keep talking to all your customers and watching how they behave with your product to see if you need to shrink or grow your product line.

6.2.3 Branding and Protecting Your Product's Name and Identity

Any brand name, term, sign, symbol, design, or a combination of these that is intended to identify the goods or services of one seller or group of sellers and to differentiate them from competitors is known as a **brand. Brand names** are the part of the brand that can be vocalized. **Brand mark** is the part of the brand that is recognized but is not utterable, such as a symbol, design, or distinctive coloring or lettering.

The primary function of the brand is to identify the product and to distinguish it from those of competitors. From the buyer's perspective, it may simply be consistent quality or satisfaction, or shopping efficiency. A distinctive brand may also call attention to new products. Selecting a brand name is one of the key new product decisions and reflects the overall position and marketing program desired by the firm. Satisfied customers associate quality products with an established brand name. It is through its brand that a product can:

▲ Be meaningfully advertised and distinguished from substitutes
▲ Make it easier for the customer to track down products
▲ Be given legal protection

As with new product development, branding involves generating new names, screening them, and selecting the best. The basic branding strategy may be one of the following:

▲ **Manufacturer's branding policy:** The producer refuses to manufacture merchandise under brands other than his own, although he may sell seconds or irregulars on an unbranded basis.
▲ **Exclusive distributor's brands policy:** The producer does not have a brand of his own but agrees to sell his products only to a particular distributor and carry his brand name (private brands).
▲ **Mixed brand policy:** Elements of both extremes are used so that the manufacturer's and the distributor's brands are produced. For example, Firestone sells tires under their own brand names and under private labels.

Brand names are mandatory if the manufacturer or distributor intends to use mass advertising, and they also make word-of-mouth advertising effective.

You can gain legal protection for your brands by using, and getting legal recognition for, a unique identifier for your product, a line of products, or even for your entire company. For most companies, both brand names and trademarks are vital in the identification of products. Legal protection can apply to names, short verbal descriptions, and visual symbols. All these forms of identification are marks that can represent the identity of the thing you apply them to:

▲ **Trademark:** A tangible product's name and/or visual symbol; it protects a name or logo

▲ **Service mark:** A service name, which U.S. law treats similarly to a trademark

▲ **Trade name:** A business name, with similar protection under the law

You should also know these:

▲ A **patent** protects a design.

▲ A **copyright** protects writing, artwork, performances, and software.

In the United States, you establish and protect your rights to exclusive use of any unique trademark by using it. You should register it (with the U.S. Patent and Trademark Office — contact any law firm handling intellectual property to find out how). But registering the trademark isn't nearly as important as using the trademark.

In other countries, usage and registration also matter, but sometimes governments reverse the emphasis — without registration, usage gives you no protection. So check with local authorities in each country where you plan to use a trademark. Also, contact your lawyer, any experienced ad agency that does brand marketing, or a name lab.

SELF-CHECK

- Define **product line, morpheme,** and **trade name.**
- State the difference between a trademark and a service mark.
- What is meant by depth and breadth of product lines?
- State what a patent, trademark, or copyright protects.
- Name the three types of brand policies.
- Can product lines be changed?

6.3 Packaging and Labeling

A customer enters a grocery store, pulls a package down, and carries it to the register. A customer opens a catalog, flips through, selects an item, and dials the toll-free number. A customer goes on-line to purchase airplane tickets and make a hotel reservation. At all these points of purchase, the marketer is out of the picture. The product must sell itself.

But to do so, the product must be noticeable, enticing. It must appear better than (and a better value than) the competition. To prepare your product for its solo role at this vital point-of-purchase stage, think carefully about how you display and present it. **Point of purchase** (POP) is the time and place at which the purchase is made.

You cannot play this all-important role for your product, but you can select the stage and design the set and costume. The stage is made up of the store, catalog, or other meeting place; the set includes the shelving, signs, display, or other point-of-purchase designs; the costume is the exterior package you give your product. Together, they make up what marketers refer to as the **package**, or the product as the customer first sees it.

The package provides protection, containment, communication, and utility for the product. Every product, whether tangible or not, sold in a store or not, has packaging. Marketers must give careful thought to package design, regardless of the product. Services, ideas, and even people (like musicians, job seekers, and political candidates) are included because they can all be products in the right context.

The packaging makes the sale in the majority of purchase decisions (along with any additional point-of-purchase influences to draw attention to the product). Your packaging may well be the most important part of your marketing plan. In spite of the vast sums of money and attention lavished elsewhere — on advertising, marketing research, and other activities — it all comes down to the package.

Does the prospective customer see the package and choose it over others? Studies of the purchase process reveal that people rarely know just what they will buy before the POP. The majority of consumers are ready and willing for your product to sway them at point of purchase, as the findings in Table 6-1 (from a study by the Point-of-Purchase Advertising Institute) reveal.

Table 6-1: The Point-of-Purchase Decision-Making Process

Nature of Consumer's Purchase Decision	Percent of Purchases, Supermarket	Percent of Purchases, Mass-Merchandise Stores
Unplanned	60%	53%
Substitute	4%	3%
Generally planned	6%	18%
Total = Product selection made at point of purchase	70%	74%

As Table 6-1 shows, unplanned purchases make up the biggest category. Furthermore, specifically planned purchases (those purchases not included in the table) are less than a third of all purchases — all the rest can be influenced at least partially by the package and other point-of-purchase communications. (The study is for packaged goods in stores, but service purchases can also be strongly influenced by the brochure, sales presentation, or Web site that packages the service.)

If more than half of final decisions about what to buy are made at point of purchase, then the package may be more important than any other marketing element. You may even want to consider dispensing with all other forms of marketing communication, and invest only in packaging and point-of-purchase promotions and displays.

If your target customer is open to a point-of-purchase decision, then this extreme is at least a possibility. And by focusing 90 to 100 percent of your marketing attention there, you can handle the point of purchase better than less-focused competitors. The radical nature of this idea means your competition probably won't think of it. See Section 8.3 for more on point-of-purchase sales. In addition, here are some ways to make sure your packaging makes the sale:

▲ **Bump up the visibility of the package.** Increasing the size of the brand name, the brightness or boldness of the colors and layout, or the size of the package itself helps make it more visible, as does arranging (or paying) to have stores display it more prominently.

▲ **Choose a color that contrasts with competitors.** Nabisco chose green when they introduced their SnackWells brand of healthy but delicious cookies a few years ago. Green isn't typically used on the cookie aisle of the grocery store, so their products really stand out.

▲ **Improve the information on the package.** Less is more when it comes to clarity, so can you cut down on the number of words you use? Also, ask yourself if the shopper may find any additional information useful when making a purchase decision.

▲ **Use the Web to package a product in information.** Many Web sites give you enough information to compare options and actually make a purchase decision without having to go into a store and look at the product. In this case, the Web page provides *virtual packaging* for the product.

▲ **Let the packaging sell the replacement, too.** Make some aspect of your packaging (if only a label on the bottom) be so permanent that it sends the user to your Web page or phone number for a reorder when the time comes.

▲ **Give your package or label emotional appeal.** Warm colors, a friendly message, a smiling person, and a photo of children playing are all ways to make the product feel good when someone looks at it. Purchases are about feelings, not just logic, so give your packaging a winning personality.

> ### FOR EXAMPLE
>
> #### Coca-Cola
>
> The Coca-Cola bottle is recognized throughout the world for its unusual shape, which was actually trademarked by the Coca-Cola Company. The wave shape of its logo appears on all Coca-Cola cans around the world and was taken from the contour of the original Coca-Cola bottles. Coca-Cola is one of the best-known brands, appearing in every country. And its packaging is unmistakable and immediately recognizable by people who speak languages other than English.

▲ **Add some excitement to the package.** Try to make your packaging dynamic. A wave is exciting. A box is not. Put a wave on your box! Do you have a symbol of movement, achievement, or excitement somewhere in your packaging? Sometimes consistency in appearance between your products isn't as important as having eye-catching packaging.

▲ **Increase the functionality or workability of the package.** Can you make your packaging protect the product better? Can you make it easier to open, useful for storage, or easier to recycle? Packages have functional roles, and improving functionality can help increase the product's appeal.

These ideas and tips all fall into a popular framework for designing packaging, called VIEW.

▲ **VIEW:** Visibility, information, emotion, and workability

Use these ideas or your own to improve the VIEW by upgrading your packaging. Also, make sure you comply with any regulations that govern packaging in your industry.

SELF-CHECK

- List ways to improve your packaging.
- What does POP stand for?
- What does VIEW stand for?

6.4 Product Mix Strategies

Very few products are so perfect that they fit naturally with their customers. With product management, you are competing on a changing playing field. Your competitors are trying hard to make their products better, and you have to do the same.

As more brands enter the marketplace, it becomes more difficult to win and hold buyers. In a competitive market, several strategies can be employed that involve either changing the product to further distinguish it from other products, or designing a strategy that will eliminate the product and make way for new products.

You should modify your products to improve performance, value, and quality with each new season and each new marketing plan. Always seek insights into how to improve your product. Always look for early indicators of improvements your competitors plan to make and be prepared to go one step further in your response. And always go to your marketing oracle — the customer — for insights into how you can improve your product.

6.4.1 Modifying a Product

These are tests that a product must pass to remain viable. If your product does not pass, you need to improve or alter it in some way.

▲ **When it is no longer special:** At the point of purchase — that place or time when customers make their actual purchase decisions — your product needs to have something special. It has to reach out to at least a portion of the market. Your product needs to be better than its competition on certain criteria because of inherent design features. Or it needs to be about as good as the rest, but a better value, which gives you a sustainable cost advantage. Marketers generally underestimate the rarity of those cost advantages. Or the product needs to be the best option by virtue of a lack of other options. Do not assume your lack of special features means that your product isn't special. You can be special just by being there when customers need the product. You can justify keeping a product alive just by having a way of maintaining your distribution advantage. But a product at point of sale has to have at least some special distinction if you expect it to generate a good return in the future. Otherwise, it gets lost in the shuffle. If your customers do not think your product is unique in any way, then you may need to delete that product. But do not set up the noose too quickly. First, see if you can work to differentiate it in some important way.

FOR EXAMPLE

Volvo Diehards

"I'd never drive anything but a Volvo. They're comfortable and safe, they do not break down, and they last longer than American cars." Some U.S. customers say just that when asked about their Volvos, so Volvo has an excellent base of repeat buyers. For that reason, it doesn't vary its models as much from year to year as other car companies do. The existence of customer champions gives Volvo the luxury of selling virtually the same car to people time after time, while competitors are madly retooling their factories every year or two.

▲ **When it lacks champions:** Champions are customers who really love your product, who insist on buying it over others, and who tell their friends or associates to do the same. But such loyal champions are rare. The championship test is tougher than the differentiation test. Many products lack champions. But when a product does achieve this special status — when some customers anywhere in the distribution channel really love it — then that product is assured an unusually long and profitable life. Such high customer commitment should be your constant goal as you manage the life cycle of your product. Products with champions get great word of mouth, and their sales and market shares grow because of that word of mouth. Even better, champions faithfully repurchase the products they rave about, providing your company with high-profit sales, compared with the higher costs associated with finding new customers.

The hook is that the repeat buyer must want to repeat the purchase. They need to be converts, true believers, fans. Otherwise, you need to think of each sale as a new sale, and the sale costs you almost as much as selling to someone who's never used the product before. How do you know if you have champions rather than regular, ordinary customers? Because when you ask them about the product, they sound excited and enthusiastic.

6.4.2 Positioning Your Product

Product **positioning** is a strategic management decision that determines the place a product should occupy in a given market — its market niche. The word "positioning" includes several of the common meanings of position: a place, a rank, a mental attitude, and a strategic process. Positioning can be applied at any stage of the product life cycle. Approaches range from gathering sophisticated market research information to the intuition of the product manager.

A product or idea can be positioned by the following:

▲ **Attributes:** Crest is a cavity fighter.
▲ **Price:** Sears is the value store.
▲ **Competitors:** Avis positions itself against Hertz.
▲ **Application:** Gatorade is for after exercising.
▲ **Product user:** Miller is for the blue-collar, heavy beer drinker.
▲ **Product class:** Carnation Instant Breakfast is a breakfast food.
▲ **Services provided:** Circuit City backs up all its products.

Products are constantly being repositioned as a result of changes in competitive and market situations. Repositioning involves changing the market's perceptions of a product or brand so that it can compete more effectively in its present market or in other market segments. That may involve changing the product itself, its price, or just its promotional message.

SELF-CHECK

- Define **champions, positioning,** and **repositioning.**
- Name some ways that a product can be positioned.
- How can you tell when somebody is a champion of a product?
- What's the differentiation test?

6.5 Deleting a Product

Unlike people and companies, products do not die on their own. They never had a pulse anyway, and product bankruptcy just doesn't exist. Consequently, the marketer needs to have the good sense to know when an old product has no more life in it and keeping it going just wastes resources that ought to go to new products, instead.

Yet often you see weak products hanging around. Companies keep them on the market despite gradually declining sales because everybody, from manufacturer to retailer, hates to face reality. Worse, you sometimes see marketers investing treasured resources trying to boost sales of declining brands through renewed advertising or sales promotions. If the product has one foot in the grave, anyway, you should put those resources into introducing a radically improved version or a replacement product.

You need to face facts: Many products would be better put out of their misery and replaced with something fresh and innovative. "But," you rightly object, "how do we know when our particular product reaches that point of no return?" Here are the warning signs that you are due to replace a product:

▲ The market is saturated and you have a weak/falling share.
▲ A series of improvements fails to create momentum.
▲ Something is wrong with your product.

6.5.1 The Market Is Saturated

What if you do not have many new customers around to convert? Growth slows, limited by the replacement rate for the product, plus whatever basic growth occurs in the size of the target market. This means the market is saturated. **Saturation** means that you and your competitors are selling replacement products.

Saturation alone is no reason to give up on a product — many markets are saturated. An obvious one is the U.S. automobile market. You find very few adults who do not already own a car if they have the means to buy one and the need for one. So manufacturers and dealerships fight for replacement sales and first-time sales to young drivers, which can still be profitable for some of the competitors — but usually not all of them.

If you have a product that has a share of less than, say, 75 percent of the leading product's market share, and if your share is falling relative to the leader, then you are on a long, slow, downward slide. (Market share means the percentage of all product sales that one company captures for itself.)

Better to introduce a replacement and delete the old product than to wait it out. (*Product* is used here in the marketing sense, to include whatever you are offering, whether a good, service, idea, or person. Services, ideas, and even people sometimes need to be withdrawn from the market, just as goods do.) You have to replace the product eventually, and the sooner you do, the less your share and reputation suffer. Whatever else happens, you cannot afford for customers to see you as a has-been in a saturated market!

6.5.2 A Series of Improvements Fails to Create Momentum

Often, companies try a series of "new and improved" versions, new packages, fancy coupon schemes, contests, and point-of-purchase promotions to breathe life into products after they stop generating year-to-year sales growth.

Sometimes these ploys work and help to renew growth. Sometimes they do not. Consider this rule from baseball, which seems to work: Three strikes and you are out. Do not bother trying for a fourth time. It's time for a new player to approach the plate.

FOR EXAMPLE

Deadly Painkiller

Pharmaceutical giant Merck developed the painkiller Vioxx for arthritis patients. The company lost a multimillion dollar lawsuit in 2005 when a Texas widow sued, claiming the drug contributed to her husband's death. During the trial, documents were produced showing company insiders had concerns about the drug's safety before it was released, but those concerns were ignored in favor of a quick push to market. To send a message, the jury awarded the plaintiff the exact dollar figure that Merck's marketers had estimated it would lose if they delayed the drug's release. Merck had to withdraw the drug and face a battery of lawsuits, as well as damaged public relations. Merck (and its customers) would have been better off delaying the drug's release.

6.5.3 Something Is Wrong with Your Product

All too often, marketers discover some flaw in a product that threatens to hurt their company's reputation or puts its customers at risk. If your engineers think that the gas tank in one of your pickup trucks can explode during accidents, should you pull the model immediately and introduce a safer version or keep selling it and put the technical report in your paper shredder?

A major auto company chose the second option. In the long run, the faulty gas tank killed some of its customers, and the company had to stage an extremely unprofitable recall, along with a repair-the-damage publicity campaign, topped by several lawsuits. Marketers should learn a lesson from this, but many do not.

Brand equity and profits take a licking whenever your customers do. But many marketers lack the stomach or the internal political clout to delete a bad product, even when the product may kill customers. Pull the product if you find out it may cause cancer, give people electrical shocks, choke a baby, or even just not work as well as you say it does.

Pull the product immediately and ask questions later. Write a press release announcing that you are acting on behalf of your customers, just in case the rumors are true. By taking this decisive step immediately, you let the market know that you have a great deal more integrity than most. That can only make your brand equity stronger, not weaker. You may be able to tally up some losses if you delete the product, but you cannot put a price on the customer goodwill that you will generate.

Pulling a product takes courage, but it is the best option, when the dust settles. If you always invest creative energy and funds in your product development efforts, you should have something better to offer as a replacement.

6.5.4 How to Delete or Replace a Product

Getting rid of old products is the least of your troubles, because liquidators are happy to sell your inventory below cost to various vendors. Contact some of your distributors or your trade association for referrals.

But you may want to use a more elegant strategy — one that avoids the negativity of customers seeing your old products offered for a tenth of their normal price: Stage some kind of sales promotion to move the old inventory to customers through your normal distribution channels.

This is more positive, especially if it also introduces consumers to the new product. But this method only works if you get started before the old product loses its appeal. So you have to aggressively replace your products. Do not wait for the market to delete your product; do the deed yourself. The **coattails strategy** is a great promotional device for replacing an old product with a new one. Use it whenever you want to delete an old product in order to make room for a new one. *Room* can mean room in the customer's mind, room on the store shelf, room in the distributor's catalog, or room in your own product line.

The variety of ways to put this strategy to use is limited only by your imagination. You can offer a free sample coupon for the new product to buyers of the old product. You can package the two together in a special two-for-one promotion. You can do special mailings or make personal or telephone sales calls to the old customers. If the two products are reasonably similar from a functional perspective, you can call the new product by the old product's name and try to merge it into the old identity as if you wanted to introduce an upgrade rather than something brand new.

In other words, you can dress the new product in the old product's coat instead of just attaching it to the coattails. You need to be able to defend this stealth strategy from a commonsense perspective, or your customers get angry. If you can make the argument that customers are getting a "more and better" version of the same product, then the strategy should work.

Products take up space, and physical or mental space can give you an important resource. But you do take a big risk. When you make room for your new product, competing products can try to take that space, instead. Why? Any customers still faithful to the old product have to reconsider their purchase patterns, and they may choose a competitor over your new option.

Similarly, retailers, distributors, or other channel members may give your space to another product. So you need to hold on to your space, even as you eliminate your product. Avoid any gaps in the availability of your products.

▲ **The product-line placeholding strategy:** Using *product lines* to create clear product niches and hold them for replacement products

You should use price lining when you do this. (Other pricing strategies are discussed in Chapter 9.)

▲ **Price lining:** Keeping pricing consistent with product positions in your product line

For example, a bank may offer a selection of different savings options to its retail customers — a mix of straight savings accounts, savings with checking, mutual-fund accounts, and certificates of deposit. If the bank organizes these options into a coherent range of named products and lists them in a single brochure in order from lowest-risk/lowest-return to highest-risk/highest-return, then it creates a clear product line with well-defined places for these products. Each product sits in a unique place on that spectrum, with no overlaps.

Now, when the bank wants to introduce a new product, it can substitute the new one for an old one, and consumers accept that this new product fills the same spot in the product line. The bank can also extend the line in either direction or fill gaps with new products. Whatever the bank does, the product line can act as a placeholder to ease the entry of new products.

But few banks use this strategy. As a result, you are always confused when you try to understand their offerings, and they therefore lose some business that they should have won. Make sure your offerings fall into a clear product line with an obvious logic and clear points of difference anyone can understand at a glance. Product lines are a very important part of any marketing strategy, yet marketers often neglect them. Clarify the options you give customers and ensure your branding and product offerings make good sense to everyone.

SELF-CHECK

- Name three reasons to delete a product.
- What's the risk in the product-line placeholding strategy?
- Why is price lining useful?
- What's your best option when you have a bad product?
- Explain the coattails strategy.

SUMMARY

Introducing and naming new products is an ongoing process. Developing a brand identity and protecting it is necessary. Packaging and labeling can spur sales, so that POP is a bigger factor in a product's success than many marketers realize. Know when to modify or delete a product. Product-mix strategies such as positioning and modifying products are used to differentiate your product in a competitive marketplace. Price lining helps when introducing a new product.

KEY TERMS

Brand	Any brand name, term, sign, symbol, design, or a combination of these that is intended to identify the goods or services of one seller or group of sellers and to differentiate them from competitors is known as a brand.
Brand mark	The part of the brand that is recognized but is not utterable, such as a symbol, design, or distinctive coloring or lettering.
Brand names	The part of the brand that can be vocalized.
Breadth	Alternatives you give the customer across categories.
Category appraisal	A research technique that seeks new product opportunities within an existing category by finding out what makes the category tick.
Champions	Customers who love a product and will champion it to people they know.
Coattails strategy	A promotional device for replacing an old product with a new one.
Copyright	Legal protection for writing, artwork, performances, and software.
Depth	Alternatives you give the customer within any single category.
Morphemes	Meaningful components for a made-up name.
Packaging	Provides protection, containment, communication, and utility for the product.
Patent	This legally protects a design.
Placeholding strategy	Using product lines to create clear product niches and hold them for replacement products.
Point of purchase	The time and place at which the purchase is made.
Positioning	A strategic management decision that determines the place a product should occupy in a given market — its market niche.
Price lining	Keeping pricing consistent with product positions in your product line.
Product concept	A synthesis or description of a product idea that reflects the core element of the proposed product.

Product life-cycle concept (PLC)	A framework for planning the management of products.
Product line	Any logical grouping of products offered to customers.
Repositioning	Changing the market's perceptions of a product or brand so that it can compete more effectively in its present market or in other market segments.
Saturation	When replacement products are being sold.
Service mark	A service name, which U.S. law treats similarly to a trademark.
Trademark	A legally protected, tangible product's name and/or visual symbol.
Trade name	Protection for a business name or logo.
VIEW	Acronym that stands for visibility, information, emotion, and workability.

ASSESS YOUR UNDERSTANDING

Go to www.wiley.com/college/Hiam to evaluate your knowledge of the basics of product development and management.
Measure your learning by comparing pre-test and post-test results.

Summary Questions

1. You have a 50/50 chance of your new product making it, if you use price lining. True or false?
2. Which of the following is not legally protected?
   (a) patent
   (b) service mark
   (c) product lines
   (d) trade secret
3. VIEW stands for
   (a) visibility, information, emotion, and workability
   (b) visibility, interest, emotion, and workability
   (c) viability, information, emotion, and workability
4. Distribution can help your product pass the differentiation test. True or false?
5. Your product is no longer special if it lacks champions. True or false?
6. The best sources for new product ideas come from basic research. True or false?
7. Which is the correct order for the product development process?
   (a) screening product development ideas, business analysis, manufacturing planning, technical and marketing planning, test marketing, commercialization
   (b) screening product development ideas, technical and marketing planning, manufacturing planning, test marketing, business analysis, commercialization
   (c) screening product development ideas, business analysis, technical and marketing planning, manufacturing planning, test marketing, commercialization
8. The product life-cycle concept has eight stages. True or false?
9. Avis is positioned by which criteria?
10. New products won't sell in saturated markets. True or false?

Review Questions

1. What's the most important factor in the average purchasing decision, according to marketing research?
2. What's price lining and why is it important to use it?
3. What are three situations in which deleting a product is a good idea?
4. List five ways of improving your packaging and labeling. What does VIEW mean in terms of packaging?

Applying This Chapter

1. When is it okay, in business, to use somebody else's idea?
2. You are marketing a clothing line that has failed to catch on for several years. Yet you have other successful products that are doing well. What are some possible reasons for this? Explain some ways to improve the situation.
3. Explain the new product development process for a new laundry detergent. What steps would the new product have to go through?
4. You've launched a successful product line of bedding. Everyone loves your monogrammed sheets and sales are strong. How can you increase the depth and breadth of your product line?

YOU TRY IT

Better-Tasting Fiber

You are introducing a high-fiber cereal, and you want to replace your old cereal, which consumers tell you tastes bad. You hope to use a coattails strategy to gain acceptance for your product. What risks will you encounter? How can you handle them?

A New Wrinkle in Ironing

You are an innovative manufacturer of appliances, including irons. All your products, which use the latest technologies, are doing well, except for your irons. You know that many people hate to iron, although they dislike wrinkles in their clothes. Brainstorm some ways to differentiate your product from the other irons on the market.

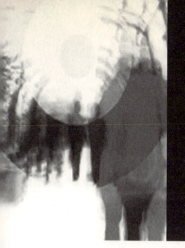

7

MARKETING-CHANNEL MANAGEMENT
Getting Your Product or Service to the Market

Starting Point

Go to www.wiley.com/college/Hiam to assess your knowledge of the basics of marketing-channel management.
Determine where you need to concentrate your effort.

What You'll Learn in This Chapter

▲ Market-channel structure
▲ Direct versus indirect channels
▲ The components of supply-chain management

After Studying This Chapter, You'll Be Able To

▲ Demonstrate how to reduce transactions through intermediaries
▲ Investigate sources of potential distributors
▲ Differentiate between vertical and horizontal marketing

Goals and Outcomes

▲ Assess the efficiency of a channel structure
▲ Compare pros and cons of distribution intensities
▲ Predict the channel-management issues for a company

INTRODUCTION

Your product reaches the consumer through many decisions about intermediaries. How you make these decisions can reduce inefficiencies, save you money, and increase sales. This chapter will explore how you can make the most of your marketing channels, whether it be finding more distributors, streamlining your channel, or using a new channel system.

7.1 Understanding Marketing Channels

Did you ever wonder about how all the different products in stores actually get there, and why some stores are always running out of the things that you want? **Distribution-channel management** is the answer. Improving distribution is one of the few ways that marketers can still cut costs.

Distribution, also known as placement, is considered one of the marketing Ps (see Section 1.1 for more about the marketing P's). The companies with the widest distribution are often the most successful, because that distribution system gives them access to so many potential customers. Channel selection is not a static, once-and-for-all choice, but a dynamic part of marketing planning.

7.1.1 Channel Functions

The channel acts like a bridge to connect the producer of a product and the user of it, whether located in the same community or in different countries across the world. The channel facilitates the transaction, and the physical exchange. An institution, or **channel member,** will be one of these types:

▲ Producer of the product — craftsman, manufacturer, or farmer
▲ User of the product — an individual, household, business buyers, institution, or government
▲ Middlemen at the wholesale or retail level

Indirect channels are the most common, where middlemen are necessary to get the product to the ultimate user. See Figure 7-1 for an example of how an electrical cable manufacturer gets its products to shops and other users.

A channel performs three important types of functions:

▲ Transactional — buying, selling, and risk assumption
▲ Logistical — assembly, storage, sorting, and transportation
▲ Facilitating — postpurchase service and maintenance, financing, information dissemination, and channel coordination or leadership

Figure 7-1

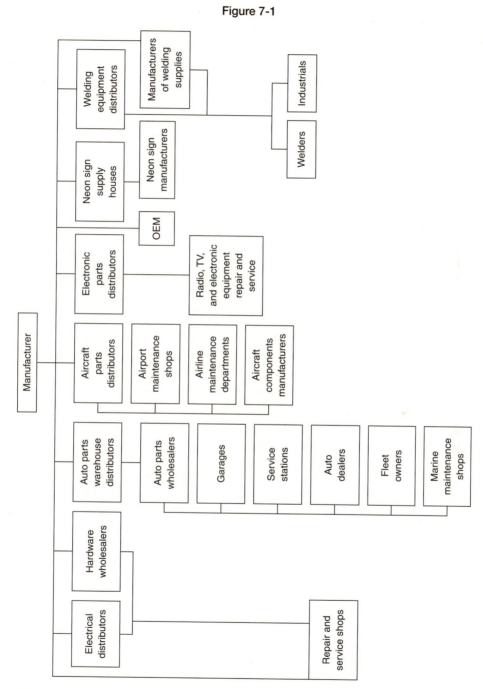

Marketing channels of a manufacturer of electrical wire and cable.

FOR EXAMPLE

Imagine that a producer of custom hunting knives decides to sell through direct mail instead of retail outlets. The producer absorbs the sorting, storage, and risk functions; the post office takes on the transportation function; and the consumer assumes more risk in not being able to touch or try the product before purchase. But the producer gains more control over his or her channel and cuts costs, and the consumer gains the convenience and possibly lower prices of buying direct. Eliminating the middleman doesn't eliminate his functions — it just shuffles them around.

Not every channel performs every function, of course, but all channel members are part of many transactions at any point in time. The complexity can be overwhelming, which is why routinization in the channel is needed. **Routinization** means that the right products are always found in places where the consumer expects to find them, comparisons are possible, prices are marked, and payment methods are available.

Another thing to remember is that although you can eliminate or substitute channel institutions, as when you go direct to the user with a direct channel such as a catalog or Internet sale, you cannot eliminate channel functions. Somebody has got to do it! So if you remove the wholesaler or retailer from the channel, the function that member performs will either be shifted forward to a retailer or the consumer, or shifted backward to a wholesaler or the manufacturer.

Channels can also apply to service products such as health care or air travel. Service marketers also face the strategic problem of delivering their products in the form and at the place and time that their customers demand. Banks have responded by offering ATMs and on-line banking. The medical community provides emergency medical vehicles, outpatient clinics, and home-care providers. Even the performing arts employ distribution channels. See Figure 7-2.

7.1.2 Types of Channel Members

Unless you have a direct channel, several different parties will participate in a given marketing channel.

▲ **Producers and manufacturers:** These firms extract, grow, or make products. Firms range from a one-person operation to a multinational corporation with several thousand people that generates billions of dollars in sales.

Figure 7-2

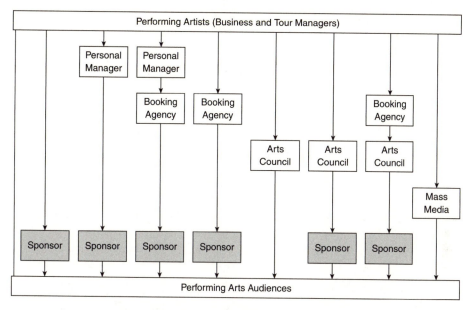

The marketing channels for the performing arts.

All are in business to satisfy the needs of markets, which means that their products must get there. Most of these firms cannot perform all the tasks that would be necessary to distribute their products directly. A computer manufacturer may know everything about designing the finest, fastest computer, but know nothing about sales.

In many cases, the expertise and availability of other channel members make it possible for a producer or manufacturer to even participate in a market. A company like Frito-Lay has immense leverage with various supermarket chains. If you developed a new snack chip, what do you think your chances are of taking shelf space away from Frito-Lay? Zero. Luckily, a specialty catalog retailer is able to include your product for a fee.

It's rare for a manufacturer to have expertise in all the channel functions. Other channel members can be useful to the producer in designing the product, packaging it, pricing it, promoting it, and distributing it.

Retailers are another important channel member.

▲ **Retailers:** Retailing includes all activities necessary to market consumer goods and services to ultimate users who are buying for individual or family needs, as opposed to business, institutional, or industrial use.

Not just traditional stores are involved in retailing — retailing is done by mail order and the Internet, by vending machines, by door-to-door salespeople, and by hotels and motels. Outlets vary in size, also, from small mom-and-pop corner stores to planned shopping centers and malls. (See Chapter 8, Retailing, for more on types of retailers and their functions.)

Retailers often depend upon

▲ **Wholesalers:** Wholesaling includes all activities required to market goods and services to businesses, institutions, or industrial users who are buying for resale or to produce and market other products and services.

Here are three examples of wholesale transactions:

▲ A bank buys a new computer for data processing.
▲ A school buys audio-visual equipment for classroom use.
▲ A dress shop buys dresses for resale.

The vast majority of goods sold in an advanced economy, such as in the United States, have wholesaling involved in their marketing. Even a centrally planned socialist economy needs a structure to handle the movement of goods from the point of production to other production activities or to retailers who distribute to consumers. The types of wholesalers are shown in Figure 7-3.

Retail establishments in the United States outnumber wholesalers; however, the total wholesale sales volume is more than 1 trillion dollars a year, higher than retail sales. Why? Wholesale volume includes sales to industrial users as well as merchandise sold to retailers for resale.

Wholesale functions include the following:

▲ **Warehousing:** Receiving, storing, packaging, and other functions necessary to maintain stock for their customers
▲ **Inventory control and order processing:** Managing inventory and processing transactions to ensure a smooth flow of merchandise from producers to buyers and payment back to producers
▲ **Transportation:** Arranging the physical movement of goods
▲ **Information:** Supplying information about markets to producers and information about products and suppliers to buyers
▲ **Selling:** Personal contact with buyers to sell products and services

Wholesaling activities cannot be eliminated, but they can be taken on by manufacturers and retailers. Merchant wholesalers who have remained in business — despite pressure to reduce intermediaries — have been successful because they provide improved service to suppliers and buyers. Modern technology has been increasingly integrated into wholesaling.

Figure 7-3

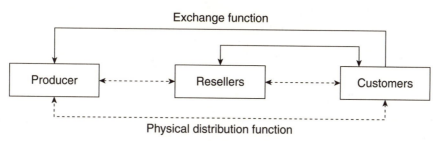

Types of modern wholesalers

SELF-CHECK

- Define **distribution, channel management, channel member, routinization, producers and manufacturers, retailers,** and **wholesalers.**
- What are the three types of channel members?
- What are the three types of channel functions?
- Which is greater — wholesale or retail volume?

7.2 Channel Design

For your channels to be effective, your distribution needs to be efficient. Efficiency is the driving principle behind distribution-channel design. So, having efficient pathways is your goal. Here are some general questions to ask when you are trying to improve distribution:

▲ Can you add distributors or expand your distribution network? If so, your product may become available to more people, and sales may rise.

▲ Can you improve the visibility of your product within its current distribution channel, for example, by displaying it better, if it's a product, or communicating it better, if it's a service? That will boost sales, too.

▲ Can you shift your distribution slightly to give you access to more desirable or larger customers? One large contract can be as valuable as 10 or 20 smaller clients.

▲ Can you increase the availability of your products in your distribution channel? Getting more inventory out there and speeding the movement of products to customers can have a dramatic impact on sales.

▲ Can you find ways to strengthen your business relationships with companies that help you make sales or service customers? Do not take these relationships for granted. Even a gift basket at the holidays can be a good investment in these relationships.

7.2.1 Supply-Chain Management

Supply-chain management is something every businessperson does, whether or not he or she uses the term. It means moving goods or services from one place to another efficiently.

In traditional manufacturing, for example, the supply chain starts at the factory with the production of goods and continues through to the warehousing and distribution channels, ending up in a retail store and, finally, in the consumer's hands.

The typical supply chain has four components:

▲ **Production:** How much, where, and which suppliers are used by other members of the chain
▲ **Inventory:** Where and how many products are kept
▲ **Distribution:** Moving and storing products from place to place
▲ **Payments:** How to pay suppliers and get paid by consumers

7.2.2 Finding Distributors

Major conventions in your industry are the best places to find distributors. Hop on a plane, bring product samples and literature, put on comfortable shoes, and walk around the convention hall until you find the right distributors! Distributors want items that are easy to sell because customers want to buy them. It's that simple.

Here are the steps to gaining distribution:

1. Make sure your product is appealing. A brilliant product and a clear way of presenting that product so its brilliance shines through is a great investment for growing any distribution system. You may still have to go out and tell distributors about it and work to support them, but if you start with a good product, it will be a lot easier to expand your distribution.

2. After you are confident that you have something worth selling, ask yourself what distributors may be successful at selling it. Who's willing and able to distribute? Are wholesalers or other intermediaries going to be helpful? If so, who are they and how many can you locate? Phone companies publish business-to-business telephone directories by region for most of the United States, and these directories often reference the category of intermediary you are looking for in their Yellow Pages sections.

3. You can also find several helpful trade associations and trade shows special-izing in distributors in specific industries. For example, the International Food Distributors Forum puts on an annual conference for food distributors.

4. Who are the retailers that may help you sell? You can much more easily identify retail stores for the simple reason that they're in the business of being easy to find. The Yellow Pages phone directories list retail stores. These stores also have their own trade associations. Consult any directory of associations for extensive listings.

5. Finally, consider wearing out a little shoe leather and tire rubber to find out who the leading retailers are in any specific geographic market. Just visit high-traffic areas and see which stores are prominent and successful to iden-tify the leading retailers.

7.2.3 Getting Closer to the Customer

Traditionally, channels have evolved to minimize the number of transactions, because the fewer the transactions, the more efficient the channel. As Figure 7-4 shows, a channel in which four producers and four customers do business directly has 16 (4×4) possible transactions. In reality, the numbers get much higher when you have markets with dozens or hundreds of producers and thousands or mil-lions of customers.

You lower the number of transactions greatly when you introduce an interme-diary because then you do not have to do all the selling directly. In the example shown in Figure 7-4, you only need 8 ($4 + 4$) transactions to connect all four cus-tomers with all four producers through the intermediary. Each producer or cus-tomer only has to deal with the intermediary, who links him to all the producers or customers he may want to do business with.

Although intermediaries add their markup to the price, they often reduce overall costs of distribution because of their effect on the number of transactions. Adding a level of intermediaries to a channel reduces the total number of transac-tions that all producers and customers need to do business with each other.

This example is simplistic, but you can see how the logic applies to more com-plex and larger distribution channels. Introduce a lot of customers and producers, link them through multiple intermediaries (perhaps adding a second or third layer of intermediaries), and you have a classic indirect marketing channel. Many indus-tries have some channels like this.

These traditional, multilevel channels can be problematic. The longer and more complex they grow, the more types of intermediaries they have. The more times a product is handed from intermediary to intermediary, the more room for problems. Only one layer between you and your customers, if possible, works best. Traditional, many-layered channels separate you too much from the end consumer. Some modern business trends make running lean and mean channels easier:

▲ Improved transportation
▲ Computerized links between channel members (through *electronic data interchange* or *EDI*)
▲ Just-in-time inventory systems in which suppliers bring only what's needed, when it's needed
▲ Direct-marketing technologies and practices

Figure 7-4

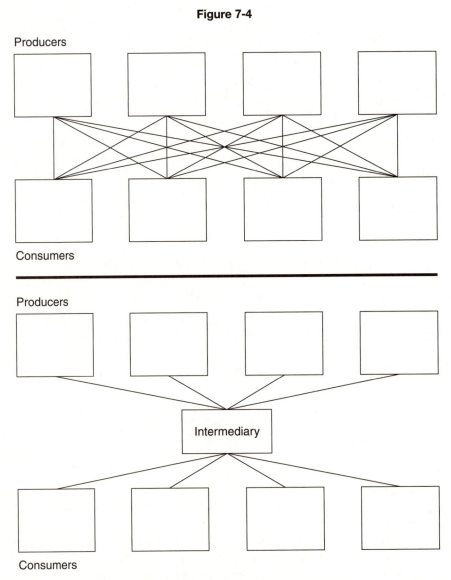

Reducing transactions through intermediaries.

Just as big companies are delayering to become more efficient and get closer to their customers, the big distribution channels in many industries are trying to do the same thing. The trend is toward simpler and more direct channels, and marketers need to be prepared to handle a large number of customer transactions on their own without as much help from intermediaries. Database-management techniques alone do much to make this future possible.

So think hard about how to get closer to your customer. Can you reduce the layers in your channel or begin to develop direct channels (by mail, phone, or Internet) to supplement your traditional indirect channels? If so, balance the advantages of being close to the end customer with the benefits of broad reach from having many distributors. One way to do this is to add more distributors in the horizontal direction, where each new distributor buys directly from you, not through another distributor who then bundles their purchase with others and sends it on to you. Think broad distribution, not deep, if you want modern reach without traditional layers and all of the complexities and costs of those layers.

7.2.4 Channel-Marketing Systems

Whether they are planned or not, distribution channels have an observable structure. We'll talk about the three most common types here.

▲ **Conventional channels:** Channel members who are working independently without a central leader

A group of independent businesses, each motivated by profit, and having little concern about any other member of the distribution sequence, is the typical situation. Informally organized and ran, these channels share no common goals.

The problems with conventional channels are that tasks can go undone, power struggles can be rampant, and ineffective channel relationships can persist for years. It some cases, however, the problems can be worked out.

▲ **Vertical marketing systems:** When a member of the channel, typically the manufacturer, takes a leadership role and coordinates the efforts of the channel so that mutually beneficial goals can be attained

Vertical marketing systems, or VMS, have emerged to solve the problems of conventional channel structures.

VMS has three forms:

▲ **Administered VMS:** Very close to the conventional network, but informally guided by goals and programs developed by one or a few firms in the existing channel. The **channel captain** can be the driving force of the channel. Dominant brands such as Proctor & Gamble are able to get this kind of cooperation. The advantages are higher profits, greater product exposure, better-organized inventory management and promotional activities, and better-functioning channels. Yet a single person cannot always handle the responsibility of managing it, and channel members can become polarized when some try to remain independent of the system.

▲ **Contractual VMS:** If channel members formalize their relationship with a contractual agreement, the most popular form of VMS occurs. It creates additional control by spelling out the marketing functions to be performed by all members of the channel.

▲ **Corporate VMS:** If channel members on different levels are owned and operated by one organization, it's known as a corporate vertical marketing system. There are two variations:

- **Forward integration:** When a manufacturer owns the various members of its channel network
- **Backward integration:** When a retailer takes over the wholesaling and manufacturing tasks

Manufacturers who have integrated through to the retail level are Dannon Yogurt and Pepperidge Farms. Sears and Safeway are examples of backward integration. Total integration is also being used.

▲ **Horizontal channel systems:** When two companies get together and establish a relationship to work with each other, usually because they do not have the capital or the technical or production know-how to market their products themselves.

Such a relationship can be permanent or temporary. For instance, two small producers may combine their shipments to common markets in order to gain full-carload transportation rates that each could not obtain separately. Another common scenario is for a large retailer to buy out several competing small retailers in order to gain entry into certain markets or with certain customers.

7.2.5 Channel-Design Strategies

When looking at your marketing channels, the following big-picture strategic issues will come up. How you set up and manage your distribution channel or channels affects each issue. Consider market coverage and speed to market.

When considering market coverage, look at how well your channel reaches your target customers. If you go direct, doing everything yourself, you may be unable to cover the market as intensely as you want. By adding even one layer of intermediaries, you suddenly have many more warm bodies or storefronts out there. As you add more layers to the channel, the bottom of the channel grows ever larger, allowing you to achieve increasingly good market coverage. In short, market coverage increases as you add layers and members to your distribution

FOR EXAMPLE

The Popularity of Catalogs

The reasons for the trend toward catalog direct shopping in the clothing industry are not mysterious. Customers can obtain their choice of style and size from a large assortment within a few days, if the shipper uses UPS, or the next day, if the shipper uses an overnight air service. You may think that you can shop in a department store more quickly because you can walk out with your purchase. But you may not have time to visit a department store for days or weeks whereas you can take care of a late-night call to Lands' End today. Catalog clothing sales are gaining over retail sales, in part because many consumers perceive catalog shopping as the quicker and easier alternative.

channel. As you increase market coverage, you increase your availability to customers, which in turn maximizes your sales and market share. You cannot fight that. So sometimes building a channel, rather than delayering it, makes sense. Just make sure that you really do get better coverage and that the coverage translates into increased sales. Otherwise, those intermediaries aren't pulling their weight.

In terms of speed to market, the longer the channel, the slower the product's trip from producer to customer. A relay team can never beat an individual runner in a sprint. If your customers need or want faster delivery and service, you have to prune the distribution channel until it's fast enough to satisfy the consumers. You may even need to replace physical distributors with a Web site where everything can be ordered immediately, for next-day delivery. Catalog shopping is a good illustration of this.

SELF-CHECK

- Define **supply-chain management, conventional channels, vertical marketing systems, forward integration, backward integration,** and **horizontal channel systems.**
- What is the driving principle behind channel design?
- What are the four supply-chain components?
- What are the three types of channel systems?
- Backward and forward integrating systems fall into what category of systems?

7.3 Understanding Channel Dynamics

The way many channels are organized, each channel member is only concerned with the channel members immediately next to it — the ones each buys from and sells to. Ideally, everyone would cooperate with everyone else and the channel would run smoothly all the time. In the real world, this rarely happens.

The tendency is for these channel members to try to exhibit their independence as separate business operations. Because channels involve people, channels have interpersonal dynamics. These four things need to be taken into account:

▲ Roles
▲ Communication
▲ Conflict
▲ Power

7.3.1 Roles

A major issue in channel management is defining the roles of various participants to achieve desired results. The tasks to be performed must be carefully appraised and clear communication given to each member about what it is supposed to be doing.

Most channel members participate in several channels. Establishing the role for each member means defining what its behavior should be. For example, the manufacturer should maximize the sales of his or her particular brand of product. This means actively competing for market share and aggressively promoting the brand.

The roles of independent wholesalers, on the other hand, are quite different. Because they are likely to represent several competing manufacturers, the role would be to build sales with whatever brands are most heavily demanded by retailers. This may conflict with the role of a particular manufacturer, but it is necessary for the system to function.

7.3.2 Communication

▲ Channel communication is sending and receiving information relevant to operating the channel. Each channel member must help create an effective flow of communication within the channel. The **channel captain** is the person leading the channel.

The channel manager should try to detect any behavioral problems that inhibit the flow of communication and try to solve them before communication becomes seriously distorted. Members will only communicate if they perceive it to be in their own interest to do so, so the channel manager must keep communication going.

> ## FOR EXAMPLE
>
> ### Power Plays between Channel Members
>
> A large retailer may want the manufacturer to either modify the design of the product or perhaps to be required to carry less inventory. Both parties may attempt to exert power in an attempt to influence the other's behavior. The ability of either of the parties to achieve the outcome he or she prefers will depend on the amount of power that each can bring to bear.

7.3.3 Conflict

Managing the inevitable conflicts in the channel is necessary. Conflict can be personal and direct, and it is pervasive in distribution, where members' interests often collide. To manage conflict, a mechanism must be established for detecting it, appraising the effects of, and resolving the conflict. This last consideration is the most difficult part to accomplish.

Some techniques that are used:

▲ Implementing a channel committee
▲ Joint goal setting
▲ Bringing in an outside arbitrator

In some cases, conflict is necessary. This is the case in the e-marketplace. Anne Mulcahy, President of Xerox General Markets, notes, "Those that do not aggressively embrace multiple channels for multiple products will get left behind. The inherent conflict in this business model is not only a reality of business; it's a sign of a healthy company."

SELF-CHECK

- Define **channel manager.**
- What are the four channel dynamics?
- Who is the person who can work toward efficient communication in the channel?

7.4 The Channel-Management Process

Channels, like products, promotions, and pricing, need management. Channels are made up of people, as already noted, and managing channels requires skill and finesse. The five steps of the channel-management process are

Step   1: Analyze the consumer

Step   2: Establish the channel objectives

Step   3: Specify distribution tasks

Step   4: Evaluate and select intermediaries

Step   5: Evaluate channel-member performance

7.4.1 Step 1. Analyze the Consumer

This is the first step in the channel-management process. Two questions need to be answered:

▲ Who is the ultimate user and buyer of the product or service?

▲ Who is the immediate purchaser of the product or service?

Sometimes, if you have a direct channel, the two buyers are identical. But in any event, you need to know who they are, what they need, when they buy, and how they buy. Let's first look at the ultimate user. The buyer of a high-definition television may be described in this way:

▲ Purchases only from a well-established, reputable dealer

▲ Purchases only after considerable shopping to compare prices and merchandise

▲ Willing to go to some inconvenience, spending time and traveling, to locate the most acceptable brand

▲ Purchases only after extended conversations involving all interested parties, including dealer, users, and other purchasers

▲ Purchases only from a dealer equipped to give prompt and reasonable product servicing

This illustrates the kinds of requirements — what the buyer demands — that you must know about if you are manufacturing high-definition televisions. Usually this kind of information is fairly obvious and can be discovered without much research.

But, in some cases, it's more complicated. Consider that certain people will not dine at restaurants that serve alcohol and that some people will only go to supermarkets that have ethnic merchandise. When you know what the consumer wants, you can decide on which wholesaler and retailer you should use.

For the immediate purchaser, or reseller, you need to ask from whom your retail outlets prefer to buy. Some retailers may prefer to buy directly from manufacturers, but not all. Some prefer to buy from local distributors who have lenient credit terms, offer a wide assortment of merchandise, and can deliver the product quickly.

7.4.2 Step 2. Establish the Channel Objectives

When a company is just getting started, or an older company is trying to carve out a new market niche, the channel objectives may become dominant — more important than overall marketing strategy and long-term goals. Think about a small manufacturer that wants to expand out of its local market. Its immediate obstacle is that it receives limited shelf space. Without this exposure, the product is doomed. So, overcoming these obstacles becomes its channel objective.

Channel objectives can be of several types:

▲ To grow sales by reaching new markets or increasing sales in existing markets
▲ To maintain or improve market share by educating or assisting channel members to increase the amount of product they handle
▲ To achieve a pattern of distribution by structuring the channel differently
▲ To create an efficient channel by modifying various flow mechanisms

7.4.3 Step 3. Specify Distribution Tasks

Each channel member has a function within the channel system. Sometimes they take on more than one function. You, or the channel manager, need to decide what they will do, by evaluating all phases of the distribution network. This means identifying tasks and their costs accurately and precisely.

How do intermediaries earn their cut? In deciding how to distribute your product, draw up a list of tasks you want distributors to do. For example, you may want distributors to find you more customers than you can find on your own. That's just one of the functions distributors may be able to perform.

Decide what you'd like them to do, and then seek out distributors who say they want to do those things for you. That way, you will be more likely to get a good match. Here's a starting list of functions you may want your intermediaries to perform. One or more of these functions may be important to you:

▲ Finding more customers for your product than you can on your own
▲ Researching customer attitudes and desires

▲ Buying and selling
▲ Breaking down bulk shipments for resale
▲ Setting prices
▲ Managing point-of-purchase promotions
▲ Advertising at the local level (**pull advertising,** which is designed to bring people to a store or other business)
▲ Transporting products
▲ Inventorying products
▲ Financing purchases
▲ Separating poor-quality leads from serious customers (marketers call this **qualifying sales leads**)
▲ Providing customer service and support
▲ Sharing the risks of doing business
▲ Combining your products with others to offer appropriate assortments

7.4.4 Step 4. Evaluate and Select Intermediaries

Once you've decided what the channel members will need to do, you need to choose who is best equipped to perform these tasks. Your intermediaries can do several useful things for you, and you should decide who can best do which of these things. You need to evaluate the following options, which we discuss in this section:

▲ Number of levels
▲ Intensity at each level
▲ Types of intermediaries
▲ Who should lead

Channels can range from two to many, but five is a typical number. In some industries everyone does it the same way because of tradition, but in others, this is more flexible and subject to rapid change. Thinking about the issue of market coverage in terms of intensity is useful.

▲ **Intensity:** The extent of your geographic coverage of the market

Your level of intensity can help you figure out how many and what types of distributors to use. Conventional wisdom says that three practical strategies exist.

1. **An intensive distribution strategy.** This attempts to put every customer within reach of your products by using as many intermediaries and layers as needed to create maximum coverage.

You should use this strategy in mature markets where your competitors are trying to do the same thing, or in markets where the customer makes a convenience purchase, because intensive distribution makes your product convenient. This strategy is costly, and you may not need it in other circumstances.

Advantages are increased sales, wider consumer recognition, and considerable impulse purchasing. Disadvantages are low prices, low margins, and smaller order sizes, and the difficulty of trying to stimulate and control a large number of intermediaries.

2. **A selective distribution strategy.** This targets the most desirable areas or members of your market.

For example, the business-to-business marketer may decide to target a geographic region where many users of her technology are headquartered. The consumer-products marketer may decide to market to zip-code areas or counties where he finds heavy users of his product. You need to consider market potential, density of population, dispersion of sales, and competitors' distribution policies. It's difficult to determine the optimal number of intermediaries in each market.

3. **Exclusive distribution.** This is the strategy of cherry picking to find the best intermediaries and customers.

This strategy is appropriate when you do not have any really serious competition and you have a specialty product that you want to keep providing at the same profitable level. This method doesn't grow your market or boost share significantly, but it does maximize profit margins!

Exclusive distribution is also appropriate as you introduce an innovative new product, whether a good or a service. With a limited number of early adopters in any market, a massive effort to mass-market a new innovative product usually fails. Start with exclusive distribution to those customers most interested in trying new ideas and then work up to selective distribution as competition builds and the product goes mainstream.

Finally, push toward intensive distribution as the market matures and your emphasis shifts from finding first-time users to fighting over repeat business. Ethan Allen and Drexel Heritage Furniture use this strategy. The advantages are high dealer loyalty, greater control, and considerable sales support. But you sacrifice potential sales, and the success of your product depends (for better or worse) on the performance of a single intermediary.

The intensity decision is extremely critical, because it is an important part of the firm's overall marketing strategy. Companies such as Coca-Cola and Timex watches have been successful with intensive distribution strategies.

After you gather information on the distribution tasks that potential intermediaries perform, you can eliminate alternatives. Then you can narrow it down further using a few other factors, for instance:

▲ Environmental trends
▲ Reputation of the reseller
▲ Level of experience of reseller
▲ Geographic factors

More information on finding distributors is in Section 7.2.2.

Regardless of which channel framework you select, channels work better if somebody is providing some kind of leadership. You need a channel member to coordinate the goals and efforts of the channel members. Historically, before 1920, the role of the wholesaler was the most vital, and wholesalers led most channels.

Today, manufacturers and retailers try to exert power through their sizes. In a type of business "cold war," both have tried to gain dominance through matching the others' size, leading to business warfare over who will lead the channel. Here are some general points:

▲ The manufacturer should lead if control of the product is critical for things like merchandising and repair and if the design and redesign of the channel is best done by the manufacturer.
▲ The wholesaler is better suited when the manufacturers and retailers are small, numerous, relatively scattered geographically, financially weak, and lacking in marketing expertise.
▲ The retailer should lead when product development and demand stimulation are relatively unimportant and when personal attention to the consumer is paramount.

7.4.5 Step 5. Evaluating Channel-Member Performance

The failure of one component can cause everyone to fail. Channels are normally evaluated by their sales performance. You want to look at current sales compared with historical sales, compare sales with other channel members, and also consider whether they are meeting quotas. Other possible performance criteria:

▲ Maintenance of adequate inventory
▲ Selling capabilities
▲ Attitudes toward the product
▲ Competition from other intermediaries and from other product lines carried by the manufacturer's own channel members

FOR EXAMPLE

Avon Lady Gets Distribution Makeover

Avon Products Inc. decided to get serious about reducing distribution costs after losing sales in early 2005. The international company announced it was spending $200 million on new technology to streamline its global supply chain. Avon noted, however, that restructuring might be necessary to do this. One of Avon's target markets is China, where in 1998 it was banned from selling door-to-door — its successful business model — but was given permission to use direct selling again. This way of selling has allowed it to grow in countries where retail networks are less developed. (Reported in the *Wall Street Journal,* September 2005.)

You should think hard before making changes to existing channels. Channel relationships tend to be long term, and terminating members for performance should be done only as a last resort because of its profound effect on the rest of the system. If you can correct deficiencies, this is far less destructive and will maintain goodwill among channel members.

New competition, technology, or market potential can force changes to the structure. Sometimes a producer will need to add an entirely new channel or delete an existing one. If you make camera accessories, for instance, and you want to reach the skilled amateur market, as well as the professional photographer market, you'll need to design a different channel and learn about a new set of intermediaries.

SELF-CHECK

- Define **pull advertising, qualifying sales leads, and intensity.**
- Name some possible channel objectives.
- What are the five steps of the channel-management process?
- What are the three types of distribution strategies?

SUMMARY

Channels have various structures. Channel members can take on different functions when the channel design is modified, but all the functions need to be accomplished. Channel dynamics can get in the way of efficiency, so channel-management systems are sometimes employed. Your goal is to reduce inefficiency in the channel.

KEY TERMS

Backward integration	When a retailer takes over the wholesaling and manufacturing tasks.
Channel captain	The driving force of the channel.
Conventional channels	Channel members who are working independently without a central leader.
Exclusive distribution	When you cherry pick to find the best intermediaries and customers.
Forward integration	When a manufacturer owns the various members of its channel network.
Horizontal channel system	When two companies get together and establish a relationship to work with each other, usually because they do not have the capital or the technical or production know-how to market their products themselves.
Intensity	The extent of your geographic coverage of the market.
Intensive distribution strategy	This attempts to put every customer within reach of your products by using as many intermediaries and layers as needed to create maximum coverage.
Producers and manufacturers	These firms extract, grow, or make products. Firms range from a one-person operation to a multinational corporation with several thousand people that generates billions of dollars in sales.
Retailers	Retailing includes all activities necessary to market consumer goods and services to ultimate users who are buying for individual or family needs, as opposed to business, institutional, or industrial use.
Routinization	The right products are always found in places where the consumer expects to find them, comparisons are possible, prices are marked, and payment methods are available.

Selective distribution strategy

When you target the most desirable areas or members of your market.

Vertical marketing system

When a member of the channel, typically the manufacturer, takes a leadership role and coordinates the efforts of the channel so that mutually beneficial goals can be attained.

Wholesalers

Wholesaling includes all activities required to market goods and services to businesses, institutions, or industrial users who are buying for resale or to produce and market other products and services.

ASSESS YOUR UNDERSTANDING

Go to www.wiley.com/college/Hiam to evaluate your knowledge of the basics of marketing-channel management.
Measure your learning by comparing pre-test and post-test results.

Summary Questions

1. You can eliminate the functions of the channel members, but you cannot eliminate the members. True or false?
2. Indirect channels are the most common in business. True or false?
3. Which would **not** be a channel objective?
   (a) sales growth
   (b) maintaining market share
   (c) restructuring the channel
   (d) direct marketing
4. Conventional channels are usually managed by the wholesaler. True or false?
5. The first step of the channel-management process is to analyze the consumer. True or false?
6. The most popular form of VMS is
   (a) backward integration
   (b) forward integration
   (c) corporate
   (d) contractual
7. The extent of your geographic coverage of the market is called *intensity*. True or false?
8. Outside arbitrators are sometimes used for managing channel conflict. True or false?
9. Distribution is one of the five P's of the marketing mix. True or false?
10. Which type of distribution would be appropriate for a tire manufacturer?
    (a) intensive
    (b) exclusive
    (c) inclusive
    (d) direct

Review Questions

1. When are channel objectives a dominant consideration for a company?
2. List the four components of the supply chain.
3. What are the three types of functions carried out by a marketing-channel member?
4. Explain the advantages and disadvantages of using intermediaries.

Applying This Chapter

1. Assume you are a manufacturer of children's car seats. Who do you think is the ultimate user of a child's car seat? Name two probable purchase requirements that this person might have that would affect your choice of distributors. Are there any special things you need to determine when you are analyzing this buyer and deciding where to distribute this product? Under what circumstances would direct channels be a good idea?
2. You own a small bakery. You bake most of your goods on the premises, but you purchase some of the bread from a wholesale baker. The prices have gone up twice in the last year, and you think the quality is slipping. You think you can take over all the baking yourself and do it better. What would this move be called in marketing terms? Name one possible disadvantage of losing your wholesaler.
3. You are manufacturing a new type of snowboard that is designed to be easier to turn. It looks a little different from other snowboards on the market already, but you know it performs better based on your tests. What are the functions your distributors will need to provide for you, that you cannot do yourself (without opening your own stores)?

Too Much Luxury

You are selling luxury goods, and you've noticed that your sales are better in stores in certain geographic areas. You have decided to rethink your intensive distribution strategy of being in every possible store and add a direct-marketing component to your marketing by publishing an annual catalog. What type of distribution strategy would you now be pursuing? Why is this a better strategy for you?

8

RETAILING
Measuring Your Marketing

Starting Point

Go to www.wiley.com/college/Hiam to assess your knowledge of the basics of retailing.
Determine where you need to concentrate your effort.

What You'll Learn in This Chapter

▲ Different types of retailers
▲ Direct marketing strategies
▲ Criteria for a strong POP display
▲ Merchandising strategies

After Studying This Chapter, You'll Be Able To

▲ Apply an understanding of consumer behaviors
▲ Analyze the components of successful retailing concepts
▲ Improve your odds with direct-marketing techniques
▲ Find a unique selling proposition for your POP display

Goals and Outcomes

▲ Utilize different merchandising strategies
▲ Put together effective direct-response ads
▲ Choose a retail location with good potential

INTRODUCTION

Retailing, the final destination of your supply chain, is the endgame for the marketer. You can measure your marketing success by how well you do at the retail level. We discuss what matters in retail, from creative concepts to point-of-purchase displays to drawing traffic. The right merchandising strategies can drive the success of your retail effort. Use direct-marketing techniques to sell directly to your customer.

8.1 Types of Retailers

When you think of retailing, you may typically think of a store. But retail sales are also made by door-to-door salespeople, over the Internet (*e-tailing*), through mail-order catalogs, by vending machines, and at hotels and motels. Although most retail sales are still made in brick-and-mortar stores, the convenience of other types of retailing has boosted their popularity.

Retailers vary in size, in services provided, in the assortment of merchandise they carry, and in many other ways. Most retailers have sales of under $500 a week, but some have exceeded $1 million on special days. The types of retailers include the following:

▲ **Department stores.** Have very wide product mixes and their merchandise is typically displayed in a different section or department within a store.

▲ **Chain stores.** Able to buy a wide variety in large quantity discounts. They can buy at a discount, and undercut the prices of smaller competitors. Also have an advantage at getting the best locations.

▲ **Supermarkets.** Large self-service stores with central checkout facilities. They boast extensive food selections and low-cost distribution methods. Lately supermarkets have been getting larger and including more prepared foods, nonfood goods, and outside services, such as banking.

▲ **Discount houses.** Developed with the growth of the suburbs. These emphasize price as their sales appeal. Limited assortments of the most popular goods, with long hours, free parking, and simple fixtures.

▲ **Warehouse retailing.** Catalog showrooms are the largest of this type, which had enormous growth in the 1970s, with more than $10 billion in annual sales today. Includes Home Depot and Staples.

▲ **Franchises.** These originated as a response to large chain stores from small business owners. Franchises allow small businesses to compete by giving them the resources of a national operation. Common examples are oil companies such as Mobil and automobile dealerships.

> ## FOR EXAMPLE
>
> ### The Mall Fights Back
>
> Malls face increasing competition from on-line shopping and from discounters. Yet they aren't going away. Consumers may have less time and may like the bargains they find at Wal-Mart, but shopping is still a form of entertainment for many. And malls are responding by researching their customers and giving them what they want. Upscale malls have services such as valet parking and car washes. The mall has become a high-quality environment for the delivery of high-touch, high-experience, high-margin retail goods and services: a place you go for the entertainment shopping experience.

▲ **Boutiques or specialty shops.** Stores or Internet sites, usually single proprietorships, that specialize in unique goods. Shoppers generally are not as price sensitive because they do not know if they can get the same thing somewhere else.

▲ **Planned shopping centers or malls.** Exploded with the growth of suburbia. These range from *local clusters* to *regional centers* that have major department stores as their anchors. Facing increasing challenges from discount giants such as Wal-Mart and more convenient options such as e-tailing.

▲ **Nonstore retailing.** This is a growing, important sector of the market. Used often for products such as life insurance, cigarettes, magazines, books, CDs, and clothing. Includes *in-home sellers* such as Avon and Electrolux, vending machines and kiosks, mail-order and catalog marketing, and on-line marketing or e-tailing. See Chapter 13 for a full discussion of on-line marketing. In Section 8.4 we talk about direct marketing, which enables you to market directly to your customer and eliminate distribution channels (for more on distribution, see Chapter 7.)

SELF-CHECK

- Local clusters and regional centers are what type of retailer?
- What is nonstore retailing?
- A catalog showroom is considered what type of retailer?

8.2 Merchandising Strategies

Whether you retail services or goods, you need to think about your merchandising strategy. You do have one, whether you know it or not — and if you do not know it, then your strategy is based on conventions in your industry and needs a kick in the seat of the pants to make it more distinctive.

▲ **A merchandising strategy** is the selection and assortment of products offered.

This tends to be the most important source of competitive advantage or disadvantage for retailers. What should be your merchandising strategy? To answer this, you need to recognize your own strengths — what makes you especially notable — and make sure you translate that uniqueness into visible, attractive aspects of both exterior and interior store design. Take a creative approach to merchandising, and think about ways to entertain customers and make them want to stay longer. The majority of success stories in retailing come about because of innovations in merchandising.

You need to think about what product lines you offer, and in what depth and breadth. Designing product lines is explained in Section 6.2.2.

So you should be thinking of new merchandising options daily — and trying out the most promising ones as often as you can afford to. The following sections describe some existing strategies, which may give you ideas. Perhaps no one has tried them in your industry or region, or perhaps they suggest novel variations to you.

8.2.1 General Merchandise Retailing

This strategy works because it brings together a wide and deep assortment of products, thus allowing customers to easily find what they want — regardless of what the product may be. Department stores and variety stores fall into this category.

FOR EXAMPLE

That's Entertainment

Examples of entertaining retail concepts include The Rainforest Cafe and the Hard Rock Cafe, two ways of combining a restaurant with entertaining extras. Likewise, Sharper Image mall stores display lots of interesting gadgets, including massage chairs people can try out — a form of entertainment. And some Barnes & Noble bookstores create comfortable, enclosed children's book sections with places to play and read or be read to, so that families with young children can linger and enjoy the experience.

Hypermarkets, the European expansion of the grocery store that includes some department store product lines, are another example of the general merchandise strategy. In the United States, Wal-Mart is a leader because it offers more variety (and often better prices) than nearby competitors. The warehouse store (such as OfficeMax) gives you another example of general merchandise retailing. And as this varied list of examples suggests, you can implement this strategy in many ways.

8.2.2 Limited-Line Retailing

Limited-line retailing emphasizes depth over variety. In New England, the Bread & Circus chain of grocery stores specializes in natural and organic food products; as a result, the chain can offer far greater choices in this specialized area than the average grocery store. Similarly, a bakery can offer more and better varieties of baked goods because a bakery sells only those baked goods.

Limited-line retailing is especially common in professional and personal services. Most accounting firms just do accounting. Most chiropractic offices just offer chiropractic services. Most law firms just practice law. Innovation in the marketing of services is rare.

Perhaps you can combine several complementary services into a less limited line than your competitors. If you can expand your line without sacrificing quality or depth of offerings, you can give customers greater convenience — and that convenience should make you a winner.

After all, the limited-line strategy only makes sense to customers if they gain something in quality or selection in exchange for the lack of convenience. Regrettably, many limited-line retailers fail to make good on this implied promise — and they're easily run over when a business introduces a less-limited line nearby.

What makes, say, the local stationery or shoe store's selection better than what a Staples or Wal-Mart offers in a more convenient setting? If you are a small businessperson, you should make sure that you have plenty of good answers to that question! Know what makes your merchandise selection, concept, or location different and better than that of your monster competitors.

8.2.3 Scrambled Merchandising

With a **scrambled merchandising strategy,** the merchant uses unconventional combinations of product lines. Consumers have preconceived notions about what product lines and categories belong together. Looking for fresh produce in a grocery store makes sense these days because dry goods and fresh produce have been combined by so many retailers. But 50 years ago, the idea would seem radical because specialized limited-line retailers used to sell fresh produce. When grocery stores combined these two categories, they were using a scrambled merchandising strategy.

Today, the meat department, bakery, deli section, seafood department, and many other sections combine naturally in a modern grocery store. And many are adding other products and services, such as a coffee bar, bank, bookshop, dry cleaners, shoe repair, hair salon, photographer, flower shop, post office, and so on! In the same way, gas stations combine with fast-food restaurants and convenience stores to offer pit stops for both car and driver. These scrambled merchandising concepts are now widely accepted.

You can use scrambling as a great way to innovate. It gets at the essence of creativity because many people define creativity as the search for unexpected but pleasing combinations of things or ideas. But you should never employ this strategy just for your convenience as a marketer. Too often, retailers add a novel product line just because doing so is easy. They know someone in another industry who can handle the line for them, or they have a chance to buy a failed business for peanuts. Those reasons are the wrong sort to justify scrambling.

Scrambling only works if you approach it from the customer's point of view by seeking new combinations that may have special customer appeal. For example, several innovators around the United States have stumbled independently upon the concept of combining a coffee shop and an Internet access service into one retail store. The result is a natural — a coffee shop where you can enjoy your espresso while cruising the Internet or flirting with another customer on-line. This new combination adds up to more than the sum of its parts, giving customers a pleasurable new retail experience.

8.2.4 Price and Quality Strategies

Retail stores generally have a distinct place in the range of possible price and quality combinations. Some stores are obviously upscale boutiques, specializing in the finest merchandise — for the highest prices. Others are middle class in their positioning, and still others offer the worst junk from liquidators but sell it for so little that almost anybody can afford it. In this way, retailing still maintains the old distinctions of social class, even though those class distinctions are less visible in other aspects of modern U.S. and European society.

As a retailer, this distinction means that customers get confused about who you are unless you let them know where you stand on the class scale. Does your store have an upper-class pedigree, or is it upper-middle, middle, or lower-middle class? Do you see your customers as white collar or blue collar? And so on.

After you make a decision about how to place your store, you are ready to decide what price strategy to pursue. In general, the higher class the store's image, the higher the prices that the store can charge. But the real secret to success is to price just a step below your image. That way, customers feel like they're buying first-class products for second-class prices. And that makes them very happy, indeed!

8.2.5 Pursuing Retail Sales

After choosing a merchandising strategy, many retailers take a passive approach. They put the products on the shelves or display racks and wait for customers to pick them up and bring them to the counter. Other retailers are a bit more proactive. They have staff walking the aisles or floors, looking for customers who may need some help. But few retailers go all the way and actually put trained salespeople on the floor to work the customers. Less than half of all retailers make active efforts to close a sale. Even approaching customers to ask whether they need help is rare.

Sometimes a hands-off approach makes sense, but in general, if people walk into a store, they're considering making a purchase, which makes them likely prospects. Somebody should find out what their wants or needs are and try to meet them! The effort doesn't need to be pushy — in fact, the effort shouldn't be pushy or you reduce return visits — but you should make a friendly effort to be helpful.

Find out what customers are looking for, offer them whatever you have that seems relevant, and ask them if they want to make a purchase. The last part, asking them for the purchase, is especially important. In selling, you call that the close, and when you attempt to close sales, you usually up the sales rate. See Section 10.2 for more details on personal selling.

8.3 Creative Retailing

If you decide to improve sales at a retail store and you bring in a specialized retail consultant, you may soon be drawing *planograms* of your shelves and counting *SKUs*.

▲ **Planograms:** Diagrams showing how to lay out and display a store's merchandise

▲ **SKUs or stock-keeping units:** A unique inventory code for each item you stock

You may also examine the statistics on sales volume from end-of-aisle displays (higher sales) versus middle of the aisle (lower sales), and from eye-level displays (higher sales) versus bottom or top of the shelf (lower sales). Although a technical approach has its place, you cannot use this method to create a retail success story.

Yet your work will not be over. The real winners in retail are the result of creative thinking and good site selection, in that order. Those points are the two big-picture issues that determine whether your store has low or high performance. A creative, appealing store concept, in a spot that has the right sort of traffic, and a lot of it. **Traffic** is the flow of target customers near enough to the store for its external displays and local advertising to draw them in.

You want a great deal of traffic, whether it's foot traffic on a sidewalk, automobile traffic on a road or highway, or virtual traffic at a Web site. Retailers need to have people walking, driving, or surfing into their stores ("virtual" stores on Web sites need to have traffic in the form of lots of clicks and visitors; see Section 13.3). Customers do not come into a store or onto a site in big numbers unless you have plenty of people to draw from, so you need to figure out where high traffic is and find a way to get some of it into your store.

An old saying about retailing goes like this: "The retail business has three secrets of success — location, location, and location." Pick a location carefully, making sure that you have an excess of the right sort of traffic nearby.

Think of designing a retail store like digging a pond. You wouldn't dig a pond unless running water was nearby to fill it. Yet people dig their retail ponds in deserts or up steep hills, far from the nearest flow of traffic, all the time. You also wouldn't dig a huge reservoir beside a small stream. You must suit your store to the amount and kind of traffic in its area, or move to find more appropriate traffic.

Any retailer has to find a way to appeal to a broad cross section of that traffic or has to find something so compelling to sell that people flock from out of town to visit the store.

A **pull or draw** attracts shoppers to your retail establishment. Few retail concepts are so unique that they can draw traffic from beyond their immediate area. But some do. For example, a jewelry store with an outstanding selection of merchandise may draw far more traffic than the surrounding stores. And if its owner carefully stimulates this traffic through a direct-mail program and by giving the store a unique and highly visible appearance, by putting it in a striking building with sidewalk appeal, it can shine.

▲ This strategy focuses on more than location — it requires that you have a store concept. A **concept** is a creative mix of merchandising strategy and atmosphere that you can use to give your store higher-than-average drawing power.

An exciting concept, well executed, makes shopping an enjoyable event and can boost traffic and sales tenfold.

8.3.1 Creating Atmosphere

A store's atmosphere is the image that it projects based on how you decorate and design it. Atmosphere is an intangible — you cannot easily measure or define it. But you can feel it. And when the atmosphere feels comforting, exciting, or enticing, this feeling draws people into the store and enhances their shopping experience.

Sophisticated retailers hire architects and designers to create the right atmosphere and then spend far too much on fancy lighting, new carpets, and racks to implement their plans. Sometimes this approach works, but not always. At any point in time, most of the professional designers agree about what stores should look and feel like. And that means your store looks like everyone else's.

Instead, try to develop the concept for your store yourself. If you think a virtual tropical forest gives the right atmosphere, then hire some crazy artists and designers to turn your store into a tropical forest! Rainforest Cafe did so a few years ago, creating a fantasy environment they call "a wild place to shop and eat." Their first store, in the Mall of America in Minnesota, was so successful that they've expanded.

Maybe you really like old-fashioned steam engines. Make that the theme of your children's toy store or men's clothing boutique. Run model train tracks around the store, put up huge posters of oncoming steam engines, and incorporate the occasional train whistle into your background music. Some people will love it; others will think you are nuts. But nobody will ever forget your store. Atmospherics are important because consumers increasingly seek more from retail shopping than just finding specific products.

In consumer societies, shopping is an important activity in its own right. Surveys suggest that less than a quarter of shoppers in malls went there in search of a specific item. Consumers often use shopping to alleviate boredom and loneliness, to avoid dealing with chores or problems in their lives, to seek fulfillment of their fantasies, or simply to entertain themselves. If that's what motivates many shoppers, you need to take such motivations into consideration when you design your store.

Perhaps you can honestly and simply provide some entertainment for your customers. Just as a humorous ad entertains people and, thereby, attracts their attention long enough to communicate a message, a store can entertain for long enough to expose shoppers to its merchandise.

FOR EXAMPLE

Selling a Lifestyle

Abercrombie & Fitch is a retailer that has raised the idea of atmosphere to a new level, often courting controversy in the process. Marketing to a young, well-heeled crowd, it aggressively promotes the "A&F lifestyle" with its advertising and Web site showing tanned, muscled, (white) all-American models frolicking in the ocean and playing football bare-chested on the beach. Its stores play loud, edgy music and are staffed with young workers wearing the clothing they sell. But Abercrombie's catalogs have drawn fire for displaying more skin than clothing, leaving the company defending itself from charges of promoting teenage pornography. Abercrombie also settled a lawsuit alleging that its hiring practices discriminated against Asian Americans, Hispanics, and Blacks. The lesson for marketers is clear: Cultivate atmosphere, but stay within the law and the bounds of good taste.

8.3.2 POP! Stimulating Sales at Point of Purchase

Point of purchase, or **POP,** is the place where customer meets product. It may be in the aisles of a store, or even on a catalog page or computer monitor, but wherever this encounter takes place, the principles of POP advertising apply. Table 8-1 gives you percentage figures relevant to retail design and point-of-purchase marketing, according to the Point of Purchase Advertising Institute (whose members are professionals working on POP displays and advertising, so the Institute researches shopping patterns and how to affect those patterns at points of purchase.

Customers plan some purchases outside of the store — 30 percent of supermarket purchases and 26 percent of mass merchandise purchases fall into this category. In these cases, customers make a rational decision about what stores to go to in order to buy what they want. Because they have a clear idea of what they want to purchase, their purchases aren't highly subject to marketing influence.

Even so, the right merchandise selection, location, atmosphere, and price strategy can help get customers to choose your store for their planned purchases rather than a competing store. And the right store layout and point-of-purchase displays help customers find what they want quickly and easily. So even with so-called specifically planned purchases, you do have an influence over what happens.

Furthermore, you have a far greater influence over the majority of purchases than you probably realize. Many studies, including the statistics shown in Table 8-1 (and also the statistic that three-fourths of people visiting malls aren't looking for a specific item), demonstrate the startling conclusion that shoppers are remarkably aimless and suggestible!

This fact makes point-of-purchase marketing important to all marketers of consumer goods and services. Whether you are a retailer, wholesaler, or producer, you need to recognize that customers make an impulse decision in most cases. And that suggests that you should do what you can to sway that decision your way at point of purchase. Otherwise, the sale goes to the competitor who does.

Table 8-1: Nature of Consumer's Purchase Decision

	Supermarkets Percent of Purchases	Mass Merchandise Stores Percent of Purchases
Unplanned	60%	53%
Substitute	4%	3%
Generally planned	6%	18%
Specifically planned	30%	26%

8.3.3 Designing POP Displays

You can boost sales by designing appealing displays from which consumers can pick your products. Freestanding floor displays have the biggest effect, but retailers do not often use them. They take up too much floor space. Rack, shelf, and counter-based signs and displays aren't quite as powerful, but stores use these kinds of displays more often than free-standing displays.

Customers are likely to use any really exciting and unusual display, which means that display works very well because it has a general impact on store traffic and sales, as well as boosting sales of the products it's designed to promote. Exciting displays add to the store's atmosphere or entertainment value, and store managers like that addition. Too often, POP displays are lacking. They do not work well unless they do the following:

▲ **Attract attention.** Make them novel, entertaining, or puzzling to draw people to them.

▲ **Build involvement.** Give people something to think about or do in order to build their involvement in the display.

▲ **Sell the product.** Make sure that the display tells viewers what's so great about the product. Simply putting the product on display isn't enough. You have to sell the product, too, or the retailer doesn't see the point.

Retailers can put products on display without a marketers' help. Retailers want help in selling those products. The display must communicate the positioning and USP, or unique selling proposition. A **unique selling proposition** is the feature that makes your product stand out from the competition.

FOR EXAMPLE

Vicks Shows Its USP

When Procter & Gamble introduced a new formulation of its Vicks 44 cough syrup, it created a point-of-purchase display with a rotating frame with two clear bottles displayed. Each had some red syrup in it — one with Vicks 44, the other with a competing product. When customers rotated the frame to turn the bottles over, they could see that the Vicks 44 coated the inside of the bottle and the competition's syrup sloshed to the bottom. This interactive display shows the unique selling proposition, or *USP*, that Vicks 44 coats your throat better than the competition. It also gave customers something interesting to do to build their involvement. It boosted retail sales and won design awards for its originality.

Why should you care whether retailers like and use POPs? This concern is a major issue for marketers because between 50 and 60 percent of marketers' POPs never reach the sales floor. If you are a product marketer who's trying to get a POP display into retail stores, you face an uphill battle. The stats say that your display or sign needs to be twice as good as average, or the retailer simply tosses it into the nearest dumpster.

8.3.4 Answering Questions about POP

The following questions and answers about POP will give you some facts to help develop and implement a POP program.

▲ **Who should design and pay for POP — marketers or retailers?** In some cases, marketers design POPs and offer them to retailers as part of their marketing programs. Some retailers develop their own POPs. Retailers directly purchase half of all POP displays, and marketers who offer their materials to retailers make up the other half.

▲ **What kinds of POPs do marketers use?** The Point-of-Purchase Advertising Institute's surveys reveal that salespeople spend the most on POPs for permanent displays (generally, retailers). Next in spending are in-store media and sign options. Temporary displays come in third. Yet marketers generally think about temporary displays first when talking about POP. Maybe marketers need to rethink their approach and redesign their programs to emphasize permanent displays and signs first and temporary displays second.

▲ **How much can POP lift your sales?** Researchers compare sales with and without POP to calculate **lift,** or the increase in sales of a product attributable to POP marketing.

You need to estimate lift in order to figure out what return you can get for any particular investment in POP. Generally, accessories and routine repurchases have the highest lifts. Also, significantly new products have high lifts if their POPs effectively educate consumers about their benefits.

▲ **How much of your marketing budget should you allocate to POP?** Every program has to be shaped by its unique circumstances. POP advertising ranks third in spending among measured media in the United States. (Television is first at around $30 billion, print second at about $25 billion, and POP third at $12 billion.) Most marketers do not realize the large size of the POP medium.

Partly because retailers, distributors, wholesalers, and producers spread this spending out broadly between them, POP doesn't get the attention that other media does in most marketing programs and plans. Try to identify who in your distribution channel is involved in POPs that affect your sales, and work toward an integrated strategy and plan so that you can bring this hidden medium into the spotlight and make it work more effectively for your plan.

POP is just one example of proactive marketing. It's not enough just to get a distributor to agree to sell your product, or to write a sale to a retailer. Now you have to get to work making sure that your product moves faster than others so that you win the enthusiastic reorders and loyalty that make for durable, profitable distribution channels.

Channel management (see Section 7.4) is an important part of most marketers' jobs and requires attention and a generous share of marketing imagination. One good way to do this is to offer a varying selection of good point-of-purchase options to help your distributors succeed in selling your product.

SELF-CHECK

- Define planogram, SKU, traffic, pull or draw, concept, point of purchase, and lift.
- Explain the difference between pull and lift in retailing.
- What three things does POP need to do to be effective?

8.4 Direct Marketing

You may choose to eliminate the middleman by selling directly to your customer. **Direct marketing** enables you to do this, and the Internet has made direct marketing easier than ever, helping direct marketing achieve tremendous growth. (See Chapter 13 for more on on-line marketing.) Here we discuss conventional media used in direct marketing: direct mail, telemarketing, and direct-response ads.

▲ Direct marketing allows the consumer to purchase directly from the manufacturer. The manufacturer and the marketer become the same.

The odds of success in direct marketing are not particularly good. The average direct appeal to consumers or businesses goes unanswered, yet if you can improve the response rate even slightly above the average, you can do well with direct-response marketing. Start slowly with a modest program to minimize your downside risk and start growing from there.

Direct marketing can work whether you're big or small, a retailer or wholesaler, or a for-profit or not-for-profit business. When Levi Strauss & Co. started a direct-marketing initiative, they started simply, by including a registration card with each pair of jeans they sold. Equipment marketers know this technique well, but no one in other markets has used it very much. As cards came back, Levi Strauss & Co. built up a database of customers that they could use in their direct marketing.

No matter what direct marketing you do, always keep it civil and polite, and you get much better results. Avoid impolite calls, errors on labels, and anything else that may offend the average person. Cull lists to eliminate duplications and errors. It costs just a bit more to do it well, but you get far better results. You have to make a positive impression if you want to achieve high response rates. Here's the most important principle of direct marketing: It's better to contact a hundred people well than a thousand people poorly.

8.4.1 Using Databases to Keep Track of Customers

Every effective direct-marketing program needs a well-managed database of customer and prospect names. Almost all direct marketers use computerized databases. You should make the transition to this technology eventually if you do not already use it. But you do not absolutely need a computerized database unless you have thousands of names in your database, so if you're a small-time direct marketer, you can postpone the transition.

In fact, a drawer of customer folders and a box of index cards make up the simplest forms of databases, which can work well for many smaller businesses. But if your business has a lot of contacts, consider using one of the major database-management programs. Here are some things database programs should do:

▲ Report on and sort by recency of purchase

▲ Report on and sort by frequency of purchase

▲ Report on and sort by total value of past purchases in a selected period

▲ Support list management (merging and purging functions)

▲ Permit integration of new fields (including data from purchased lists or marketing research)

▲ Support name selection (through *segmentation,* which is dividing the list into similar sub-groups; *profiling,* which is describing types of customers based on their characteristics; and *modeling,* which is developing statistical models to predict or explain response rates)

▲ Make sorting, updating, and correcting easy

▲ Make tracking and analyzing individual responses to specific communications easy, in order to test the effectiveness of a letter or script

▲ Allow operators at **call centers** (central collections of equipment and staff for handling incoming and/or outgoing calls more efficiently) to quickly pull up and add to profiles of all customers (or at least customers designated as members of a club or continuity program)

8.4.2 Using Direct-Response Ads and Direct Mail

Direct-response ads, or direct-action ads, are ads that stimulate people to respond with an inquiry or purchase. The registration cards that some companies now include with each purchase fall into this category, although you see direct-response ads more commonly in print media — magazines and newspapers — and now on the fax machine and the Web, as well. And the ads and purchased listings on Web search engines give you a new, and often highly effective, form of direct-response advertising. See Chapter 13 for details of Internet advertising.

The people who respond to such advertising have self-selected as customers or prospects. You need to do two things with them:

▲ Try your best to close the sale by getting them to buy something.

▲ Find out as much as you can about them and put the information in your database for future direct-marketing efforts.

Many businesses build a direct-marketing capacity through this very process. They place ads in front of what they hope is an appropriate target market and wait to see who responds. Then they attempt to build long-term direct-marketing relationships with those who respond (for example, by sending them catalogs or direct-mail letters). Over time, the businesses add respondents to their direct-marketing databases, information about the respondents builds up, and many of those respondents become regular direct purchasers.

Make sure that your direct-response ad does the following:

▲ **Appeals to target readers:** A good story, a character they can identify with and want to be more like — these factors make up the timeless elements of true appeal.

▲ **Supports your main claim about the product fully:** Because the ad must not only initiate interest but also close the sale, it has to give sufficient evidence to overcome any reasonable objections on the reader's part. If you think the product's virtues are obvious, show those virtues in a close-up visual of the product. If the appeal isn't so obvious (as in the case of a service), then use testimonials, a compelling story, or statistics from objective product tests.

▲ **Speaks to readers in conversational, personal language:** Your ad must be natural and comfortable for readers. Write well, polish, and condense, but do not be stiff or formal.

▲ **Targets likely readers:** Your ad's readership dramatically affects your response rate. In fact, the same ad, placed in two different publications, can produce response rates at both ends of the range. So the better you define your target consumers, the easier it becomes to find publications relevant to those target consumers, and the better your ad performs. Highly selective publications work better for direct-response advertising. A special-interest magazine may deliver a readership far richer in targets than a general-interest magazine or newspaper. If you're focusing on women, select a publication read by them. That specification ups your response rate 50 percent. *Good Housekeeping,* for example, reaches more than 5 million readers — most of them women.

▲ **Makes responding easy:** If readers can make a purchase easily, ask them to do so. If it is complicated or difficult to buy (because the product is technical, for example), then just ask people to contact you for more information and try to close the sale when they do so. Sometimes, you need an intermediate step. When in doubt, try two versions of your ad — one with an intermediate step and one that tries to make the sale on the spot. Then see which one produces the most sales, in the long run.

Direct mail is the use of personalized sales letters. Direct mail is really no more or less than a form of print advertising. So before you design, or hire someone to design, a direct-mail piece, please think about it in this context (see Section 11.1 on print advertising). Actually, a direct-mail piece is not like a print ad. It's like two print ads.

▲ **The first ad is the one the target sees when the mail arrives.** That ad has to accomplish a difficult action goal: to get the viewer to open the envelope rather than recycling it. Most direct mail ends up in the recycling pile without ever getting opened or read! Keep this fact in mind. Devote extra care to making your envelope.

  • Stand out — it needs to be noticeable and different.

  • Give readers a reason to open it. (Sell the benefits or engage their curiosity or, even better, promise a reward!)

  • Or send a color catalog with a stunning front and back cover they can't resist. Make sure the recipient can see the catalog's exterior. Do not hide it under a dull envelope.

▲ **The second ad goes to work only if the first succeeds.** The second ad is what's inside, and it needs to get the reader to respond with a purchase or inquiry. In that respect, this ad is much the same as any other direct-response ad.

The most effective direct-mail letters generally include several elements, each with its own clear role:

▲ **Bait:** You should include some sort of bait that catches the reader's eye and attention, getting him or her to read the letter in the first place.

▲ **Argument:** You then need to provide a sound argument — logical, emotional, or both — as to why your great product can solve some specific problem for the reader. Marketers devote the bulk of many letters to making this case as persuasively as possible, and you should keep this sound practice in mind when drafting your direct-mail letter.

▲ **Call to action:** Finally, you should make an appeal to immediate action, some sort of hook that gets readers to call you, send for a sample, sign up for a contest, or place an order. If they act, you can consider the letter a success. So this hook is really the climax of the letter, and you need to design everything to ensure that this hook works.

8.4.3 Responsible Telemarketing

Telemarketers need to have a call center — the place where telephone calls from your customers are answered. It can be a real, physical place — a room full of phones staffed by your employees. It can also be a virtual place, a telephone number that rings to whatever subcontractor you're currently using to handle telemarketing.

Effective telemarketing means being accessible to desirable customers when they want to call you. If you service businesses, then you can use business hours to answer business calls (but make sure that you cover business hours in the business's time zones, not just your own). If you service consumers, however, be prepared to take calls at odd hours. Some of the best customers for clothing catalogs do their shopping late at night. Being accessible means more than just having staff by the phones. You need to make sure that nobody gets a busy signal. If you answer your phone faster than the competition does, you can gain some market share from them. Here are ways to be effective and responsible:

▲ **Measure and minimize customer wait time.** Do not leave people sitting on hold for more than what they perceive to be a moderate amount of time. Depending on the nature of your product and customer, that time limit is probably less than two perceived minutes. A *perceived minute* is the time period a customer on hold thinks he has waited for a minute — and that time typically comes out to be closer to 40 seconds on the clock. You have to convert actual wait times to perceived wait times to appreciate the customer's perspective.

▲ **Capture useful information about each call and caller.** One of the most important functions for your call center is to field inquiries or orders from new customers as they respond to your various direct-response advertisements — such as magazine ads, letters to purchased lists, and your Web page. These callers are hot leads. You do not want their order as much as you want their data. Make sure that your operators ask every caller for her full name and address, how she heard of your company, and perhaps a few other qualifying questions, as well.

▲ **Have your operators on-line, so that they can enter the data directly into your database as they obtain it.** At the very least, give them a printed information form they can fill in — or, if you're the one answering those customer calls, make yourself a form so you do not forget to capture useful information about the prospects, their needs, and how they found your number. You will capture call-ins for your customer database and recognize repeat customers. Repeat customers' names pop up on-screen for the operator's reference. That way, the operators do not have to ask stupid questions, and they can surprise customers with their knowledge.

▲ **A toll-free number is useful for inbound telemarketing, in which customers call you in response to direct-response advertising.** And every direct-response ad should have a phone number as one of the contact options — with a trained telemarketing sales force or an eager entrepreneur at the other end. (You can post a toll-free phone number prominently on your Web site and print it on packaging, brochures, business cards, and so on, in case someone prefers to talk rather than e-mail or mail you. Add a toll-free fax number, if customers in your industry like to fax in orders, too.)

There is, in the United States, a growing momentum behind legal restrictions over telemarketing. Consumers can put themselves on a do-not-call list to block inbound telemarketing. If you buy lists, ask whether the broker or supplier is up-to-date and has pulled any names that are illegal to call. If you get any complaints from people who say they are on the do-not-call list when you use a purchased list, stop and recontact the list supplier to find out what went wrong. In business-to-business marketing, fewer restrictions apply, but the need for respect and courtesy remains.

FOR EXAMPLE

Theater Tickets and Telemarketing

The Steppenwolf Theatre in Chicago prefers to sell subscriptions. Doing so guarantees an audience (or at least a box office take) for each show in its season. Theatre marketers discovered that a 16-week phone campaign to its in-house list (a list of current and past customers and qualified leads), supplemented with any other appropriate names they could find, was very effective at selling subscriptions. The telemarketing effort happens in-house by properly trained, knowledgeable staff and has a fairly high hit rate. Note that this telemarketing program successfully generates sales, and it doesn't risk legal and financial liability or expose prospects to incompetent — and possibly rude — telemarketers. Best of all, it actually completes the sale, instead of requiring follow-up. Outbound telemarketing does not have to be unwelcome.

8.4.4 Boosting Sales from Direct Marketing

Here are a few ways to generate high responses to your direct marketing:

▲ Send out a letter, special announcement, small catalog, or brochure by first-class mail once in a while to find out how well your list responds. The U.S. Post Office returns undeliverables if you use first class, so you can remove or update out-of-date addresses.

▲ Run a very small display ad because they are the least expensive. Limit it to 15 words or less. Describe in a simple headline and one or two brief phrases what you have to sell and then ask people to contact you for more information. (Include a simple black-and-white photo of the product to eliminate the need for a wordy description.)

▲ Replace your existing advertising copy (your words) with *testimonials* (quotes praising your product or firm) from happy customers or with quotes from news coverage of your firm or product. These comments attract more buyers because they seem more believable than positive things you say about yourself.

▲ Give away a simple, useful, or fun gift in exchange for placing an order, or include an inexpensive premium (see Section 12.3.2) in your mailing. Customers love this.

▲ Trade customer lists with another business to boost your list size for free.

▲ Send a thank-you note or card to customers by mail or e-mail after they place a purchase. This polite gesture often wins a repurchase. It also lets you test your contact information and habituates the customer to reading your messages so that they are more likely to pay attention to a sales-oriented message later on.

▲ Send out birthday or holiday greetings in the form of cards or gifts to your in-house list. If you consider them valuable customers, let them know it. You may be surprised how many contact you afterward to place a new order, even though your mailing was noncommercial.

▲ Change your communication sometimes. If you always send out a sales letter, try a color postcard or an e-mailed newsletter. Variations like this can increase customer interest, and you may also find that different customers respond best to different forms of communication.

▲ Use a photograph of a person's face, looking directly at the viewer with a friendly expression. The person should represent a user or an expert on the product, or relate to the product or offer in some other way. A face attracts attention and increases sales for most direct-response ads and direct-mail letters.

▲ Use a clear, appealing photo of the product. Showing what you have to sell attracts appropriate customers simply and effectively. And if some details do not show up in the photo, add close-up photos. Visual direct-response ads can outsell wordy ones by a wide margin.

▲ Try an old-fashioned radio advertisement using a lot of amusing sound effects and asking people to call a toll-free number or visit a Web site. Radio ads can be fun.

▲ Run your direct-response ad in Yellow Pages phone directories. Get a local number for each directory you list your ad in.

SELF-CHECK

- Define **direct marketing, direct-response ads, direct mail,** and **call center.**
- Name four ways to conduct telemarketing well.
- List five useful functions of database programs for direct marketing.

SUMMARY

Different retail stores entail different strategies. Merchandising innovations, based on a strategy, will help you define your store's concept and drive its success. Creative retailing involves designing POP displays and creating atmosphere, no matter what type of storefront you have. Direct marketing lets you eliminate the middleman and can be successful when done properly.

KEY TERMS

Call centers	Central collections of equipment and staff for handling incoming and/or outgoing calls more efficiently.
Concept	A creative mix of merchandising strategy and atmosphere that you can use to give your store higher-than-average drawing power.
Direct marketing	When the consumer purchases directly from the manufacturer.
Direct mail	The use of personalized sales letters.
Direct-response ads	Ads that stimulate people to respond with an inquiry or purchase.

Inbound telemarketing	Customers call you in response to direct-response advertising.
Lift	The increase in sales of a product attributable to POP marketing.
Limited-line retailing	A strategy emphasizing depth over variety.
Merchandising strategy	The selection and assortment of products offered.
Planogram	Diagrams showing how to lay out and display a store's merchandise.
Point of purchase (POP)	The place where customer meets product.
Pull or draw	The thing that attracts shoppers to your retail establishment.
Scrambled merchandising strategy	Using unconventional combinations of product lines.
SKU (stock-keeping unit)	A unique inventory code for each item you stock.
Traffic	The flow of target customers near enough to the store for its external displays and local advertising to draw them in.
Unique selling proposition (USP)	The feature that makes your product stand out from the competition.

ASSESS YOUR UNDERSTANDING

Go to www.wiley.com/college/Hiam to evaluate your knowledge of the basics of retailing.

Measure your learning by comparing pre-test and post-test results.

Summary Questions

1. Automobile dealerships are examples of franchises. True or false?
2. Which is the **least** important to the success of a retail store?
   (a) pull
   (b) temporary displays
   (c) traffic
   (d) the concept
3. Which type of retailer is able to buy a wide variety in large quantity discounts and has an advantage in location?
   (a) department stores
   (b) supermarkets
   (c) chain stores
   (d) franchises
4. Discount pricing accounts for most retail successes. True or false?
5. A combination coffee shop and Internet café is a good example of scrambled merchandising. True or false?
6. In-store media and signs are the most popular type of POP. True or false?
7. Professional services usually use which type of strategy?
   (a) general merchandise retailing
   (b) limited-line retailing
   (c) scrambled merchandising
8. Your odds of success are poor in direct marketing. True or false?
9. Limited-line retailers are vulnerable to competition because of their lack of
   (a) breadth in their product lines
   (b) depth in their product lines
   (c) convenience
10. A direct marketing appeal that doesn't close the sale is worthless. True or false?

Review Questions

1. What percentage of purchases in mass-merchandise stores (not supermarkets) are planned beforehand by the consumer who makes them?
2. Are more purchases made on-line and by catalog, or do more occur in retail stores?
3. Explain the difference between the following strategies: general merchandise retailing, limited-line retailing, and scrambled merchandising.
4. What's the difference between inbound and outbound telemarketing?

Applying This Chapter

1. You are opening a health food store. How can you *pull* traffic from outside your general vicinity? Explain what will make your store successful or not in attracting customers.
2. Think of an exciting POP display for your film-developing service that will *lift* your sales. What three things will it need to do?
3. You want to open a store to sell just high-end pet supplies. What kind of merchandising strategy would you be utilizing, and what are the pros and cons of that strategy?
4. Think of a product that is popular on-line, such as books or clothing. How would you market this product in a retail store? Explain some ways to get customers to prefer buying your product in your store, rather than on-line.

Location, Location, Location

You are opening a restaurant and you have a choice of two sites. One potential location is at a mall and gets lots of traffic on weekends, and the other is downtown, with many office workers around during the week, but a much higher rent. How would you make your decision?

Scrambled Stores

Can you think of the perfect new combination of stores? How about a gym and a laundromat, so people can work out while washing their clothes? Coming up with novel combinations isn't hard — give it a try! Explain what to avoid.

9

PRICING
Mastering Pricing Concepts

Starting Point

Go to www.wiley.com/college/Hiam to assess your knowledge of the basic pricing concepts.
Determine where you need to concentrate your effort.

What You'll Learn in This Chapter

▲ How pricing affects customer perceptions of your product or service
▲ Factors to consider when setting a price
▲ How to avoid illegal pricing practices
▲ Understanding discount structures and general pricing approaches

After Studying This Chapter, You'll Be Able To

▲ Demonstrate ways to raise prices while increasing sales
▲ Effectively employ special offers and discounts
▲ Interpret customer perceptions of pricing

Goals and Outcomes

▲ Estimate how price sensitive your customers are
▲ Predict the redemption rate for your marketing offer
▲ Set prices that take into account multiple factors

INTRODUCTION

Establishing a price is one of the toughest things anybody does in business. In this chapter, we'll take you through the pricing process logically, step by step. Price setting has many factors, including customer perceptions and your own objectives. The pricing process generally has five steps.

9.1 The Facts of Price

Some marketers believe that businesses fail most often for two simple reasons: Their prices are too high, or their prices are too low! Getting the price just right is the hardest task marketers face, but finding the right pricing approach makes success a lot easier. The bottom line of all marketing activities is that the customer needs to pay — willingly and, you hope, rapidly — for your products or services.

But how much will they pay? Should you drop your prices to grow your market? Or would raising the price and maximizing profits be better? What about discounts and special promotional pricing? Getting the price part of your marketing plan right is hard. And several trends have been forcing prices downward:

▲ Foreign competition has put pressure on American companies. Foreign-made products are often higher in quality but cheaper to produce.

▲ Competitors try to gain market share by lowering prices. Customers may be more price sensitive than ever.

▲ New products are far more common today than in the past. Pricing new products is tougher, because there's no history to draw upon.

▲ Technology has caused rapid turnover of products. Marketers face pressure to price products to recover cost more quickly.

Most companies fall prey to the myth that customers choose a product based only on its list price. They set their list prices lower than they need to. Or when they need to boost sales, they do so by offering discounts or free units. If you insist on selling on the basis of price, your customers buy on the basis of price.

But alternatives always exist. To raise your price and still sell more, you can:

▲ **Build brand equity.** Better-known brands command a premium price.

▲ **Increase quality.** People talk up a good product, and that word of mouth earns it a 5 to 10 percent higher price than the competition.

▲ **Use prestige pricing.** Giving your product a high-class image can boost your price 20 to 100 percent.

▲ **Create extra value through time and place advantages.** Customers consider the available product worth a lot more than one you cannot get when you need it. (That's why a cup of coffee costs twice as much at the airport — are you really going to leave the terminal, get in a taxi, and go somewhere else to save a couple of bucks?)

Sure, price is important, but it doesn't have to be the only thing — unless the marketer doesn't know this price fact.

9.1.1 Exploring the Impact of Pricing on Sales

You need to estimate how price-sensitive your customers are. **Price sensitivity** is the degree to which purchases are affected by price level.

The following list is a series of qualitative indicators of price sensitivity. Ask the following questions about your customer, product, and market. Then add up the number of "yes" answers and see which way they lean. This study isn't scientific, but it gives you a good idea.

▲ **Does the customer view the price as reasonable?** If you are operating within an expected price range, customers aren't very price sensitive. Outside of the expected price range, they become more sensitized.

▲ **Is the product valuable at (almost) any price?** Some products are unique, and customers know that finding a cheaper substitute may be hard. That lowers price sensitivity.

▲ **Is the product desperately needed?** I do not care how much fixing a broken arm at the emergency ward of a hospital costs — if my arm is broken! And I'm not too price sensitive about roadside repair and towing services if I've broken down on the highway at night. These products meet essential needs. But if your product is a nonessential, meaning they do not have to have it right now, the customer is more price sensitive.

▲ **Are substitutes unavailable?** If the customer purchases in a context where substitute products aren't readily available, price sensitivity is lower. Shopping for price requires that substitutes at different prices be available. (For example, if you are the only local company offering plumbing repairs on weekends, you can command a high price for your services.)

▲ **Is the customer unaware of substitutes?** What the customer doesn't know costs him. And shopping is a complex, information-dependent behavior. The Internet makes it easier to compare prices — but not everything is convenient to buy that way. Not everyone is willing to shop around.

▲ **Does the customer find comparing options difficult?** Even where options exist, the consumer can have much difficulty comparing some products. What makes one doctor better than another? It's hard to say. The technical complexity of their work, plus the fact that you cannot consume medical care until after you make the purchase decision, makes comparing options hard. And that difficulty makes health-care consumers less price sensitive — and doctors richer.

▲ **Does the product seem inexpensive to customers?** Customers do not worry too much about price when they feel like they're getting a good value. However, if customers feel the pinch on their pocketbooks when they buy, they pay close attention to prices. That's why you negotiate so hard when you buy a car or a house. Even products that cost far less can seem expensive if they're at the high end of a price range. For example, you are more price sensitive if you shop for a fancy, high-performance laptop computer than for a simple, basic desktop unit because the former probably costs 50 to 100 percent more than the latter, making the laptop expensive by comparison.

The more of these that apply, the less price sensitive your customer is. If more than one is true, you probably can raise prices without hurting sales significantly. You can supplement your estimate of price sensitivity (from this list) with actual tests.

For example, if you think a 5-percent increase in prices won't affect sales, you can try that increase in a test market or for a short period of time, holding the rest of your marketing constant. If you were right, you can roll out the increase in your entire market.

9.1.2 Finding Profits without Changing Prices

When you think about profits, you may assume that your focus should be on the price. But many factors drive your company's cash flows and profits, not just the list price of your products. If your manager tells you to figure out how to raise prices because profits are too low, do not assume she's going at it from the right angle.

Lowering a price is easier than raising it. In general, you want to set price a bit high and see what happens. You can take back any price increase with a subsequent price cut. You can take back price increases much more easily (if they do not work) than price decreases. Customers may not be as price sensitive as you fear. They may tolerate an increase better than you think, and they may not respond to a discount as much as you need them to in order to make that decrease profitable. They may assume that price correlates with quality — in which case, they do not buy your product unless the price is high enough.

Instead of assuming that cutting your price is the only way to boost profits, try experimenting with a price increase. Be a contrarian. If that doesn't work, here are some ways to boost profits without raising prices:

FOR EXAMPLE

Apple iPod — High Price, High Sales

This is a success story every marketer would love to duplicate. Apple's iPod MP3 player so dominates the market, that the word iPod is better known than the generic name for the product, MP3 Player. At this writing, iPod had 70 percent of the MP3 Player market, and its combination of brand equity with the Apple name, award-winning advertising, and high quality (an intuitive product design that others have tried but failed to duplicate) enables it to command higher prices — yet still sell more than its lower priced rivals.

▲ Check to see how quickly you are making collections — are vendors paying in 65 days? If so, cutting that time by 25 days may make up the needed profits without any price increase.

▲ All the discounts and allowances your company offers affect its revenues and profits, so you look at these factors before you assume that price is the culprit. Are customers taking advantage of quantity discounts to stock up inexpensively and then not buying between the discount periods? If so, you have a problem with your sales promotions, not your list prices.

▲ If you are in a service business that charges a base price, plus fees for special services and extras, then look hard at the way you assess fees. Perhaps your company is failing to collect the appropriate fees, in some cases.

▲ Maybe your fee structure is out of date and doesn't reflect your cost structure accurately. For example, a bank that charges a low price for standard checking accounts, plus a per-check processing fee, may find its profits slumping as customers switch to automated checking over the bank's computers — because banks often set the introductory fees for this service low or waive them to stimulate trials. If so, the problem isn't with the base price of a checking account, it's with the nature of the fee structure.

SELF-CHECK

- Define **price sensitivity**.
- Name four ways to sell more, even at a high price.
- Name four ways to boost profits without raising prices.

9.2 Factors to Consider When Setting a Price

Setting prices may seem complicated at first, but when you understand all the factors you need to consider, the process begins to make sense. (Figure 9-1 illustrates the process that you should use.)

9.2.1 Step 1: Figure Out Who Sets Prices

This step isn't obvious. You, as the marketer, can set a list price. But the consumer may not ultimately pay your price. Distributors, wholesalers, and retailers all take their markups. Furthermore, the manufacturer generally doesn't have the legal right to dictate the ultimate selling price. The retailer gets that job. So your list price is really just a suggestion, not an order. If the retailer doesn't like the suggested price, the product sells for another price.

Start by determining who else may be setting prices along with you, and involve them in your decision making by asking some what they think about pricing. You may have constraints to consider that you must know before you start.

For example, if you are setting the price for a new book, you find that the big bookstore chains in the United States expect a 60 percent discount off the list price. Knowing that, you can set a high enough list price to give you some profit, even at a 60 percent discount rate. But if you do not realize that these chains expect much higher discounts than other bookstores, you may be blind-sided by their requirement.

Marketers who operate in or through a multilevel distribution channel (meaning that they have distributors, wholesalers, rack jobbers [companies that keep retail racks stocked], retailers, agents, or other sorts of intermediaries) need to establish the *trade discount structure*. **Trade discounts** (also called *functional discounts*) are what you give your intermediaries.

These discounts are a form of cost to the marketer, so know the discount structure before you move on. Usually, marketers state the discount structure as a series of numbers, representing what each of the intermediaries get as a discount. But you take each discount off the price left over from the discount before it, not off the list price. Here's how to compute prices and discounts in a complex distribution channel:

1. Say that you discover that the typical discount structure in the market where you want to introduce your product is 30/10/5. What does that mean? If you start with a $100 list price, the retailer pays at a discount of 30 percent off the list price ($0.30 \times \$100 = \$70$). The retailer, who pays $70 for the product, marks it up to (approximately) $100 and makes about $30 in gross profit.

Figure 9-1

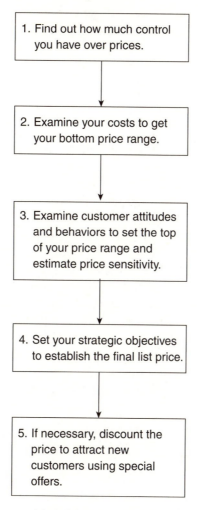

A helpful pricing process.

2. The discount structure figures tell you that other intermediaries exist — one for each discount listed. The distributor, who sells the product to the retailer, has a discount of 10 percent off the price that she charges the retailer (that's $0.10 \times \$70 = \$7$ of gross profit for the distributor). This distributor must have paid $70 – $7, or $63, for the product to another intermediary (probably a manufacturer's representative or wholesaler). The marketer sells to this intermediary. And the 30/10/5 formula shows that this intermediary receives a 5 percent discount: $0.05 \times \$63 = \$3.15$ in profit for him.

3. Subtracting again, you can also determine that the marketer must sell the product to this first intermediary at $63 – $3.15, or $59.85. You, as the marketer, must give away more than 40 percent of that $100 list price to intermediaries if you use this 30/10/5 discount structure. And so you have to calculate any profit you make from a $100 list price as costs subtracted from your net of $59.85. That's all you ever see of that $100!

9.2.2 Step 2: Examine Your Costs

How do you know your costs? You may not have accurate information on the true costs of a specific product or service. Take some time to try to estimate what you are actually spending, and remember to include some value for expensive inventories if they sit around for a month or more.

After you examine your costs carefully, you should have a fairly accurate idea of the least amount you can charge. That charge is, at a bare minimum, your actual costs. Sometimes you want to give away a product for less than cost in order to introduce people to it — but do not use this ploy to take customers from competitors or you could be sued for dumping. See Section 9.4.

More often, you need a price that includes the cost plus a profit margin — say, 20 or 30 percent. So that means you have to treat your cost as 70 or 80 percent of the price, adding in that 20 or 30 percent margin your company requires. This cost-plus-profit figure is the bottom of your pricing range (see Figure 9-2). Now you need to see if customers permit you to charge this price — or perhaps even allow you to charge a higher price!

Figure 9-2

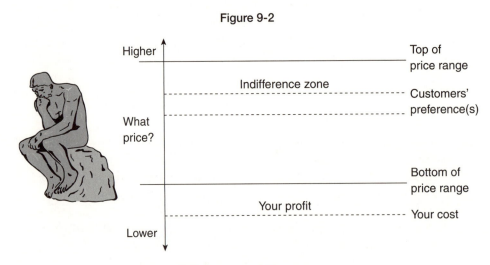

Defining your pricing range.

9.2.3 Step 3: Evaluate Customer Perception of Price

Your costs and profit requirements impose a lower limit on price. But your customers' perceptions impose an upper limit. You must define both of these limits to know your possible price range. So you need to figure out what the market will bear.

In Figure 9-2, the price that customers favor is the customers' preference. Note that customer preference may not be the upper limit. If customers aren't too price sensitive, they may not notice or care if you set your price somewhat higher than their preferred price. The **indifference zone** is the difference between the customer's desired price and a noticeably higher price. Within the indifference zone, customers are indifferent to both price increases and price decreases. However, the zone gets smaller (on a percent basis) as the price goes up.

How big or small is the zone of indifference in your product's case? Go back to the price-sensitivity list. The zone is small if your customers are highly price sensitive, and the zone is large if they aren't that price sensitive. Just make some assumptions that seem reasonable for now. At worst, your errors may be random, in which case they cancel each other out.

You can also get at customer preference by looking at the current pricing structure in your market:

▲ What are people paying for comparable products?
▲ Does a downward trend exist in the prices of comparable products?
▲ An upward trend?
▲ Or are they stable?

Go shopping to figure out the existing price structure; you get excellent clues as to how customers may react to different prices for your product. You need at least back-of-the-envelope figures for the customers' preferred price and how much higher you can price without drawing attention. That means you have established the top of your price range.

The simplest approach to pricing is to set your price at the top of the range. As long as the price range is above the bottom limit (as long as your preferred price plus the indifference zone is equal to or greater than your cost plus your required profit), you are okay. But you cannot always set your price at the top of the range. Keep reading to find out why.

9.2.4 Step 4: Examine Secondary Influences on Price

Your costs and the customers' upper limits are the two primary considerations in setting a price range. But you need to consider many other factors, too. These factors may influence your decision by forcing you to price in the middle or bottom of the price range rather than at the top, for example.

Carefully examine each of the following:

▲ **Consider competitive issues.** Do you need to gain market share from a close competitor? If so, either keep price at parity and do aggressive marketing, or adjust your price to be slightly (but noticeably) below the competitor's price.

▲ **Consider likely future price trends.** Are prices trending downward in this market? Then you need to adjust your figures down a bit to stay in synch with your market. Similarly, currency fluctuations may affect your costs and, thus, your pricing options. If you are concerned that you may take a hit from the exchange rate, better to be safe and price at the high end of the range.

▲ **Consider product-line management** — it may dictate a slightly lower or higher price. For example, you may need to price a top-of-the-line product significantly higher than others in its line just to make it clear that this product is a step above its competition.

9.2.5 Step 5: Set Your Strategic Objectives

Your pricing strategy will have certain objectives. Your objectives in pricing can be one or more of the following:

▲ **Survival:** If revenue falls below cost for a long period of time, the firm cannot survive.

▲ **Profit:** Closely linked to survival. Making a certain profit may be a pricing objective for a firm. For many businesses, long-term profitability allows the business to satisfy its stockholders. Lower-than-expected or no profits will drive down stock prices and may prove disastrous.

▲ **Sales:** Profit requires sales. Marketing aims to increase sales, which is done by managing demand.

▲ **Market share:** Firms must maintain an adequate share of the market so that their sales volume will keep the firm going. Many marketers price near the bottom of their price range to increase their market share.

▲ **Image:** Price is a highly visible communicator of image. The right price can convey good value, reliability, fairness, and stability.

Ideally, you would price at the top of the range and use the extra revenues to invest in quality and brand-building marketing promotions in order to increase market share (see Section 2.1 for details on these and other strategy options).

▲ **Price wars:** These occur when a business believes that price cutting produces increased market share, but it does not have a true cost advantage.

Typically, price wars are overreactions to threats that either aren't there at all or are not as big as they seem. If you can stick to nonprice competition, rather than price competition, you ought to because it is more difficult to match nonprice characteristics. And profits are safer that way.

Yet, you may not be able to do that. If you are in a highly competitive market, you may have to go along.

▲ **Competitive pricing:** Pricing relative to an important competitor or set of competitors.

Decide which competing products the customers may view as closest to yours and then make your price sufficiently higher or lower to differentiate your product. How much difference is enough depends on the size of the customers' indifference zone.

Should you price above or below a tough competitor? That decision depends on whether you offer more or fewer benefits and higher or lower quality. If you offer your customer less or about the same, you need to make your price significantly lower so that you look like a better value. If you offer greater benefits, you can make your price a little higher to signal this fact — but not too high because your product must seem like a better value.

In general, a business can price itself to match its competition, price higher, or price lower. Each has its own strategy:

▲ **Pricing to meet competition.** Sometimes you should just price exactly at the competitor's price. You may want to match prices if you plan to differentiate your product on the basis of some subtle difference, because this way, customers focus their attention on the difference rather than on price. This strategy means that you use price as an indicator or baseline. The key is to have an accurate definition of your competition and knowledge of competitors' prices. A maker of handcrafted shoes is not in competition with mass producers and will be unprofitable if it tries to compete with mass producers on price because it will have higher production costs.

▲ **Pricing above competitors.** Profits will be good, but the marketing mix must be strategically used for this to work. You must have a clear advantage on some nonprice element of the marketing mix. You must prove to customers that your product justifies a premium price. To appear significantly superior to the competition, make sure that your prices are significantly higher. Do not put a prestigious image at risk by underpricing.

FOR EXAMPLE

Tiffany Goes Downmarket

Tiffany & Company risked its prestigious name and lost some of its luxury image when it was acquired by Avon. Why? Avon tried to mass-market the Tiffany name by putting it on a line of inexpensive jewelry. Millions of dollars of losses later, Avon sold out and Tiffany went back to success — by going back to exclusively high prices.

▲ **Pricing below competitors.** This strategy works if the market is price-sensitive and/or your company's cost structure is lower than competitors. Costs can be cut by increasing efficiency, by economies of scale, or by reducing credit, delivery, and advertising. A high market share later will probably provide more profits, so low pricing is an investment strategy. With certain volume goals — such as needing to run a factory near its capacity level — pricing in the low end of the range will maximize unit sales, even if doing so doesn't maximize net profits per unit.

SELF-CHECK

- Define **trade discounts,** the **indifference zone,** price wars, and **competitive pricing.**
- Name the five steps in the pricing process.
- List some possible pricing objectives.

9.3 General Pricing Approaches

Why play with the price? If you think the price should be lower, why not just cut the price permanently? As explained in Section 12.3 under Sales Promotions, a price cut is easy to do, but hard to undo. A special offer allows you to temporarily discount the price while still maintaining the list price at its old level. When the offer ends, the list price is the same — you haven't given anything away permanently.

Here are some cases in which maintaining your list price can be important:

▲ When your reason for wanting to cut the price is a short-term one, like wanting to counter a competitor's special offer or respond to a new product introduction.

▲ When you want to experiment with the price (to find out about customer price sensitivity) without committing to a permanent price cut until you see the data.

▲ When you want to stimulate consumers to try your product, and you believe that after they try it, they may like the product well enough to buy it again at full price.

▲ When your list price needs to stay high in order to signal quality (**prestige pricing**) or be consistent with other prices in your product line (**price-lining strategy** — see Section 6.5.4).

▲ When your competitors are all offering special lower prices and you think you have no choice because consumers have come to expect special offers.

9.3.1 Coupons and Other Special Offers

Many marketers have trained their customers to expect special offers and only buy in response to them. This mistake is the biggest and dumbest one that marketers make, and they've been making it for many years.

Consequently, customers purchase many product categories on the basis of price more than on the basis of quality and benefits. As a result, the rates of coupon redemptions keep climbing in the United States, Canada, and many European countries. Ultimately, special offers take up a bigger and bigger share of marketing budgets every year and often eat unnecessarily into profits.

What happens when competitors get too focused on making and matching each other's special offers? They flood the customers with price-based promotions. Sometimes marketers will reduce prices temporarily, by offering discounts or special offers. **Special offers** are temporary inducements to make customers buy on the basis of price or price-related factors. Special offers play with the price, giving consumers (or intermediaries) a way to get the product for less — at least while the offer lasts.

Special promotions can, and do increase customer sensitivity to price. They encourage people to become price switchers, thus reducing the size of the core customer base and increasing the number of fringe customers. So special offers have the potential to erode brand equity, reduce customer loyalty, and cut your profits. This slope is slippery, and you can easily lose your footing on it!

But you still may have legitimate reasons to use special offers, or you may not have the power to change practices in your market. You can offer coupons, refunds, premiums (or gifts), extra products for free, free trial-sized samples, **rebates**, sweepstakes and other event-oriented premium plans, and so on — just check with your lawyers to make sure that the promotion is legal. (You cannot mislead consumers. A sweepstakes or contest has to be open to all, not tied to product purchase. See Section 9.4 for more on marketing legal caveats.)

If you are promoting to the trade, as marketers collectively term intermediaries like wholesalers and retailers, then you can also offer your intermediaries things like free-goods deals, buy-back allowances, display and advertising allowances, and help with their advertising costs (called **cooperative**, or **co-op advertising**).

▲ A large (and growing) majority of all special offers takes the form of *coupons*. A **coupon** is any certificate entitling the holder to a reduced price.

That's a pretty broad definition — giving you a lot of room for creativity. To get a good feel for the options and approaches to coupons, just collect a number of recent coupons from your own and other industries.

9.3.2 Estimating Redemption Rates and Costs

Designing a coupon isn't the hard part. The hard part comes when you try to guess the redemption rate. The **redemption rate** is the percentage of people who use the coupon.

And you raise the stakes when you use big offers, which are riskier to forecast. As we explain in Section 12.3.1, in North America, customers redeem a little over 3 percent of coupons (and the average coupon offers a bit under 40 cents off list price). So you can use that as a good starting point for your estimate. But the range is wide — some offers are so appealing, and so easy to use, that customers redeem 50 percent of those coupons. For others, the redemption rate can be close to zero.

So how do you find out if your coupon will have a high or low redemption rate?

▲ **Look at your offer compared to others.** Are you offering something more generous or easier to redeem than you have in the past? Than your competitors do? If so, you can expect significantly higher than average redemption rates — maybe twice as high or higher.

▲ **Look at your past data for excellent clues**. If you have ever used coupons before, your company should have rich information about response rates. Just be sure that you examine past offers carefully to pick ones that truly match the current offer before assuming the same response rate can be repeated.

▲ **Look at price sensitivity.** A lower price isn't always better. Your offer really just shifts the price on a temporary basis — at some cost to the customer because of the trouble they need to go to in order to redeem the coupon. So the real new price is something less than the discount you offer on the coupon — adjust it a little to reflect how much the customer thinks it costs him to redeem the coupon. Now ask yourself if this real price is lower than the list price enough to alter demand. Does the price fall outside of most customers' indifference zones or not?

Many coupons do not shift the price very far beyond the indifference zone — that's why they generally attract those fringe customers who buy on price but do not attract the core customers of other brands. And that's why redemption rates are only a few percent, on average. However, if your coupon does shift the price well beyond the indifference zone, you are likely to see a much higher redemption rate than usual.

Coupon deals gone wild is the most common reason for marketers to lose their jobs. So always check the offer against what you know of customer perception and price sensitivity to make sure that you aren't accidentally shifting the price so far that everyone and her brother wants to redeem coupons. Say you believe that 4 percent of customers will redeem a coupon offering a 10 percent discount on your product.

To estimate the cost of your coupon program:

1. Decide whether this 4 percent of consumers accounts for just 4 percent of your products' sales over the period in which the coupon applies. Probably not. They may stock up in order to take advantage of the special offer. And so you have to estimate how much more than usual consumers will buy.

2. If you think they'll buy twice as much as usual (that's a pretty high figure, but it makes for a simple illustration), just double the average purchase size. Four percent of customers, buying twice what they usually do in a month (if that's the term of the offer), can produce how much in sales?

3. Now, apply the discount rate to that sales figure to find out how much the special offer may cost you.

Is the promotion worth the money? That's for you to decide. Some marketers have their cake and eat it too when it comes to special offers. They use what they call self-liquidating premiums, which do not cost them any money at all in the long run.

▲ A **premium** is any product that you give away to customers or sell at a discount as a reward for doing business with you (see Section 12.3.2 for ideas on how to use premiums).

▲ A **self-liquidating premium** is one that customers end up paying for — at least, they cover your costs on that product.

Say you run a contest in which some of the customers who open your packaging are instant winners, able to send away for a special premium by enclosing their winning ticket plus $4.95. If your direct costs for the premium you send them are $4.95, you do not have to pay out of pocket for what the customer may see as a fun and valuable benefit.

9.3.3 Customers' Price Perceptions

When setting prices, perception can be the same as reality. You need to think as your customers think. Even if your profit margins are slim, if the consumer sees your price as too high, you have a problem. This is where odd–even pricing can come in.

If the top of your price range for a new child's toy is $10, you probably want to drop it down to $9.99 or $9.89. Why? If they're price sensitive at all, they will buy considerably more of the lower-priced product, even though the price difference amounts to only pennies. Why? People tend to perceive prices ending in 9 as cheaper — generally 3 to 6 percent cheaper in their memories than the rounded-up price.

The only problem is that customers sometimes associate this pricing with cheap products that have worse quality. Do not use odd–even pricing when your customers are more quality sensitive than price sensitive. For instance, odd–even pricing may cheapen the image of an original work of art.

▲ **Price lining.** Adjustment of your price to make it fit into your product line, or into the range of products sold by your retailers or distributors.

See Section 6.5.4 for more on this concept. The idea is to fit your product into a range of alternatives, giving the product a logical spot in customers' minds. It's generally effective for buyers and sellers.

Prices must be far enough apart so that buyers can see definite quality differences among products. Customers want and expect a wide assortment of products, and small price differences are confusing. For example, if ties are priced at $15, $15.35, and $15.75, customers cannot judge quality differences.

From your perspective, price lining offers several benefits:

▲ It's simple and efficient.
▲ It allows you to have smaller inventories.
▲ As costs change, prices can stay the same, while quality changes.
▲ Price lines make the salesperson's job easier.

You can consider costs to be the only factor, or at the other end of the spectrum, you can completely disregard costs.

▲ **Cost-based pricing.** Using your costs as the only basis for your pricing without taking other factors into consideration.
▲ **Value-based pricing.** Only the customer's perception determines your price.

FOR EXAMPLE

Better and Cheaper?

Some competitors try to convince customers that their product is better but costs less than the competitors' products. Nobody believes this claim — unless you present evidence. If you do, customers will love you — we all hope to get more for less, after all! The following scenarios are all variations of this possibility:

▲ A new antiwrinkle cream may work better but cost less if you've discovered a new formula.

▲ A retailer may be able to sell the same brands for a cheaper price because it has larger stores that do more sales volume of business.

With value-based pricing, the cost becomes whatever you think your product is worth to that customer at that time.

Value-based pricing asks two questions:

▲ **What is the highest price I can charge and still make the sale?** To answer this, you need to know how price sensitive consumers are and what sort of knowledge they have about competitors' prices. Also, if you have a market leader determining the price for your market, you'll have trouble raising your price.

▲ **Am I willing to sell at that price?** Your costs may not make it possible for you to sell at that price, but you may be able to cut costs without affecting quality. However, you may be constrained by legal considerations. (See Section 9.4.)

As long as you have — and can communicate to the customer — a plausible argument, you can undercut the competitor's price at the same time that you claim superior benefits. But make sure that you back up the claim, or the customer assumes that your lower price means the product is inferior.

Set a price that's consistent with your quality. Do not accidentally cheapen the perceived quality of your service by setting your price too low. **Price bundling** is when you group similar or complementary products and charge a total price that is lower than if they were sold separately.

A very popular pricing strategy, this can be a way of selling a less-popular product by combining it with popular ones. Industries such as financial services and telecommunications are big users of price bundling. The customer perceives a better value in many cases. This works when the increased sales generated compensates for the lower profit margin.

9.3.4 Pricing a New Product

When introducing a new product, two different pricing strategies are possible.

▲ **Skimming the market.** Selling the product at such a high price that only the very wealthy or least price-sensitive customers will buy it.

▲ **Penetration pricing.** Accepting a lower profit margin and pricing relatively low in the introduction of a product. It generates higher sales and helps the product get established in the market quickly.

Sometimes marketers even want to minimize unit volume — for example, they may not have the capacity to sell the product to a mass market and so decide to skim the market. Then they lower prices later on, when they have made maximum profits from the high-end customers and have added production capacity. CD players, fax machines, and satellite dishes for receiving TV programming all entered U.S. and European markets at high prices, using the skimming strategy.

Do not use a skimming strategy unless you are sure that you are safe from aggressive competition in the short term. Also, you need a premium product, for which demand is unusually high. A $500 ticket for the World Series or an $80,000 price tag for a limited-production sports car are two more examples. Intel and its Pentium chip possessed the advantage of legal protection for a while, which allowed it to charge premium prices. The initial high prices from skimming are usually reduced at some point, however, to match new competition and allow new customers access.

Penetration pricing works if and when you have price-sensitive customers, the opportunity to keep costs low, the anticipation of quick market entry by competitors, a high likelihood of acceptance by prospective buyers, and the adequate resources to meet the new demand.

SELF-CHECK

- Define **prestige pricing, price-lining strategy, special offers, coupon, redemption rate,** and **price bundling.**
- Distinguish cost-based pricing from value-based pricing.
- What are three ways to estimate your redemption rate?
- Name and define two different pricing strategies when pricing a new market.

9.4 Keeping It Legal

You do not have to be a legal whiz to know when pricing is illegal. Whenever a customer or competitor can make a good case for unfair or deceptive pricing, you are as good as busted. This section explains some of the more common and serious illegal pricing practices.

9.4.1 Price Fixing and Its Variants

Do not agree to (or even talk about) prices with other companies. The exception is a company you sell to, of course — but note that you cannot force them to resell your product at a specific price.

▲ **Price fixing:** Business competitors agreeing informally to push the price of a product as high as possible, leading to great profits for all sellers

Shady marketers have tried, unsuccessfully, to get around price fixing laws. If your competitors want you to require the same amount of down payment, start your negotiations from the same list prices as theirs, or use a standardized contract for extending credit or form a joint venture to distribute all your products (at the same price), you better realize that these friendly suggestions are all forms of price fixing in disguise. Just say no. And in the future, refuse even to take phone calls from marketers who offer you such deals.

This includes any exchanging of price information. You cannot talk to your competitors about prices. Ever. If it ever comes to light that anyone in your company gives out information about pricing and receives some in return, you are in big trouble, even if you do not feel you acted on that information. Take this warning seriously. Also avoid signaling.

▲ **Price signaling:** Announcing a planned price increase

This is sometimes seen as an unfair exchange of price information, because competitors may use such announcements to signal to others that everyone should make a price increase.

Believe it or not, you shouldn't even treat other marketers unfairly. Purchasers are also under this law. If purchasers join together in order to dictate prices from their suppliers, this can very well be price fixing. Have a skilled lawyer review any such plans.

In some cases, the U.S. government can charge you with price fixing, even if you didn't talk to competitors — just because you have similar price structures. After all, the result may be the same — to boost prices unfairly.

▲ **Parallel pricing:** Mirroring competitors' prices

In other cases, the law considers similar prices as natural. Here's a good-sense rule to keep in mind: Do not mirror competitors' prices, unless everyone and her uncle can see that you selected those prices on your own — especially if your price change involves a price increase.

9.4.2 Bid Rigging

If you are bidding for a contract, the same thing applies. Do not share any information with anyone. Do not compare notes with another bidder. Do not agree to make an identical bid. Do not *split* by agreeing not to bid on one job if the competitor doesn't bid on another. Do not interfere with the bidding process in any manner, or you are guilty of **bid rigging.**

9.4.3 Offenses against Competitors

Certain illegal acts involve using prices to push a competitor out of business, or to push or keep them out of a particular market. To the average marketer, these illegal acts are effectively the same (although they are tested under different U.S. regulations).

▲ Price squeezes

▲ Predatory pricing

▲ Limit pricing

▲ Dumping

FOR EXAMPLE

Big-time Bid Rigging

Bid rigging in the insurance industry is widespread, according to the New York State attorney general, Eliot Spitzer, and it hurts consumers. Eight insurance executives were indicted in 2005 on felony charges of bid rigging that totaled millions of dollars. Seven of them were from Marsh & McLennan, the largest insurance broker in the United States. These antitrust charges are taken very seriously by the government, which wants consumers to pay competitive prices for products and services. The insurance brokers allegedly colluded with major insurance companies to arrange noncompetitive bids, which were given to corporate clients (reported by the Associated Press, September 16, 2005).

For example, the classic **price squeezing** involves setting wholesale prices too high for small-sized orders. Doing so drives the independent or small retailer out of business, giving unfair advantage to the big-chain buyers that can qualify for a volume discount.

At the retail level, **predatory pricing** involves setting prices so low that local competitors cannot keep up. Predatory pricing is also used by chains and multinationals to drive locals out of business. If you are pricing at or below cost, you are probably doing predatory pricing.

Similarly, if your prices are so aggressive that they lock other competitors out of a market (even if you price above cost), then you are probably guilty of **limit pricing**. A variant is **dumping**, in which you try to buy your way into a new market by dumping a lot of product into that market at artificially low prices.

Some people throw up their hands in despair because so many pricing techniques are illegal. They say, "What can I do?" But trying to influence prices in certain ways is legal. You can offer volume discounts to encourage larger purchases, as long as those discounts do not force anybody out of the market. And although you, as a marketer, cannot force a retailer to charge a certain price for your product, you can encourage them to by advertising the suggested retail price and by listing it as such on your product.

Also, you can always offer an effective price cut to consumers through a consumer coupon or other special offer. Retailers usually agree to honor such offers (check with an ad agency, the retailer, or a lawyer to find out how to form such contracts). However, if you offer a discount to your retailers, you cannot force them to pass that discount on to your customers. They may just put the money in the bank and continue to charge customers full price.

SELF-CHECK

- Define price fixing, price signaling, and bid rigging.
- Who is hurt by predatory pricing and dumping?

SUMMARY

Pricing right means taking into account the customer's indifference zone, your costs, and secondary influences on price. The discount structure sets how much of the price you get to keep. Understand how to avoid illegal pricing practices, and understand the risks and benefits of special promotions.

KEY TERMS

Competitive pricing	Pricing relative to an important competitor or set of competitors.
Cost-based pricing	Using your costs as the only basis for your pricing without taking other factors into consideration.
Coupon	Any certificate entitling the holder to a reduced price.
Dumping	Buying a way into a new market by dumping a lot of product into that market at artificially low prices.
Indifference zone	The difference between the customer's desired price and a noticeably higher price.
Limit pricing	Pricing so aggressively that it locks other competitors out of a market.
Parallel pricing	Mirroring competitors' prices.
Penetration pricing	Accepting a lower profit margin and pricing relatively low in the introduction of a product. It generates higher sales and helps the product get established in the market quickly.
Premium	Any product that you give away to customers or sell at a discount as a reward for doing business with you.
Prestige pricing	Using a high price to signal quality.
Price bundling	Grouping similar or complementary products and charging a total price that is lower than if they were sold separately.
Price fixing	Business competitors agreeing informally to push the price of a product as high as possible, leading to great profits for all sellers.
Price lining	Keeping pricing consistent with product positions in your product line.
Price sensitivity	The degree to which purchases are affected by price level.
Price signaling	Announcing a planned price increase.
Price squeezing	Setting wholesale prices too high for small-sized orders, which drives independent or small-size retailers out of business.

Rebates	A refund of a fixed amount of money for a certain amount of time.
Redemption rate	The percentage of people who use the coupon.
Self-liquidating premium	A premium that customers end up covering your costs for.
Skimming the market	Selling the product at such a high price that only the very wealthy or least price-sensitive customers will buy it.
Special offers	Temporary inducements to make customers buy on the basis of price or price-related factors.
Trade discounts	The amount your intermediaries receive out of the total price.
Value-based pricing	When only the customer's perception determines your price.

ASSESS YOUR UNDERSTANDING

Go to www.wiley.com/college/Hiam to evaluate your knowledge of the basic pricing concepts.
Measure your learning by comparing pre-test and post-test results.

Summary Questions

1. Which of the following is **not** affecting modern pricing?
   (a) decreased price sensitivity
   (b) improved technology
   (c) foreign competition
   (d) more new products
2. With a 30/10/5 discount structure, the wholesaler is paying $70 for the product. True or false?
3. The bottom of your price range would be your cost plus your profit. True or false?
4. Possible pricing objectives are
   (a) profit, sales, and sensitivity
   (b) image, sales, and survival
   (c) costs, sales, and profits
5. A self-liquidating premium can cut into your profit margins. True or false?
6. Promotions increase price sensitivity. True or false?
7. Price signaling is always illegal. True or false?
8. It's legal to discuss your pricing with a competitor if it doesn't affect your policies. True or false?
9. Trade discounts are a form of cost to the marketer. True or false?
10. What's the best way to price your product relative to a competitor in a competitive market?
    (a) price lower
    (b) price at the same level
    (c) price according to product benefits vis a vis your competitor
    (d) price according to your costs

Review Questions

1. In what situations would a customer want to pay *more* for your product?
2. What is the *redemption rate*? How many coupons are redeemed in North America? Less than 5 percent, about 10 percent, or 32 percent?
3. Why can't you just set your price at the top of the price range, every time? Explain.

Applying This Chapter

1. Your new line of snack foods isn't making a profit, and you think you need to raise prices to cover your costs. What other options do you have that are mentioned in this chapter?
2. If your distribution channel has a discount structure of 20/15/10, how much of the $500 list price of the item are you keeping and how much are your intermediaries getting?
3. Name two products or services in which consumers are generally price sensitive. Then name two more that you think people do not shop for based on price.
4. If you estimate your customers' indifference zone at between $5 and $8 for your product, how much might you want to offer for a coupon promotion if your product is currently retailing for $6.50? What do you need to know to figure out if your promotion will pay off?

The Price of Music

Let's say you want to buy the latest CD of your favorite band but you do not want to pay full price. Price the CD at a local privately owned music store, a discount retailer, a Web site, and a national chain such as Best Buy. Whose price is the best and why do you think that is the case?

Finding the Zone

It costs you $3 to manufacture your product on average, and you've determined your customers' indifference zone is between $5 and $10. The bottom of your price range will be where?

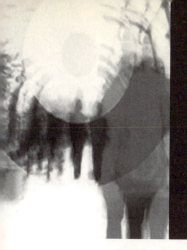

10

MARKETING COMMUNICATIONS AND PERSONAL SELLING
Making the Sale

Starting Point

Go to www.wiley.com/college/Hiam to assess your knowledge of the basics of marketing communications.
Determine where you need to concentrate your effort.

What You'll Learn in This Chapter

▲ Clear, appealing communications
▲ Great visuals and writing
▲ Attention-getting strategies
▲ The sales and service process

After Studying This Chapter, You'll Be Able To

▲ Employ "stopping power" and "pull power"
▲ Apply techniques from fiction and psychology to develop your brand personality
▲ Find and keep effective salespeople

Goals and Outcomes

▲ Create a winning personality for your brand
▲ Manage a sales force
▲ Meet customers' needs effectively

INTRODUCTION

You communicate constantly in marketing. By making your message clear and compelling, you can stand out from the clutter of ads. Developing a brand personality and using the right strategies will help you grab attention for your marketing. Personal selling is the most basic, direct way of making a sale. This chapter helps you pump up your marketing communications and understand the process of personal selling.

10.1 Developing a Recipe for Good Marketing Communications

What's the difference between good and poor marketing communications? The most important difference is **impact.** For example, suppose an educational institution wants to improve its communications with the goal of making its name and strengths better known. Everything it does, from having a representative talk to the press to designing a brochure to sending out letters or revamping its Web site, needs to make an impact and help the institution achieve its communication goal.

10.1.1 Starting with a Clear Message

Often the most exciting and creative ads fail to actually make the sale because they're not simple and clear enough. Being noticed, grabbing attention, being persuasive — marketers need to remember these important priorities. Yet, grabbing attention can distract you from the essential need to be clear in making your case. Communication has many points of influence. You need a compelling message to send out through all those influence points. How?

1. Position the product in your customers' minds. A **positioning strategy** is a detailed (but readable) statement of how you want customers to think and feel about your product. You need the right positioning strategy as a foundation — along with products that follow through on the promises you make. The strategy describes how you are positioned in their minds and hearts. See Section 2.1 for details.

FOR EXAMPLE

Whose Fries?

A Burger King TV ad campaign boasted that Burger King's French-fried potatoes had beaten McDonald's fries in a taste test. But consumers didn't pick up the nuances. They just noticed the mention of McDonald's fries, and rumor has it that sales went up at McDonald's instead of Burger King.

2. Craft a basic appeal, some motivating message that gets that positioning across. Then figure out how to convey the gist of the positioning strategy. Take the basic statement of how you want people to think of your product and convert it into a message that may actually convince them. For example, if you want to introduce a new, healthier kind of pizza made only of organic ingredients, your positioning statement may be, "healthier pizza that doesn't sacrifice taste." Then craft the basic appeal, such as: "Instead of fighting to keep your kids from eating the unhealthy junk-food pizzas they love, why not give them healthy pizzas that are actually better tasting, too?"

3. Find a creative big idea — something that packages your appeal in a message so compelling that people stop in their tracks. The message should persuade in a creative way, or nobody will pay attention. For example, the pizza's basic positioning is "organic and low-fat, so it's healthy and it also tastes good." You crafted your basic appeal above, in Number 2. Now, what creative idea can you come up with to turn this appeal into a compelling communication? Here are some options:

   • Kids stare longingly through the glass-fronted case of a candy store, in such a crowd that it's hard to even see what has drawn their attention. It's the newest flavor of the healthy pizza!

   • A journalist interviews swimmers on a remote tropical island where the average life expectancy is higher than anywhere else. In response to the question, "What is the secret to your amazing health and longevity?" a tanned and fit grandmother says, "We do not do anything special, we just order out for pizza every night." She then dives off a cliff into a tropical pool of water. The pizza is from a little old mud hut with the logo of our brand over its door and a crowd of village children in the door, happily receiving slices of the magical pizza.

4. Develop, edit, and simplify your creative idea until it's transparently clear and fits the medium. Your medium is partly determined by your message and by the creative idea you select. To tell a story, you may choose television advertising if your budget is large. A streaming-video version for your Web site or a radio-ad version of the story will cut your costs compared to TV advertising (see Section 11.3). And for much less money, have a cartoonist do a series of drawings in comic-strip format and turn them into a print ad or flier, or place them on your Web site.

These steps, when done well, create a compelling marketing message and communicate that message persuasively. The task is difficult but vital. Also, you must choose whether to build your appeal and communication strategy around a strong claim, backed by irrefutable evidence, or to make an emotional appeal that feels right to the customer but lacks hard evidence. Perhaps a balanced mix of the two is possible. (For more on marketing appeals, see Section 1.1.)

You can pitch your marketing communications at the rational or the emotional buyer. You can even segment your market based on this, and design separate marketing programs. When you design your communications, you want to emphasize one or the other. When you waffle, trying to appeal to both sides of the brain at once, your message usually gets weaker.

After you have created your basic appeal and chosen an emotional or rational approach, you need a strategy to improve the impact of your appeal, to show what makes your product great. But you cannot just tell them that your product is great, because they've heard that one before. The message must sell itself! Most appeals are ineffective. It is difficult to achieve the kind of impact you want as a marketer, so try one or more of the following strategies to improve the impact of your appeal:

▲ **Image strategy:** Shows people your product and its personality, and presents a good image of your brand, product, service, or business

For example, a day spa may develop a sophisticated logo and color scheme and work sophistication into everything, from its print ads and Web site to its decor, towels, bathrobes, and bottled water.

▲ **Information strategy:** Communicates facts that make you appealing

For example, a truck-rental company may want to let prospects know how many of what kind of trucks it has available, in what good condition it keeps those trucks, and how reasonable it makes its terms of rental. The facts should make the sale. And if you know you are particularly strong in a certain area, then communicate the facts of your brilliance instead of wasting effort on more ordinary information.

▲ **Motivational strategy:** Builds a compelling argument or feeling that should lead prospects to take action and make a purchase

For example, a life insurance company may tell some stories about people who did have insurance and others who didn't, and what happened to their loved ones after they died. Prospects often experience strong emotional responses to these stories, so this approach should lead to new sales.

▲ **Demonstration strategy:** Leverages the fundamental appeal of the product itself by simply making that product available to prospects

For some products, seeing is believing. AOL used this strategy effectively by simply mailing an access disk to prospects. Sometimes marketing really is as easy as making the product available to people — such as a car dealership offering free test-drives for a new model.

A good appeal may rely on only one of these strategies, or it can combine two or even three of them. But use at least one of these approaches when marketing.

10.1.2 Creating Great Writing and Visuals

Keep the writing direct and simple. Make it reach out and grab the reader! Great writing is always clear. Much of marketing writing, unfortunately, suffers from the following problems:

- ▲ It fails to come to the point.
- ▲ It uses passive sentences (where you cannot tell who does what to whom).
- ▲ It employs sophisticated vocabulary without sufficient cause — meaning it uses big words needlessly.
- ▲ It uses difficult verb tenses instead of the present tense ("writing would have to communicate" rather than "writing communicates," for example).

And as a result, typical marketing writing bores or confuses its readers. If you can find a novel way to make your point, do. Originality and surprise create stopping power. But above all else, make sure you write simply and clearly. You are not looking for a Pulitzer; you are just trying to communicate.

You can only get to the essence of a communication by writing, and then rewriting and rewriting. Keep reworking, keep rethinking, keep boiling your words down until you have something that penetrates to your point with startling clarity. (Nike's "Just Do It" is a strikingly simple and powerful statement of the brand's personality.)

As for visuals, pictures can truly be worth a thousand words. Imagine the following: A kid is playing tennis against a backboard when a dog runs up and steals the ball. The ball, bright yellow and fuzzy, overflows the dog's mouth as the camera zooms in to show the ball and mouth, filling the TV screen.

This visual image is simple but communicates a lot. Like how much fun kids and dogs have when playing with tennis balls. And drama — how does the kid feel when the dog takes his ball? How does the dog feel when he gets the ball? Most of all, the image reminds us that tennis is good fun for everyone, regardless of skill level, age, or even species!

The visual image comes from a television spot promoting tennis from the U.S. Tennis Association. It illustrates the power of a good visual image or sequence of images to capture attention, tell an interesting story, and communicate a point.

It also spotlights a key to successful visuals — a focus on one strong, relevant image. In this case, that image is the tennis ball, proudly framed in the dog's jaws. In your case, well, the image can be anything — as long as the image is

- ▲ Visually compelling
- ▲ Easily recognizable
- ▲ Relevant to your appeal

You need to work with artists to create effective visual imagery, unless you are an artist yourself. Gaining the technical skills and design sense to create something as simple as an illustrated brochure takes a long time, so imagine how long you would need to be able to perform more complex tasks, like a four-color print ad, a package design, or a television spot.

But still, you may find yourself having to take on some of the design tasks in your marketing department or business. Something may have to be done right now, without the budget for a creative agency or graphic designer.

Modern technology makes the technical aspects much easier and has brought costs down considerably. Yet most homemade designing off people's desktop computers and inkjet printers stinks. Sometimes these efforts waste the paper the homemade designs are printed on, insult the customer, and embarrass the profession of marketing. Doing the design work yourself is now technically easy, but if you do not know much about design, you can get into trouble really quickly with the new technologies.

A good rule of thumb in designing anything visual — brochure, Web page, logo, ad, sign, package design, label, and so on — is to know what you want people to see first, second, and third:

1. They see the visually dominant aspect of the image first. This aspect needs appeal, to stop the prospects in their tracks and draw them closer so they look at the second and third aspects of the ad.
2. The second thing they see should explain the basic appeal in a simple, clear way.
3. Finally, they should get some consistent, supporting evidence or feelings to back up what Numbers 1 and 2 tell them.

Now, with this hierarchy in mind, one image needs to be visually dominant. Have a focal point, or an entry point, for the eye. What is the number one image or design element in your ads, brochures, or other visual communications? Does it clearly dominate, or do many elements compete for the top spot? Is the dominant visual element appealing and attractive enough to deserve this top spot? And does it clearly show how your product benefits the customer? In most cases, existing marketing communications fail this hierarchy test.

Here's a simple and powerful suggestion (see Section 11.1 for details on laying out print ads and brochures): Make a visual image of your product the most visible feature of your design. Get an outstanding photo of your product and place that in a dominant position in your ad, brochure, Web page, or other marketing device.

If you provide an intangible service or process, give your service a visual identity by creating a well-done diagram, flowchart, picture of someone using or doing it, or a striking picture of something that can represent it (a rose can represent a dating service, for example).

Now place that product image as the biggest, most noticeable feature of your communication. In reality, a good picture is often worth a lot more than a thousand words.

SELF-CHECK

- Define **image**.
- What's the first thing you need to think about when communicating a message?
- What are the four types of strategies you might use?
- What are the problems with much marketing writing?

10.2 Strengthening Your Marketing Communications

Weak marketing communications can waste your company's money and erode your brand identity. You should find ways to make your products memorable and larger than life. Business is more competitive than ever, and this section discusses how to give your products personality, how to catch the customer's eye, and how to build customer traffic.

10.2.1 Giving Products Personality

You may not realize that the cars you see or drive have carefully crafted personalities, but these personalities help marketers position each auto and appeal to its intended buyers. For example, a Dodge Ram pickup truck has a tough, can-do, unfussy, masculine image. Its personality is forceful, rugged, and tough. Everyone who works on the marketing of a Dodge Ram is aware of that personality description and tries to convey that personality consistently.

Giving your brand a personal identity, as if the brand was a living thing, can create a lasting impression. The best way to think about it is to imagine that you are bringing that brand to life, particularly with an emotional appeal, because a compelling personality always attracts emotional buyers.

Even with a logical appeal, give your brand a supporting personality. If you are selling industrial design services to manufacturers, you can present the brand as a careful, thoughtful engineer. Although a supporting personality isn't as decisive as an emotional appeal, it still helps communicate with consumers and reminds them of your basic appeal.

FOR EXAMPLE

Volkswagen Gets Emotional

Volkswagen decided to reposition itself in the American market as a fun-to-drive car for Generation Xers who are moving into parenting and responsible work roles but still feel an urge to express themselves as individuals. Volkswagen's approach was to emphasize the fun of driving their cars and to convince consumers that their customers are special because of their love of driving and zest for life. This example presents a classic emotional appeal. The ads emphasize images over words and have a strongly intuitive appeal grounded in the values of Generation Xers. The advertisers tell you nothing factual about Volkswagen in those television ads, but you do get a strong emotional hit.

Define your brand's personality clearly so that you can cultivate that personality in every marketing communication. A richly scripted personality has the power to shine through all your marketing program's influence points, providing a consistent touchstone for all communications. If you know your brand well enough, you can communicate that intimacy to your customers.

So, then how do you define a personality? Psychology and fiction give us some clues:

▲ Writers will define a character's personality by his likes and dislikes. Good storytellers know how to develop characters. Sherlock Holmes, one of the most enduring fictional characters of all time, smokes strong tobacco in his pipe when thinking about a problem and also plays the violin. He has a deep interest in aspects of science that have to do with crime, and he fills notebooks with clippings about famous criminals and their doings. But he has no interest in romance and no close friends but Dr. Watson. He is a cold, rational problem solver with a touch of artistic imagination. All these facts about the man help create a characteristic image, one that publishers, game and toy makers, and movie producers have cashed in on for decades.

▲ You can draw up a list of traits or personality characteristics to associate with your brand or company name that add up to a distinct personality. Jaguar ran an effective series of ads that associated fine old country houses and estates with their vehicles.

▲ Another device borrowed from fiction involves writing a short event-based chapter about a character. Many authors give you a description of some actions or events in order to develop their characters. You can do the same. (The opening mini-movie that comes before the title and credits of a James Bond movie establishes Bond's character in just a few minutes.)

▲ Draw insights from psychology to create a personality for your product. Psychologists have studied the puzzle of human personality for decades, sometimes even making a little progress. You can use personality tests such as the *Myers-Briggs* or the *Insight Inventory*.

▲ The **trait perspective,** an approach used by psychologists, seeks to understand the variation in human personalities by identifying the various traits that make up each individual personality. Give your brands a personality by describing their essential traits. The trait perspective helps you create a product personality because it focuses on describing, rather than explaining, human behavior. And marketers are pragmatists — you do not need to know why personalities develop, you just need to figure out what personality to give your products.

You should try to achieve consistency in how you present the brand to customers. After you have developed a description of a brand's human personality, everyone can use this description as a guide by asking, whenever they do sales or marketing, whether their activities are consistent with it.

10.2.2 Stopping Power: Catching the Customer's Eye

Stopping power is the ability of an advertisement or other marketing communication to stop people in their tracks, to make them sit up and take notice. Communications with stopping power generate "What did you say?" or "Did you see that?" responses. These communications generate great attention — unlike most marketing communications, which simply do not have the ability to grab instant attention.

Thousands of marketing messages bombard customers. The high level of noise means that most efforts to communicate fail. Most ads go unnoticed by people they target.

Ask people to recall five ads they saw on television last night (if they watched TV last night, they probably saw many dozens). Watch their reactions. If you ask about print ads in a magazine or newspaper or brochures or "junk mail" letters, you may well draw a complete blank. Many people do not recall even one ad in a magazine they read yesterday unless you actively prompt them.

Or try asking about radio ads. Same problem. This puts the importance of stopping power into perspective. Your ads need to have much more stopping power than most to get a significant number of people to remember and think about your product!

According to ad agency Young and Rubicam, seven principles apply in making an ad or any marketing communication a real stopper. We've modified those principles to present this list:

▲ **The ad must have intrinsic drama that appeals to everyone.** The ad should attract many people outside of the target audience. If kids like an ad aimed at adults or vice versa, that ad fulfills this principle.

▲ **The ad must demand participation from the audience.** The ad needs to draw people into some action, whether that action is calling a number, going to a store, laughing out loud, or just thinking about something. A stopper of an ad should never permit the audience to play a passive role.

▲ **The ad needs to force an emotional response.** This principle should hold true, even if you are making a rational appeal. The heart of the ad must still contain some basic human need, something about which people feel passionately.

▲ **The ad must stimulate curiosity.** The audience should want to know more. This desire gets them to stop and study the ad — and follow up with further information searches afterward.

▲ **The ad should surprise its audience.** A startling headline, an unexpected visual image, an unusual opening gambit in a sales presentation, or a weird display window in a store all have the power to stop people by surprising them.

▲ **The ad must communicate expected information — in an *detcepxenu* way.** (*Hint:* Try reading that mystery word backward.) A creative twist, or a fresh way of saying or looking at something, makes the expected unexpected. You have to get the obvious information in — what the brand is, who it benefits, and how. But do not do so in an obvious way, or the communication doesn't reach out and grab attention and it gets ignored.

▲ **The ad may need to violate the rules and personality of the product category.** People notice things that violate expected patterns. So make your ad distinctly different from what consumers have come to expect in your product's category. If you market office-cleaning services, for example, you no doubt buy Yellow Pages ads and make up fliers with your price list and a few client testimonials. Yawn! To complement these ordinary marketing efforts, send a sponge in the mail to prospective clients with your name and phone number on one side, and, on the other, the message, "Just in case you still insist on doing the cleaning without our help."

To make an ad that has drama, that surprises people, that violates the pattern, and that says the expected in an unexpected way — requires creativity. And so perhaps the most essential secret to stopping power is creativity.

Advertising research reveals another secret of stopping power: sex. To give an ad stopping power, just give it some sex appeal. But note, sex-based ads have stopping power but do not prove very effective by other measures. Brand recall — the ability of viewers to remember what product the ad advertised — is usually lower for sex-oriented ads than other ads.

Although these ads do have stopping power, they do not seem to have any other benefits. They fail to turn that high initial attention into awareness or interest. They do not change attitudes about the product. In short, they sacrifice good communication for raw stopping power.

The only exception to the rule that sexy ads are bad communicators is when sex is relevant to the product, such as in marketing a lingerie store. But leave sexy models out of ads for hardware stores, lawn-care services, or office supplies, because they have no obvious relevance.

10.2.3 Pull Power: Building Customer Traffic

Somebody has to actually *sell* a product on the ground, in the local market, customer by customer. At this level, you just need to draw in those customers. This is why smaller or local marketers usually concern themselves with *pull power*, instead of focusing on the national advertising concerns of *brand equity* or positioning.

▲ **Pull power:** The ability of a marketing communication to draw people to a place or event.

▲ **Brand equity:** Building the value of your brand.

Pull power is the primary goal of all **local advertising,** or advertising that is focused on a specific city or county, which makes up almost half of all advertising in the United States.

Marketers use publicity, personal selling, direct mail, price-based promotions, and point-of-purchase spending to try to exercise effective pull power. Because of this pull orientation, local marketing communications are unique in these ways:

▲ Local communications tend to be part of a short-term effort, rather than a long-term campaign. Do not feel you have to do anything permanent. Short, powerful bursts usually have more pull power.

▲ You can do local communications on a shoestring budget — far smaller than the millions spent by national or multinational advertisers. Keep it simple!

▲ Local communications should generate customers in the store, make the phone ring, bring more folks to your Web site, or accomplish some other pull-oriented tactical goal. If your marketing communication isn't pulling, then pull it.

For maximum pull power, give people a strong reason to act. Tell consumers your location and that you have what they need. Ask them to come by, call, return a coupon, or visit your Web site. Keep inviting them, always in new and creative ways, so they never forget you.

SELF-CHECK

- Define **brand equity** and **local advertising**.
- What's the difference between stopping power and pull power?
- What are the seven principles for gaining stopping power?
- What type of techniques will help create personality for a product?

10.3 Sales and Service Essentials

Sometimes you need to work one on one with your prospective customer through **personal selling,** or selling face to face.

If so, you need to make sales the main focus of marketing plans and activities. Any advertising, direct mail, telemarketing, event sponsorships, or public relations has to take a back seat to sales. The following quiz in Table 10-1 helps you determine if a business should rely on sales.

If you can answer "yes" to more than one of these questions, then you can probably use personal sales (one-on-one with prospects) effectively, and you should make them an important part of your marketing plan and budget. Focus your marketing program on personal selling and good follow-up service.

Table 10-1: Are Personal Sales and Service the Key to Your Marketing Program?

Yes	No	Our typical customer makes many small purchases and/or at least a few very large ones in a year.
Yes	No	Our typical customer usually needs help figuring out what to buy and/or how to use the product.
Yes	No	Our typical customer's business is highly complex and imposes unique requirements on our products/services.
Yes	No	Our products/services are an important part of the customer's overall business process.
Yes	No	Our customer is accustomed to working with salespeople and expects personal attention and assistance.
Yes	No	Our competitors make regular sales calls on our customers and/or prospects.
Yes	No	We have to provide customized service to retain a customer.

Think of the rest of your marketing effort as support for the personal sales process. That process is going to be the key to your success. Give careful thought to how you hire, manage, organize, support, and motivate salespeople. Their performance determines whether your marketing succeeds.

10.3.1 The Sales and Service Process

The sales and service processes aren't separate. You cannot stop when you close a sale and write the order. Think of a completed sale as the *beginning* of a relationship-building process. After you close a sale, you need more sales calls, further presentations, and efforts to find new ways to serve the customer. That's real-world selling.

The sales process can be tough. But you can divide and conquer: Divide sales into multiple steps and then focus on one step at a time. Try to find the place in your process where performance is now the poorest. Focus on that weak link!

Figure 10-1 displays the sales and service process as a flowchart. Note that the chart doesn't flow automatically from beginning to end. You may be forced to cycle back to an earlier stage if things go wrong. But, ideally, you never lose a prospect or customer forever — they just recycle into sales leads, and you can mount a new effort to win them over.

10.3.2 Service Recovery

You also have to anticipate problems. No matter how good your company is, something will go wrong that upsets, disappoints, or even angers your customer. Thus, the sales process has to include a **service recovery** step.

You have to figure out how to detect a service problem — how good is your communication with that customer? Make sure that the customer knows to call his salesperson when that problem occurs. How well can the salesperson respond? If the salesperson finds himself overscheduled with sales calls, he cannot take the time to solve problems.

So budget approximately 1 in 10 sales calls as service recovery time to prepare for this contingency. The salesperson needs some resources, and time, to solve customer problems and rebuild relationships. Give the salesperson some spending authority so that he or she can make the customer whole and turn his or her anger into satisfaction.

The most faithful customers are the ones who have had a big problem that you managed to solve in a fair and generous manner. Anything that you invest in service recovery is time and money well spent!

Sales and service go hand in hand. When your business relies on personal selling, you also need great customer service. Personal selling produces new customers, but personal service *keeps* them. If you do not know how to keep new customers, you shouldn't waste your time seeking new customers. You will just lose them. If your **customer turnover rate,** or the percent of customers who leave each year, goes over 5 percent in most industries, you need to find ways to build retention.

Figure 10-1

The Sales/Service Process

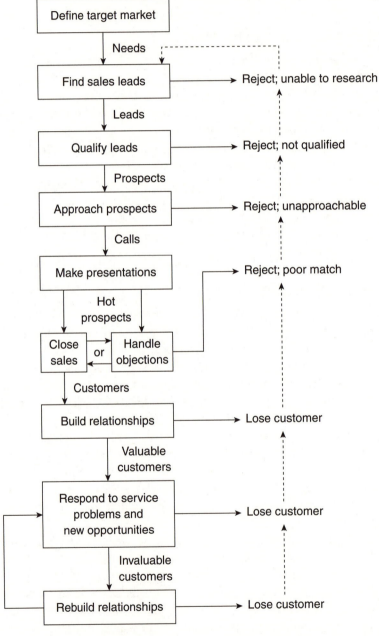

This flowchart shows you the process behind sales and service.

Service recovery starts with recognizing when service isn't going well. What makes your customer unhappy? Generate a list of the top five warning signs of an unhappy customer. Every company has a different list. Educate everyone to recognize the signs and to leap into action whenever they see one.

You can practice service recovery strategically, in the same way as sales, with the goal of winning back the customer by solving her problem or helping her feel better. Start by empathizing with the person. Listen and do not argue. The unhappy customer is always right. After he or she has calmed down a bit, then you can ask factual questions and give information.

But remember, every service recovery starts with working on the (hurt) feelings of the disgruntled customer, not on the facts. That important insight can save a lot of customer relationships and help you build a great reputation. Some other ways to serve customers and make more sales:

▲ **Smiling more often:** Even if you have to take a little "me time" to get back into a good mood, do it. If you and those you work with can maintain and project a positive attitude, customers take notice and enjoy working with you or buying from you. Smiles really do attract more and better business.

▲ **Complimenting your customers:** People like to feel noticed and appreciated. So when a natural opportunity arises, compliment your customers by offering praise for what they do. The positive feelings tend to strengthen the customer relationship, and when you are not stingy with your praise, customers aren't, either — which means they may compliment you to others who may become future customers.

▲ **Revisiting existing customers' accounts:** You can focus so hard on new customer acquisition that you ignore your old customers. Do not! Revisit them, re-research their needs, and network to meet new contacts (if the customer is a business, you need to meet as many of its employees as possible). Communicate often with existing customers — they're the backbone of your business, and without some attention, they may eventually wander off to the competition.

▲ **Installing a friendly telephone system:** Sometimes there is no way to opt out of the phone answering system and get a human being. Other annoyances include overly lengthy on-hold messages and preliminaries, no easy way to find someone's extension, no quick way to leave a voice mail, and poor or no follow-up on voice mails. If your customers have to go through hoops to call you, they just do not. You do not even know how much business you miss. If you cannot make a fancy telephone system easy to use, turn it off and go back to the old standby: When a phone rings, whoever can get to it scrambles to answer it within three rings. And if you miss it, make sure that you have a very quick and simple option for leaving a message — that you return within the hour. These standards make a phone system friendly and win you both new and repeat business.

▲ **Keeping your place clean:** A dirty window, worn-out paint, or shoddy, second-rate marketing materials send the wrong message to a company's customers. Show you care! Be meticulous about everything that the customer sees and interacts with. An airline that cannot keep its bathrooms clean and in good repair doesn't inspire confidence in its ability to maintain its engines. And a management-consulting firm that cannot keep its lobby plants fresh and healthy doesn't inspire confidence in its ability to help clients thrive. To present the best possible face to the world, you and your employees need to have pride in the company and its products.

▲ **Converting anger to purchases:** Rather than give up on angry customers, try to contact them personally by phone, letter, or card to offer an apology and see if you can turn them around. They're usually pleasantly surprised to receive a personal and polite response — and somewhat embarrassed about the angry phone call or e-mail that they dashed off in a thoughtless moment. Often, they end up responding in a friendly manner and becoming a good customer. Be an optimistic marketer — see most complaints as openings!

10.3.3 Organizing Your Sales Force

Organizational decisions can make a big difference to sales force productivity. Consider your situation. For example, how many salespeople do you need? If you have an existing sales force, examine the performance of each territory to decide whether more salespeople can help, or if perhaps you can do with less.

If some territories are rich in prospects that salespeople just do not get to, consider splitting those territories. Also consider splitting, or adding a second person to create a sales team, if you are experiencing high customer turnover. Turnover probably indicates a lack of service and follow-up visits. Alternatively, if you see some territories that have little potential, you may be able to merge those territories with other territories.

You can also use another, more systematic approach for designing a sales force from scratch. Study your market to decide how many sales calls you want to make over a year-long period. Then follow these steps:

1. Count how many potential customers you have in your entire market.
2. Decide what proportion or how many of those customers you want to call on.
3. Decide how many calls you want to make over the next year for each customer, on average (for example, 2 per month or 24 per year).
4. Multiply Step 2 by Step 3. Doing so gives you the total sales calls you need for the entire year.

5. Decide how many calls one person can reasonably make in a day. The answer depends on the nature of the call and the travel time between customers.

6. Multiply this daily figure (in Step 5) by the number of working days in your company's calendar.

7. Divide the total number of calls needed per year (from Step 4) by the number of calls one salesperson can make per year (from Step 6). Doing so gives you the number of salespeople needed to make all those calls.

For example, 10,000 sales calls needed next year, divided by 1,000 calls per salesperson per year, means that you need a sales force of 10 people to execute your plan. If you only have five on staff, you'd better hire five more or bring on some sales reps to help your staff — if you cannot get authority for or raise funding for either plan, scale back your sales goals by half. You can never sell to 10,000 customers with only five salespeople.

What about subcontracting? Good sales companies exist in most industries that will hire and manage salespeople for you. **Sales representatives** or reps usually work for a straight commission of between 10 and 20 percent, depending on the industry and how much room you have in your pricing structure for their commission.

Also, in areas where you need more work done — customer support through consultative selling and customized service — reps earn, and deserve, a higher commission. Sales reps are good if you have a small company or a short product line. They're the best option if you have scale problems that make justifying the cost of hiring your own dedicated salespeople somewhat difficult.

Scale problems arise when you have a too-short product line, which means that salespeople do not have very much to sell to customers. Each sales call produces such small total orders that those sales do not cover the cost of the call. Reps usually handle many companies' product lines, so that they have more products to show prospects when they call than your own independent salesperson would.

If you can justify hiring and running your own dedicated salespeople, then do it! You have much more control and better feedback from the market, and a dedicated sales force generally outsells a sales rep because they are focused and dependent on your product. Often, the rep doesn't care what he or she sells, as long as the client buys something. Reps tend to make the easy sales, which may not be yours!

10.3.4 Finding and Compensating Your Reps

How do you find sales reps? You cannot find them listed in any telephone directory. Rep firms prefer that you find them by networking. You have to do it on the reps' terms, which means getting word-of-mouth referrals or meeting them at a trade show or industry conference.

Here are some ways:

▲ Ask the buyers of products such as the one you sell for names of reps who currently call on them.

▲ Ask the companies that reps sell to for their opinions about the best rep firms. After all, you need the reps to sell your product to these customers, so their opinions are the most important!

▲ You can also get referrals from other companies that sell (noncompeting) products through the same kinds of reps.

▲ If you have some reps already, they can tell you about firms that cover other territories.

▲ You can network for reps at trade shows in your industry. Reps attend the trade shows, and many of them rent booths to represent their products. You can find them just by wandering the exhibition hall, and asking questions.

After you have reps lined up, your work has only just begun. You absolutely must monitor their sales efforts regularly. Which rep firms sell the best (and worst)? Usually 10 or 15 percent of the reps make almost all your sales. If you notice such a pattern developing, you can quickly put the others on notice. If they do not heat up, you probably want to replace them.

Temp agencies can fill a short-term need for experienced telemarketers, salespeople, trade-show staff, and other marketing people. Businesses do not use temporary salespeople that often, but they're a great alternative because they allow you to put a lot of salespeople on the street quickly without making a long-term financial commitment.

Use them to help you open up a new territory, introduce a new product, or follow up on a backlog of sales leads from that big trade show you exhibited at last month. Hire temps on a monthly basis to give them time to develop some continuity. Consider teaming them with your full-time salespeople to ease the transition for new accounts when the temporary period ends.

Compensation is one of the toughest and most important management decisions in marketing. Pay has a significant impact on the sales staff's motivation and performance, and their performance affects sales. Yet compensation's effect on motivation isn't always obvious.

It's worth thinking about how to have relationship-oriented salespeople, not folks who just shoot for the maximum number of transactions. Aim your commissions and also your nonfinancial incentives (recognition, praise, and so on) at both finding and *keeping* good customers, not just writing the most new business. To recruit special salespeople, you may need a special compensation plan. Differentiate yourself in your industry to make your job openings stand out.

FOR EXAMPLE

Rewarding Excellent Salespeople

In an industry in which commissions from home sales typically get split between the agent and their realty firm, Realty Executives, a Phoenix-based real estate firm, gives 100 percent of the sales commission to its realtors. And rather than offer a base salary, it charges its agents a monthly fee for use of the firm's name and facilities. This unusual approach attracts top salespeople who can earn more than the average broker would. And it weeds out low performers who would otherwise slide by on their base salaries and an occasional commission at a more conventional firm.

For example, what if you want your salespeople to take a highly consultative, service-oriented approach, with long-term support and relationship building? You need people with patience and dedication, people who are looking for a stable situation and can build business over the long term. Try offering them smaller commissions, but make compensation salary based. With sales incentives, consider bonuses linked to long-term customer retention or to building sales with existing customers. This compensation plan stands out, showing exactly what sales behavior you expect. Similarly, if you want the hottest, most self-motivated salespeople, offer more commission than the competition.

SELF-CHECK

- What is the **customer turnover rate?**
- What are some ways to find sales reps?
- What is personal selling?
- What is service recovery?
- Name some ways to serve your customers.

10.4 Generating Sales Leads and Making the Sale

In many companies, the most important steps in the sales and service process are those steps in which you find and qualify sales leads. **Qualifying** entails gathering enough information about someone or some business to make sure he or she fits a profile of a good customer. You decide on this profile, based on criteria like wealth, age, and interests (for a consumer sale), or size, industry, and location (for a business sale).

Remember the *garbage in, garbage out* rule. Do not throw garbage leads into your process. Feed your sales process with a constant flow of quality sales leads. Know what your customer profile is and seek out qualified prospects with questions or screening criteria that allow you to sift through and eliminate poor-quality prospects quickly.

Sales leads can come from any of your marketing activities. Try using as many alternatives as possible so that you can find out which works best.

▲ Your Web site may produce the best leads (see Chapter 13)
▲ Joining a professional group or association to network and meet potential clients
▲ A direct-mail campaign may produce leads
▲ Direct-response advertising to find leads
▲ Telemarketing
▲ Trade shows
▲ Event sponsorship

10.4.1 Finding New Approaches through Your Marketing

Almost any kind of marketing can produce leads. Find a good way to communicate with people who seem like good prospects and ask whether they're interested in your product or service. You also need to begin to ask for factual information: who they are, how to contact them, what they've bought or used in the past, and what their current needs are. Getting even a bit of information and an indication that someone is interested makes a lead!

Here is a very simple way to generate leads:

1. Select a magazine, newsletter, e-newsletter, or newspaper that the kind of people who should be interested in what you sell or do are likely to read.
2. Find the smallest, cheapest display ad in that publication and buy that ad space for the shortest possible time — one insertion, if you can.
3. Write a very simple, short description of what you do or sell, keeping it clear and factual. Include a clear, simple photo, if you have a relevant one (you can show the product, if you are in a product business), or use your name and logo to illustrate the ad.
4. End the ad with the following sentence: Please contact us to find out more about our offerings by calling 800-xxx-yyyy, or by using the inquiry form on our Web site at www.mywebsite.com.

You run a no-nonsense direct-response ad this way. If you already use some good lead-generation techniques, why not test something simple in a new medium? Keep experimenting. You can buy names from list brokers. Mailing and call lists are widely available. But do not make the mistake of thinking that they're leads in and of themselves. Nobody can sell you leads; you have to make them for yourself.

Write a letter describing your offer and what you do and make sure your brilliance — what you are especially good at and want to be known for — is clearly and persuasively described. Send it out to a purchased list and ask recipients to contact you if they want more information.

To increase the response rate, try including a special short-term offer and a prepaid postcard or fax form for recipients' replies. Or, try following up on the letter with a telephone call to the recipient. You may have to make two or more contacts to sort out the real leads from the rest of the list. After you get some responses and capture their names and other information, you can call them leads.

The classic retail salesperson walks a residential block, ringing doorbells. Forget that approach, which no longer works. Nobody's home in the daytime anymore, and the few people who do stay home are afraid to admit a stranger carrying a large suitcase — or should be. Some nonprofit organizations (like Greenpeace) canvas door to door at dinnertime with moderate success — if they pick neighborhoods where their name is well known and their cause popular. But mostly, cold calling door to door is dead.

So how do you reach households? Get really good at generating sales leads by using many other marketing program components to help get leads. Consider the following:

▲ *Encyclopaedia Britannica* eliminated its traditional sales force 20 years ago, and now they generate leads through advertising and referrals. They then do follow-up by telemarketing, or in person, if absolutely necessary.

▲ You can also use a Web page or on-line newsletter to reach out for prospects and generate visits and inquiries that you can turn into leads. See Chapter 13 for more ideas on how to use the Web for leads.

▲ Ask your current customers to supply you with referrals and thank them for this or even reward them with gifts or discounts. Current customers often can find you good-quality leads through their personal networks.

10.4.2 What to Avoid

One troubling trend: Many companies these days give telemarketers a survey script for those calls that they make to qualify the leads. People will answer a survey more often than they talk to a salesperson. But this practice is deceptive. The American Marketing Association's code of ethics prohibits selling or fundraising under the guise of conducting research. Why?

FOR EXAMPLE

Networking at Home

At Avon, they reach households by **networking**, using personal and professional contacts, in order to set up appointments — usually after working hours. This strategy gets through people's natural suspicions and busy schedules. In North America alone, Avon has about half a million salespeople — evidence that person-to-person selling isn't dead in the retail industry. Mary Kay uses a similar strategy with success. Its salespeople typically schedule a personal showing or a neighborhood event through their network of contacts, allowing sales representatives to sell cosmetic products in the home with success.

▲ The practice abuses the respondent's trust. (And deception in sales can run afoul of fraud laws — so it may be illegal, as well as unethical.)

▲ Deceptive prospecting irritates respondents; if it is widely done, people stop participating in legitimate marketing research. That consequence, which is beginning to happen, poses a big problem for marketers.

You can avoid deceiving people just by making your sources good, your script short and honest, and your telemarketers polite and well trained. Keep your questions short, to the point, and clear, so most decision makers take the time to answer you.

Telemarketers are the first people from your company to talk with decision makers, so consider having your salespeople select and train your telemarketers to control that vital first impression.

10.4.3 Developing Great Sales Presentations and Consultations

At the sales presentation, the salesperson must convince the prospect to become a customer. Only the truly great sales presentation can persuade most prospects to become customers. Expect to experiment and think creatively. Design the presentation to cover both basic fact needs and basic feelings needs. Your presentation should inform while also making the prospect comfortable.

Decide which type of approach best fits your company:

▲ A *consultative* approach. Begin with many questions to figure out what the customer needs, and then propose a somewhat customized solution, not just a generic purchase. This is good if you sell complex services.

▲ A *canned* approach. Write a detailed, specific script that you or your sales force follow every time you give a presentation. Use this if you have the ability to solve customers' problems, but not the time to bring a salesperson up to speed about a business.

If you do not have obvious ways to sell customized services along with your product and you just want to deliver an excellent product and let the customer worry about what to do with it, the last thing that you want your salespeople to do is to pretend that they're consultants.

You can use a simple, canned approach as effectively as a sophisticated consultative approach. Be sure to tailor your sales style to accommodate your customers' needs, purchase preferences, and habits.

SELF-CHECK

- Define **qualifying** and **networking**.
- What should you avoid with telemarketing?
- What's the difference between a canned and consultative approach?
- Name some marketing activities that can generate leads.

SUMMARY

Improving your marketing communications means being clear and compelling in your messages. You must cultivate a strong personality for your brand and use stopping power and pull power to draw attention to it. Service recovery is a strong element of the sales and service process. Avoiding deceptive marketing and organizing your sales force will help you succeed.

Key Terms

Brand equity	Building the value of your brand.
Customer turnover rate	The percent of customers who leave each year.
Demonstration strategy	Leverages the fundamental appeal of the product itself by simply making that product available to prospects.
Image strategy	A strategy that presents a good image of your brand, product, service, or business.
Information strategy	Communicates facts that make you appealing.
Local advertising	Advertising that is focused on a specific city or county.

Motivational strategy   Builds a compelling argument or feeling that should lead prospects to take action and make a purchase.

Personal selling   Selling face to face.

Positioning strategy   A detailed (but readable) statement of how you want customers to think and feel about your product.

Pull power   The ability of a marketing communication to draw people to a place or event.

Qualifying   Gathering enough information about someone to make sure he or she fits a profile of a potential customer.

Sales representative   Reps who work on commission.

Service recovery   Repairing a customer-service problem.

Stopping power   The ability of an advertisement or other marketing communication to stop people in their tracks, to make them sit up and take notice.

ASSESS YOUR UNDERSTANDING

Go to www.wiley.com/college/Hiam to evaluate your knowledge of the basics of marketing communications.
Measure your learning by comparing pre-test and post-test results.

Summary Questions

1. For a good marketing communication, you should have at least two striking visual elements. True or false?

2. Most ads do not have stopping power. True or false?

3. Once you have cultivated your brand's personality, you want to focus on
   (a) forming a demonstration strategy
   (b) forming a motivational strategy
   (c) being consistent in your communications
   (d) achieving pull power

4. During service recovery, the most important thing is to get the facts on the table. True or false?

5. One of the toughest management jobs is
   (a) finding qualified sales reps
   (b) service recovery
   (c) converting anger to purchases
   (d) compensating your reps

6. You should always have a way to opt out of the computerized phone system. True or false?

7. Never violate the rules and personality of the product category. True or false?

8. Put the following steps of the sales/service process in order:
   (a) Forming a motivational strategy, qualifying leads, building relationships
   (b) Finding sales leads, being consistent, making presentations
   (c) Defining target market, qualifying leads, building relationships

9. Sales leads can come from any of your marketing activities. True or false?

10. Calling prospects with marketing surveys is a good way to generate leads. True or false?

Review Questions

1. List three principles that will make your ad a "stopper."
2. Why is the product's personality so important?
3. What are the top five warning signs of an unhappy customer?

Applying This Chapter

1. You are opening a health and fitness club for single people. Explain how you might use four different strategies to improve the impact of your appeal.
2. Explain why service recovery is so important. What can you do to fix a damaged customer relationship?
3. If your business needs to make 20,000 sales calls a year, and each salesperson you hire can make 2 calls a day, how big of a sale staff do you need? Assume your company has 200 business days a year.

Tennis, Anyone?

Think about the visual of the dog with the tennis ball in his mouth from Section 10.1.2. The ad was for the U.S. Tennis Association, to promote tennis to the general public. How would you translate that television message into a print advertisement for a magazine? What would the headline say? Write the first paragraph for the ad.

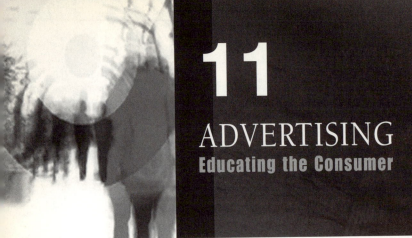

11

ADVERTISING
Educating the Consumer

Starting Point

Go to www.wiley.com/college/Hiam to assess your knowledge of basic advertising.
Determine where you need to concentrate your effort.

What You'll Learn in This Chapter

- ▲ Types of advertising
- ▲ The benefits and challenges of each type
- ▲ The parts of a print ad
- ▲ Media buying

After Studying This Chapter, You'll Be Able To

- ▲ Choose advertising types for your goals
- ▲ Distinguish between effective and ineffective ads
- ▲ Differentiate between reach, market share, and ratings

Goals and Outcomes

- ▲ Estimate advertising costs to stay within your budget
- ▲ Design an effective ad or brochure
- ▲ Evaluate an ongoing ad campaign

INTRODUCTION

In today's marketplace, consumers and marketers can have an astonishing number of choices. Advertising types include print ads, billboards, brochures, signs, and media such as radio, video, and television. Internet advertising is covered in a separate chapter, Chapter 13. This chapter will show you how to choose well from among the many forms of advertising, and how to design an effective ad.

11.1 Print Ads and Brochures

Even with all the high-tech options available today, print advertising is still where most advertising dollars are spent — except for the major national or multinational brands, which market largely on television. But for most local and regional advertising, print probably provides the most flexible and effective all-around advertising medium.

Print supports many other marketing media. You can use written brochures and other sales support materials to support personal selling (see Section 10.3) or telemarketing. Print ads also work well to announce sales promotions or distribute coupons.

11.1.1 Media Buying

Ad agencies and the marketing departments of big companies have specialists who do nothing but buy media, and some brokers specialize in it for midsized or smaller marketers. If you are a smaller-scale marketer, you can easily figure out how to buy media space on your own.

Start by checking the *rate sheets* and *schedules* for magazines or newspapers that you are sure your prospective customers read.

▲ **Rate sheet:** A table listing the prices of ads by size of ad and also showing the discount rate per ad if you buy multiple ads instead of just a single one.

▲ **Schedule:** Shows when ads for each magazine issue need to be placed and what the topics of future issues will be.

The Web sites of many publications carry this information, too. Then take a hard look at the pricing. How expensive is the average ad (in the middle of the size range for each publication)? This may be a broad number.

If a single ad costs 1/20th (5 percent) or more of your marketing budget for the entire year, forget about advertising in those publications. The business is not currently operating on a large enough scale to be able to do this kind of advertising. You need dozens of ad placements at a minimum to make a good print ad campaign, so do not begin unless you can easily afford to keep going.

▲ Advertising tends to be priced on a *cost per thousand readers* basis. The **cost per thousand readers** is the cost of buying that ad divided by the number of readers who read the publication, then multiplied by 1000.

You generally get as much exposure as you are willing to pay for. Here are some ways to economize:

▲ Consider buying multiple ads with your ad budget, rather than blowing it on a single purchase.

▲ Try smaller-circulation publications that have cheaper rates and may cater exclusively to your audience.

▲ A well-designed mailing may be better than an expensive media purchase like a magazine ad. An ad in a major magazine can cost $100,000, but buying ad space in a local publication, such as a theater program, can cost a fraction of that amount. And if your market attends the theater a great deal, you are reaching only the people you know are potential customers.

You want to minimize your risk, so small steps are generally better. A full-page ad is generally the best choice. Although larger ads attract more notice, they do not reach as many customers for your marketing dollar (see Table 11-1). It's the most economical choice, but can be risky. You can dip a toe in the water by buying a smaller ad first.

Table 11-1: Selecting the Right Size

Size of Ad	Percent of Readers Noting Ad (Median)
Fractional (partial-page) ads	24%
One-page ads	40%
Two-page spreads	55%

11.1.2 Is Your Ad Working?

A **direct-response ad** asks readers to take a measurable action like call, fax, or go to a store. You'll know whether your direct-response ad works within days of its first appearance. If nothing happens, it's not working. If your ad is an indirect response ad to create or to strengthen your company's image, you won't know immediately. In these cases, you can hire a market-research firm to get some data.

In fact, if you plan to spend more than $200,000 on print ads, you can probably consider the $20,000 or so needed to hire a research firm to pretest the ad

---

FOR EXAMPLE

Pets.com

Many dot-coms that went under spent great sums on advertising that did not pay off, such as Pets.com's hugely expensive ad during Super Bowl XXXIV. In fact, as the company was failing, its Sock Puppet dog became famous and was honored by Adweek magazine as best off-line campaign for an on-line brand. So, create great advertising, but make sure you can afford where you place it.

---

money well spent. **Pretesting** means exposing people to the ad in a controlled setting and measuring their reactions to it.

You can do it yourself by assembling a focus group of customers and asking them for feedback on your ad. Once you know what the problem is, you can change the ad accordingly. For example, maybe you need to switch from a black-and-white or two-color visual to a four-color one. Sure, you have to pay more, but the resulting ad may yield a better return, despite its higher price.

Cahners Publishing also reports from its studies that black-and-white ads and two-color ads attract the notice of about a third of readers, and four-color ads attract almost half of readers — 46 percent, to be precise.

So as with size, more is better when it comes to colors. However, you need to run the numbers to see how the extra costs and extra readers affect your cost-per-thousand figure. You should be able to reduce the options to reasonable estimates of costs and returns and then pick the highest-yielding option. Additionally, here are some inexpensive ways to test your ad:

▲ Run three variations on the ad and see which one generates the most calls or Web site visits (offering a discount based on a code number tells you which responses come from which ad).

▲ Do your own ad tests. Ask people to look at your ads for 20 seconds, and then quiz them about what they remember. If they missed much of the ad, you probably need to rewrite!

▲ Run the same ad (or very similar ones) in large and small formats and see which pulls in the largest number of consumers.

11.1.3 Designing Effective Print Advertising

Many marketers start with their printed marketing materials (such as ads, brochures, or downloadable PDF-format product literature on their Web sites), and then work outward from there to incorporate the appeal and design concepts from their printed materials or ads into other forms of marketing. (A common look and feel should unite your print ads, brochures, and Web site, for example.)

Brochures, **tear sheets** (one-page, catalog-style descriptions of products), posters for outdoor advertising, direct mail letters, or catalogs all share the basic elements of good print advertising — good copy and visuals, plus eye-catching headlines. Therefore, all good marketers need mastery of print advertising as an essential part of their knowledge base.

Great print advertising doesn't have to be expensive, just clever. Marketers generally assume that they have to work hard with colors and text to make their ads noticeable and persuasive. Statistically, they're right. But do not discount the power of imaginative design to simplify the task. You can do a simple two-color ad with very little text that actually works better than other, more elaborate ads.

You'll need to know the parts of an ad, brochure, or tear sheet:

▲ **Headline:** The large-print words that first attract the eye, usually at the top of the page.

▲ **Subhead:** The optional addition to the headline to provide more detail, also in large (but not quite as large) print.

▲ **Copy or body copy:** The main text, set in a readable size, like what printers use in the main text of a book or magazine.

▲ **Visual:** An illustration that makes a visual statement. This image may be the main focus of the ad or other printed material, or it may be secondary to the copy. Such an image is also optional. After all, most classified ads use no visuals at all, yet classifieds are generally more effective than display ads for the simple reason that people make a point to look for classified ads.

▲ **Caption:** Copy attached to the visual to explain or discuss that visual. You usually place a caption beneath the visual, but you can put it on any side or even within or on the visual.

▲ **Trademark:** A unique design that represents the brand or company (like Nike's swoosh). You should register trademarks — see Section 6.2.3.

▲ **Signature:** The company's trademarked version of its name. Often, advertisers use a logo design that features a brand name in a distinctive font and style. The signature is a written equivalent to the trademark's visual identity.

▲ **Slogan:** An optional element consisting of a (hopefully) short phrase evoking the spirit or personality of the brand.

Figure 11-1 shows each of these elements in a rough design for a print ad.

Good design is vitally important: It has to take the basic appeal of your product and make that appeal work visually on paper. So the design must somehow reach out to readers, grab their attention, and hold it long enough to communicate the appeal of the product you are advertising and attach that appeal to the brand name in the readers' memories.

Figure 11-1

May 31, 2006

FOR IMMEDIATE RELEASE

For more information, contact:
Alexander Hiam (515) 555-1212

CRAZY AUTHOR WRITES BOOK FOR DUMMIES

FIRST MARKETING TITLE TO ADDRESS REAL-WORLD NEEDS

AMHERST, Mass. — He's nearly done now. Just a section on public relations. Then the manuscript is off to production and — perhaps — history will be made. This title isn't just another book about business. This book is a redefinition of the marketing field that finally brings it up to speed with the harsh realities of business. And the book is, appropriately, by an author who straddles the boundaries between the ivory tower of business schools and the trenches of marketing management.

"What we teach about marketing on campus is pure fiction," complains Alexander Hiam, author of *Marketing For Dummies*, 2nd Edition (Wiley Publishing, 2006). "It's based on academic research, not on real-world practices and problems." Hiam threw out all his textbooks and visited past clients and other marketing practitioners before designing his new book. As a result, it...

The elements of a print ad

A memorable photograph is often the easiest way to grab the reader. And if you do not have a better idea, use a photo of an interesting face or of a child, as long as you can make the image relevant in some way to your product. Also, beautiful nature scenes are good eye-catchers.

The stages in the design process for a print ad, in order, are as follows:

▲ **Thumbnails:** The rough sketches designers use to describe layout concepts. They're usually small, quick sketches in pen or pencil — or, more recently, in design programs like Quark or PageMaker.

▲ **Roughs:** Full-size sketches with headlines and subheads drawn carefully enough to give the feel of a particular font and style (the appearance of the printed letters). Roughs also have sketches for the illustrations. The designers suggest body copy using lines (or nonsense characters, if the designer does the rough in a computer program). Ask to see the ad agency's roughs, even if they resist.

▲ **Comps (short for comprehensive layout):** A comp should look pretty much like a final version of the design. The comp may use paste-ups in place of the intended photos, color photocopies, typeset copy, and headlines. They're now done frequently on computers. Designers refer to a computer-made comp as a full-color proof.

▲ **Dummy:** Form of comp that simulates the feel — as well as the look — of the final design. Dummies are especially important for brochures or special inserts to magazines, where the designer often specifies special paper and folds. By doing a dummy comp, you can evaluate the feel of the design while you are evaluating its appearance.

11.1.4 Keeping It Simple

▲ A **font** is a particular design's attributes for the characters (letters, numbers, and symbols) used in printing your design. Font refers to one particular size and style of a typeface design (such as 10-point, bold, Times New Roman).

▲ **Typeface** refers only to the distinctive design of the letters (Times New Roman, for example).

The right font for any job is the one that makes your text easily readable and that harmonizes with the overall design most effectively. For a headline, the font also needs to grab the reader's attention. The body copy doesn't have to grab attention in the same way — in fact, if it does, the copy often loses readability.

In tests, Helvetica and Century generally top the lists as most readable (see Table 11-2), so start with one of these typefaces for your body copy; only change the font if it doesn't seem to work.

Within each typeface, you can choose different sizes and styles. Figure 11-2 shows some different Helvetica typefaces.

Table 11-2: Popular Fonts for Ads

Sans Serif	Serif
Helvetica	Century
Univers	Garamond
Optima	Melior
Avant Garde	Times New Roman

Figure 11-2

Helvetica Light 14 point

Helvetica Italic 14 point

Helvetica Bold 14 point

Helvetica Regular 14 point

Helvetica Regular 24 point

Helvetica Regular Condensed 14 point

Helvetica Bold Outline 24 point

Some of the many choices that the Helvetica typeface offers designers.

Keep in mind that you can change just about any aspect of type. You can alter the distance between lines — called the leading — or you can squeeze characters together or stretch them apart to make a word fit a space. Assume that anything is possible, and ask your printer, or consult the manual of your desktop-publishing or word-processing software, to find out how to make a change.

Research shows that people read lowercase letters about 13 percent faster than uppercase letters, so avoid long stretches of copy set in all caps. People also read most easily when letters are dark and contrast strongly with their background. Thus, black 14-point Helvetica on white is probably the most readable font specification for the body copy of an ad (or other printed marketing materials), even if the combination does seem dull to a sophisticated designer.

Generalizing about the best kind of headline typeface is no easy task because designers play around with headlines to a greater extent than they do with body copy. Although most of us know little about the design of typefaces, traditional designs are instinctively appealing. Do not go crazy with fonts, because too many changes may reduce your design's readability. Figure 11-3 shows the same ad laid out twice — once in an eye-pleasing way and once in a disastrous way.

Do not just play with type for the sake of playing (as the designer did in the left-hand version of the classified ad in Figure 11-3). Stick with popular fonts, in popular sizes, except where you have to solve a problem or you want to make a special point.

The advent of desktop publishing has lead to a horrifying generation of advertisements in which dozens of fonts dance across the page, bolds and italics fight each other for attention, and the design of the words becomes a barrier to reading, rather than an aid.

Figure 11-3

<table>
<tr>
<td>

WHEN LIFE GIVES YOU LEMONS...

What should you do? Juggle them? Make lemonade? Open a farm stand? Or give up and go home to Momma?

WHO KNOWS? It's often hard to come to grips with pressing personal or career problems. Sometimes it's hardest to see your **own** problems clearly. **Fortunately, JEN KNOWS. Jen Fredrics has twenty years of counseling experience, a master's in social work, and a busy practice in personal problem solving. Call her today to find out how to turn your problems into opportunities.**

And next time, when life gives you lemons, you'll know just what to make. An appointment.

</td>
<td>

WHEN LIFE GIVES YOU LEMONS...

What should you do? Juggle them? Make lemonade? Open a farm stand? Or give up and go home to Momma?

WHO KNOWS? It's often hard to come to grips with pressing personal or career problems. Sometimes it's hardest to see your own problems clearly. Fortunately, JEN KNOWS. Jen Fredrics has twenty years of counseling experience, a master's in social work, and a busy practice in personal problem solving. Call her today to find out how to turn your problems into opportunities.

And next time, when life gives you lemons, you'll know just what to make. An appointment.

</td>
</tr>
</table>

Which copy would you rather read?

11.1.5 Designing Brochures That Do More

Brochures are a business staple. But do not waste money by designing a brochure that has no purpose. Many brochures foolishly waste money because they do not accomplish any specific marketing goals; they just look pretty, at best. Decide who will read it, how they'll get it, and what they'll get out of it. Then list your top three uses. The most common and appropriate uses for a brochure are

▲ To act as a reference on the product, or technical details of the product, for prospects

▲ To support a personal selling effort by lending credibility and helping overcome objections

▲ To generate leads through a direct-mail campaign

Also make sure that you can answer these three questions:

▲ Who will read the brochure?

▲ How will they get the brochure?

▲ What should they discover and do from reading the brochure?

Write down and organize your **fact base,** or the information you need to accomplish your purposes, to highlight your strengths and overcome the customer's objections.

Include copy (and perhaps illustrations) designed specifically for each of the three purposes that you just listed. The appeal, with its enticing headline and compelling copy and visual, goes on the front of the brochure — or the outside when you fold it for mailing, or the central panel out of three if you fold a sheet twice. The subheads that structure the main copy respond to objections and highlight strengths on the inside pages.

Organize the fact base, needed for reference use, in the copy and illustrations beneath these subheads. If you do not know what each part of your brochure does, then you need to redesign it — otherwise, that brochure becomes a waste of time and money.

You can use the design shown in Figure 11-4 for direct mailings to generate sales leads, and you can also hand the brochure out or use it for reference in direct-selling situations. You can produce this brochure using any popular desktop publishing software, and you can even print and fold it at the local photocopy shop (if you do not need the thousands of copies that make off-set printing cost effective).

To convert this design to an even simpler, cheaper format, use 8 1/2-×-11-inch paper and eliminate the return mailer (the left-hand page on the front, the right-hand on the back, which can be returned with the blanks filled in to request information or accept a special offer). If you do remove the return mailer, however, be sure to include follow-up instructions and contact information on one of the inside pages!

Figure 11-5 shows how you can lay out such a brochure, along with dimensions for text blocks or illustrations. This format is simple and inexpensive because you print the brochure on a single sheet of legal-sized paper that you then fold three times.

The brochure fits in a standard No. 10 or No. 12 envelope, or you can tape it together along the open fold and mail it on its own. This layout allows for some detail, but not enough to get you into any real trouble. Larger formats and multipage pieces tend to fill up with the worst, wordiest copy, and nobody ever reads those pieces.

SELF-CHECK

- Define fact base, copy, rate sheet, and schedule.
- What are some ways to economize on print advertising?
- What is the difference between a headline and a subhead?
- What is a direct-response ad?
- What's the difference between a font and a typeface?

Figure 11-4

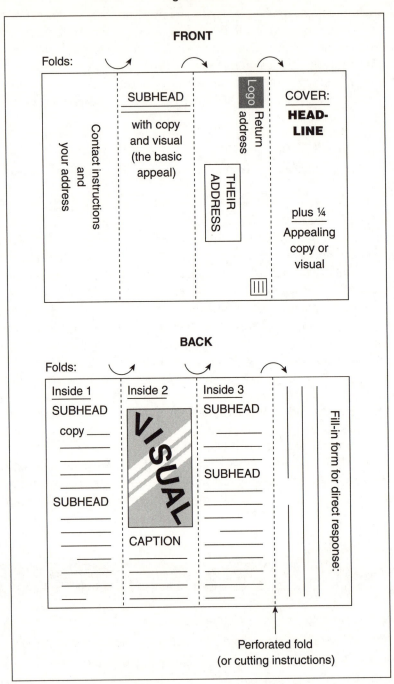

A simple, multipurpose brochure layout

11.2 Billboards, Banners, and Signs

Outdoor advertising refers to a wide variety of advertising. Signs and posters, including roadside billboards, qualify, and we include indoor signs, flags, and banners.

▲ **Out-of-home advertising:** The general outdoor advertising category. This category includes signs, flags, banners, bumper stickers, transit advertising, and even T-shirts, along with the traditional billboard formats.

The importance of outdoor advertising is underappreciated. These media are more powerful than many marketers realize — some businesses succeed by using no other advertising, in fact. Keep an inventory of your signs, posters, T-shirts, and other outdoor ads. Seek ways to increase the number and impact of these signs. When you need to make your brand identity and marketing messages visible, you can never do too much.

11.2.1 Signing Your Company's Name

Signs are everywhere, helping people find a business, and conveying important messages about that business. A well-done, handsome sign makes a great impression, while a dilapidated, chipped sign gives a business negative advertising. Do not let a sign give the public the impression that you do not care enough to maintain your signs (they may even think the company's going out of business!).

Consider having your sign designed and painted by an artist or consider hiring a cabinet-maker, stained-glass artist, oil painter, or other arts and crafts professional. Most signs have little real art, so when a business hires an artist to carve its name and logo into a big piece of mahogany, the result can have a big impact.

In fact, a really special sign, well displayed in a high-traffic area, has more power to build an image or pull in prospects than any other form of local advertising. Everybody likes free advertising, and you can get great free exposures from signs. A magnetic sign on the side of a car or truck, like those on the cars of real estate agents, can reach thousands of people a day for free.

Writing good signs is key. The writing should be clear and precise, give people a reason to stop, and communicate essential information. Before you approve any design, review the copy to make sure that the writing provides a model of clarity! *Try* misinterpreting the wording. Can you read the sign in a way that makes it seem to mean something you do not intend to say?

Try thinking of questions the sign doesn't answer that seem obvious to you — remember that the consumer may not know the answers. For example, some people have a terrible sense of direction, so a sign on the side of a store leaves them confused about how to enter that store. Solution? Put an arrow and the instructions

---

FOR EXAMPLE

Missing Signs

It's amazing how many businesses make finding themselves difficult. The town of Amherst, Massachusetts, is near the main campus for University of Massachusetts at Amherst, the biggest college in the state. Why do visitors often have to pull over in downtown Amherst and ask for directions to the campus? Well, no signs downtown point the way. Aside from their practical value (letting people know where you are), signs can and should promote your image and brand name.

"Enter from Front" on the sign! Use creativity with your signs by hand painting, using window lettering, neon, high-tech electronic displays or message repeaters, and flat-panel TVs.

Some other small ways to get your message across:

▲ **T-shirts:** Only if they are good quality. Use an exciting design, a good fabric, and an experienced, quality-conscious silk-screener.

▲ **Shopping bags:** Department stores know these are carried around, making them walking ads. Make them easy to read, with an interesting hook. If you are not in retail, you can offer to supply your bags to a retailer who doesn't want to buy bags.

▲ **Flags, banners, and awnings:** Less static and dull than a sign. Something that moves is decorative and festive. Also more readily accepted into communities that have banned billboards.

▲ **Transit ads:** Can generate leads for everyone from local real estate agents to international consulting firms. An innovative thing to try, this category includes shelter panels on buses, airport posters, and bus and taxi signs.

11.2.2 Creating Billboards That Get Noticed

Billboards are economical to rent, yet a challenge to design well. Billboards along roads need to be readable from hundreds of feet away. Viewers have to read the ad in a hurry, and often from a considerable distance.

So the ad has to be simple, yet interesting enough to be liked by people who see it every day. Outdoor ads are like print ads, but bigger. They must use far fewer words and far simpler images and, hopefully, contain an entertaining hook. The standard sizes for billboards are shown in Figure 11-5.

You can also explore the growing number of variations on these standards. Do you want your message displayed on the floor of a building lobby, on a kiosk at a mall, or alongside the notice boards at health and fitness centers? Or how about on signs surrounding the arenas and courts of athletic events? You can use all these options and more, by directly contacting the businesses that control such spaces or using one of a host of ad agencies and media-buying firms that can give you larger-scale access.

Billboards are the cheapest form of advertising. Given the high traffic rates on many expressways, you can get a pretty good buy for a billboard on a cost per thousand (CPM) viewers basis. For example, say a board in Denver delivers about 34,100 exposures.

▲ **Reach:** Number of viewers
▲ **Frequency:** How many times viewers see your ad

You do not know the **reach** versus **frequency,** but the number generally ranges from 28 to 15 times per month in surveys. That reach works out to a price of $3815 divided by 34,100, or $0.11 per thousand exposures. Although prices vary, and this is an inexpensive example, outdoor advertising gives you cheap exposure, on a CPM basis.

Figure 11-5

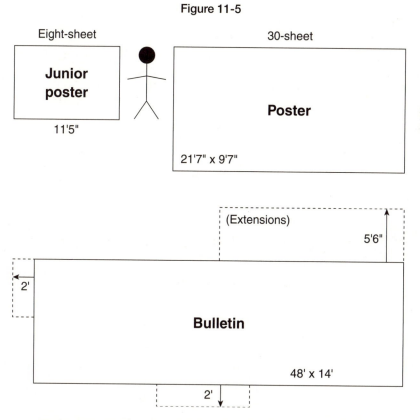

Three standard sizes for outdoor advertising in the United States.

A study from Simmons Market Research Bureau estimates the average U.S. 30-sheet poster reaches adults 18 years and older at a CPM of $1.43 per thousand. (Radio costs about twice that figure, and billboard costs are only a small fraction of TV and print costs!) You need to take into account that your target market may be smaller than all adults when you are figuring your own costs, of course.

Also, these exposures may lose value after the commuter has seen your billboard many times. Do you get the same effect from the tenth viewing of a billboard as you do from the first or second? Will anyone even bother to look at the same billboard multiple times? **Reexamination rates** are the average number of times viewers bother to read the same outdoor ad.

The best billboards have higher reexamination rates because people find them interesting enough to keep viewing.

As with all print ads, costs vary based on ad size and audience size. A bulletin costs about four times as much as the standard poster ad — because a bulletin is about four times as big as a poster. A junior poster costs about a quarter of a poster ad, being about a sixth as large. However, effectiveness does not vary with size in outdoor advertising as much as it does in standard print advertising. Location is more important.

▲ Companies that sell outdoor advertising base their rates on **traffic counts.** Traffic counts are the number of vehicles per day — or day and night if you illuminate your poster — multiplied by the average occupancy of a vehicle.

But a big difference exists between someone viewing a poster at 65 miles per hour on a freeway, someone viewing a poster at 45 miles per hour on a local road, and someone sitting next to a poster for 10 minutes in the traffic jam leading to a tollbooth or bridge. If you shop around (and possibly wait your turn) for locations with high- and low-speed traffic, you can get a billboard that many more people who pass by read more slowly and carefully!

SELF-CHECK

- Define **outdoor advertising, out-of-home advertising, reexamination rate,** and **traffic counts.**
- Name some small ways to convey your message with signage.
- What is the difference between reach and frequency?
- What is a traffic count?

11.3 Radio, Video, and Television

Radio and television are well-established, extremely powerful marketing media, and video (especially if shot in digital format) is a hot new item for streaming-video messages on your Web site. Video also offers marketing messages on television screens and computers in your booth at a trade show.

It used to be that radio and TV production and broadcasting costs were extremely steep. But new and easier ways to produce in these media are emerging all the time, along with a growing number of low-cost ways to broadcast your ads. Every year brings more radio and television channels, including cable TV, Web-based radio, and (soon) Web-based television options. More marketers are using CDs or Web sites that communicate in digital video, or with PowerPoint-type slides and radio-style voice-overs. Modern technology is making these media more flexible and affordable for all marketers.

11.3.1 On the Radio

Radio ads are 77 percent cheaper than television ads and 86 percent cheaper than newspaper ads in the United States. And radio is generally cheaper in other countries, too. You can reach a large audience for less, as with outdoor advertising.

Although local retailers frequently use radio for pull-oriented advertising (explained in Section 10.2.3), most other marketers overlook radio as a viable medium. Radio has an incredible reach. In the United States, 95 percent of teenagers and adults listen to radio each week (according to Arbitron National Radio Database), and 81 percent are listening on any given day. Your target audience is in there somewhere! Also consider radio talk shows for publicity purposes.

Arbitron Inc. is the leading source of audited information about audience size and composition for television and radio stations in the United States and is also now providing information and assistance for those who want to purchase radio and video ad time on Webcasts.

The radio and TV stations or networks hire Arbitron to survey their audiences, and those stations or networks share the information with you and other potential advertisers for free.

Radio has a broader reach than that of other media in the United States (and many other nations, as well). Table 11-3 shows the daily reach figures for U.S. radio, TV, and newspapers.

Theoretically, radio can deliver a larger audience for your ads than print or TV can. Radio definitely gives you a good medium for broad-reach goals. You can also target radio advertising quite narrowly — both by type of audience and by geographic area. This fact helps make radio a very good buy. Radio stations make a real effort to target specific audiences — just as advertisers try to do.

Table 11-3: Reach Out and Touch Someone

Advertising Medium	Daily Reach (Percentage of U.S. Population 18 Years Old and Over)
Radio	81%
Television	76%
Newspapers	69%

You can get good data, both demographic and lifestyle- or attitude-oriented information, on radio audiences. And you can often find radio stations (or specific programs on those stations) that reach a well-defined audience, rich in those people you want to target, making radio an even better buy. The general lack of appreciation for this medium also helps by keeping ad prices artificially low.

Radio is a great support medium, if you use it right. You can often perform the same basic plot on radio as on TV. You want to try to generate mental images for the listener. Try to:

▲ Favor direct over indirect action goals for radio ads. The most effective radio ads call for direct action.

▲ Give out a Web address (if the listener can remember that address easily) or a toll-free number in the ad.

▲ Use sound effects and scripts to provide context.

Good radio allows you to *see* the action clearly as it unfolds. The script and sound effects (*SF* or *SFX* in radio lingo) create a string of powerful visual images in your mind as the story unfolds. Just be sure that your script identifies all sound effects. Sound effects are wonderful and evocative, but in truth, many sound just about alike. Without context, rain on the roof can sound like bacon sizzling in a pan.

So the script must identify that sound, either through direct reference ("Oh no, a storm's coming!") or through context. You can provide context with the script, the plot, or simply by other sound effects. Would you recognize the sound of sizzling bacon? Add the sounds of eggs cracking and hitting a hot pan, coffee percolating, and someone yawning to help identify that sizzle as the breakfast bacon.

11.3.2 The Emotional and Visual Appeal of TV

Television looks simple when you see it, but do not be fooled — it is not simple at all. Hire an experienced production company to help you do the ad, or do what many marketers do and hire a large ad agency (and budget accordingly) to design and supervise the production of your ad.

> ## FOR EXAMPLE
>
> ### The Power of Great Writing
>
> If you can create truly great, compelling TV, your ad may never die. Some lines like "Where's the beef?" have staying power because they are such great shorthand for many situations that we can all relate to. The classic Prudential commercial ("Own a piece of the rock") is a strictly emotional appeal, designed to convey a feeling of permanence and dependability about the company's products. People remember these ads.

This choice costs you, but at least you get quality work. If you do it yourself at a local cable station, you'll get what you pay for. The ads will look cheap when shown on the local network affiliate right next to expensive ads. If you are going to do TV, do it right. Either become an expert yourself or hire an expert. Without high-quality production, even the best design doesn't work.

As for the script, your spot will be only as good as the writing. Think of all the memorable scenes from movies, commercials, and television you've seen and you'll realize that it mainly comes down to great writing — lines that you remember and quote for years.

Be sure to take full advantage of TV's great strength: its ability to show. You can demonstrate a product feature, show a product in use, and do a thousand other things just with your visuals.

In any ad medium, you want to show as well as tell. Some people in your audience think visually, although others favor a verbal message, so you have to cover both bases by using words and images. But in TV, showing is the most important thing (see Table 11-4). Visuals are also important because many viewers will mute their sets during commercials.

It is especially easy to evoke emotions in TV and video, just as in traditional theater. Emotions, especially positive ones such as love, family, or friendship,

Table 11-4: Showing vs. Telling

Medium	What It Does
Television	**Show** and tell
Radio	Show by **telling**
Print	**Show** and **tell**

make TV ad messages far more memorable. In tests, viewers recall emotional-appeal TV ads about as easily as rational-appeal ads. But in-depth studies of the effectiveness of each kind of ad tend to show that the more emotionally charged ads do a better job of etching the message and branding identity in viewers' minds.

First think about what emotion you want your audience to feel. Then use the power of imagery to evoke that emotion. Always use the emotional power of TV to prepare your audience to receive that appeal, whether your appeal is emotional or rational.

Designers prepare rough storyboards to help visually think through and discuss various ad concepts.

▲ **Storyboard:** A way to show the key visual images of film, using pictures in sequence.

The sketches run down the center of a sheet of paper or poster board in most standard storyboard layouts. On the left, notes are made about how to shoot each image, how to use music and sound effects, and whether to superimpose text on the screen. On the right, a rough version of the script appears (see Figure 11-6).

What kind of ad should you produce? Most studies show that humorous and celebrity endorsement styles work best. See Table 11-5. On the other hand, making ads that are the exception to the rule may give you an edge, so do not give up hope on other types of spots. Just make sure that your ad is well above average if you do not want the rule of averages to apply to it.

Table 11-5: It Don't Mean a Thing if It Ain't Got That Swing

More-Effective Styles	Less-Effective Styles
Humorous commercials	Candid-camera style testimonials
Celebrity spokespeople	Expert endorsements
Commercials with children	Song/dance and musical themes
Real-life scenarios	Product demonstrations
Brand comparisons	

11.3.3 Video Production Tips

Video can cost $2000 per minute to produce — or even $20,000 if you are making a sophisticated national TV ad. But it can also cost $100 a minute or less. Many marketers do not realize that the limiting factor in inexpensive or homemade video is usually the sound quality, not the picture quality.

Figure 11-6

VIDEO

AUDIO

Lightning and thunder. Rabbit pops out of top hat. Zoom in.

Surprise!

Cut to dark room. Lights come up on birthday party. Zoom in on cake.

Many voices: Surprise!

Cut to dark. Sudden flash of lightning illuminates new product. Zoom in.

Even more voices: SURPRISE!

Inset product in slide.

(SLIDE)

Company name and logo

ANNCR: Until you try the new *** from ***, you don't know what a surprise is!

Roughing out a TV ad on a storyboard.

A good handheld video camera with a high-quality microphone is actually capable of producing effective video for your marketing, especially for use on the Web, where low-resolution video files are usually used, making camera quality less important. We offer some tips for shooting video yourself:

▲ Write a simple, clear script, and time it before you bother to shoot any video.

▲ Clean up the background. Most amateur efforts to shoot video presentations or ads for marketing are plagued by stuff that shows up in the background. Eliminate trash cans, competitors' signs, and anything else that's unsightly.

▲ Use enough light, and try to have multiple light sources. A digital video camera is just a fancy camera, and it needs light to work. Normal indoor lighting is too dim for quality video. Instead, add more lights, including bright floodlights and open windows. And make sure light shines from both sides so that you fill the shadows. (Shadowed areas get darker in the video.)

▲ Shoot everything more than once. Editing is easy (well, easier) as a result of the many software programs you can use on your own PC to edit video. But editing is much easier if you have lots of footage to select from. Repeat each short section several times. Then, in editing, choose the version that came out best. That's how they make movie stars look good, and it can work well for you, too!

▲ You can produce radio ads or sound-only messages for your Web site using the same digital recording and editing capabilities as you use to do homemade digital video. The key is a quiet environment and a good microphone for recording. Or you can go into a production studio's sound booth and let the technicians there worry about the technical aspects.

▲ If you want actors, consider recruiting them locally and even asking people to volunteer.

For editing and production, you can learn to do it yourself, or hire a media production firm that can do high-quality work at moderate rates. With plenty of smaller production firms around, try interviewing some in your area and getting samples of their work plus price quotes — you may find that by the time you master the software and come up to speed, you are spending as much doing your own work!

11.3.4 Buying Ad Time

Which television venues work best for your ad? Should you advertise on a network or cable station? Should the ad run in prime time, evening, or late-night slots? Which programs provide the best audience for your ad?

Buyers rely on demographic studies to find out about audience size and characteristics. The Simmons Market Research Bureau and Mediamark Research both provide useful data in publications, and *SRDS's TV and Cable Source* gives you an excellent source of data.

A. C. Nielsen provides the key data for North American television markets. The Nielsen Television Index rates programs based on **sweeps,** which are quarterly surveys of viewership in major media markets.

The surveys require participants to keep logs of what they watch. And now a high-tech improvement over this approach has appeared on-line: in-home boxes called *people meters* that record what a household watches and relays that information to Nielsen (or to Arbitron, Nielsen's main competitor in this business). The resulting ratings tell you how many television sets tune in to any particular program in any geographic market.

However, advertisers and the television industry argue about the accuracy of the Nielsen ratings constantly because slight differences in ratings make a big difference in the cost of advertising!

Rating surveys provide the following statistics by geographic area:

▲ How many TV sets are in the market in all (**television households** or *TVHHs*)?

▲ How many TV sets are turned on at any given time (**households using TV** or *HUTs*)?

▲ What percentage of the HUTs are tuned to a specific program (**audience share**)?

▲ What percentage of the TVHHs are tuned to a specific program (**rating**)?

Say a city has 800,000 TVHHs. If 200,000 (or 25 percent) of these TVHHs are tuned to a particular program, then that program gets a rating of 25. If half of all televisions are on, then HUT equals 400,000 households (or 50 percent), and that program's share of market is 200,000 out of 400,000, or a 50 percent share. In general, advertisers pay more attention to ratings than to share of market data, because ratings tell them how big the audience is, and they usually try to reach the largest audience possible with their ads.

More repetitions increase the certainty and usability of the attitudes your ad forms in the viewer's mind. So plan on more repetitions if you need to reinforce these aspects of attitude. But one or a few repetitions can generally form the initial attitude, so you do not need many repetitions when you think the viewer will quickly agree with your ad's message and have no trouble remembering it in purchase situations.

▲ A **gross rating point (GRP)** is the total rating points achieved by your media schedule.

▲ A **media schedule** is all the times you run an ad over a specific period.

When media buyers purchase a series of time blocks on TV for your ad, they add up all the ratings from each of the times/places where your ad runs and give you the total — your campaign's GRPs. The number is big, but it doesn't tell you very much.

The GRP number doesn't distinguish between reach and frequency, but you should. Maybe your ad reached 10 million television households, but did it reach the same 1 million households, 10 times over — or did it reach 10 million households, 1 time each? The answer probably lies somewhere in between. But how can you find out the exact answer?

Obtaining reach and frequency estimates for any TV ad schedule helps you interpret the GRP figure. In some campaigns, you may want 10 or 20 repetitions. In others, one or two may be your goal. Let your agency or media buyer know what your goal is.

You need to find out how rich in target viewers a television audience is to figure out whether an ad in that space is a good buy or not. Rating points emphasize the size of the program's audience, not the match between the audience and your target market.

So be sure to convert — or ask your agency to convert — ratings into figures that represent reach into your target market and exclude those households outside of your target market that you do not need to advertise to. When you look at the TV-buying decision in this way, you often end up advertising on a wider variety of channels and programs than if you relied on straight rating points.

SELF-CHECK

- Define **sweeps, audience share, rating, gross rating point (GRP), and media schedule.**
- What is the difference between rating and audience share?
- What is a storyboard?
- Cite three video production tips.
- What should be your three goals when using radio?

SUMMARY

Print ads and brochures are the most common form of advertising, whereas billboards, banners, and signs are somewhat overlooked. Radio, video, and television, when done well, can bring your message to life. Always monitor the results of your advertising to see what's working and how you can make your marketing dollars go further.

KEY TERMS

Caption	Copy attached to the visual to explain or discuss that visual.
Comps	The design stage preceding a final version of the design.
Copy or body copy	The main text, set in a readable size, like what printers use in the main text of a book or magazine.
Cost per thousand readers	The cost of buying an ad divided by the number of readers who read the publication, then multiplied by 1000.
Direct-response ad	Asks readers to take a measurable action like call, fax, or go to a store.
Dummy	A form of comp that simulates the look and feel of the final design.
Fact base	The information you need to accomplish your purposes.
Font	A particular size and style of a typeface design (such as 10-point, bold, Times New Roman).
Frequency	How many times viewers see your ad.
Gross rating point (GRP)	The total rating points achieved by your media schedule.
Headline	The large-print words that first attract the eye, usually at the top of the page.
Media schedule	All the times you run an ad over a specific period.
Outdoor advertising	A wide variety of advertising, including signs, posters, roadside billboards, and indoor signs, flags, and banners.
Out-of-home advertising	The general outdoor advertising category. This category includes signs, flags, banners, bumper stickers, transit advertising, and even T-shirts, along with the traditional billboard formats.
Pretesting	Exposing people to the ad in a controlled setting and measuring their reactions to it.
Rate sheet	A table listing the prices of ads by size of ad and also showing the discount rate per ad if you buy multiple ads instead of just a single one.

Reach	Number of viewers that see an ad.
Reexamination rates	The average number of times viewers bother to read the same outdoor ad.
Roughs	Full-size sketches with headlines and subheads drawn carefully enough to give the feel of a particular font and style (the appearance of the printed letters).
Schedule	Shows when ads for each magazine issue need to be placed and what the topics of future issues will be.
Signature	The company's trademarked version of its name. Often, advertisers use a logo design that features a brand name in a distinctive font and style. The signature is a written equivalent to the trademark's visual identity.
Slogan	An optional element consisting of a (hopefully) short phrase evoking the spirit or personality of the brand.
Storyboard	A way to show the key visual images of film, using pictures in sequence.
Subhead	The optional addition to the headline to provide more detail, also in large (but not quite as large) print.
Sweeps	Quarterly surveys of viewership in major media markets.
Thumbnails	The rough sketches designers use to describe layout concepts.
Traffic counts	The number of vehicles per day — or day and night if you illuminate your poster — multiplied by the average occupancy of a vehicle.
Typeface	The distinctive design of the letters.
Visual	An illustration that makes a visual statement.

ASSESS YOUR UNDERSTANDING

Go to www.wiley.com/college/Hiam to evaluate your knowledge of basic advertising. *Measure your learning by comparing pre-test and post-test results.*

Summary Questions

1. How can you save money in print advertising?
   (a) Use the Helvetica typeface.
   (b) Target your mailings.
   (c) Use brochures rather than signs.
2. The rough is the second stage of the storyboarding process. True or false?
3. Billboards are the cheapest form of advertising. True or false?
4. What's the most important thing for a billboard's success?
   (a) reexamination rates
   (b) slogan
   (c) location
5. Most effective radio ads call for direct action. True or false?
6. The stages of a print ad are, in order,
   (a) thumbnails, roughs, comps
   (b) roughs, thumbnails, comps
   (c) thumbnails, roughs, comps
7. The best value in advertising is brochures. True or false?
8. The gross rating point (GRP) does not tell you what you need to know about your media schedule. True or false?
9. Nielson ratings accurately assess the match between audience and target markets. True or false?
10. Television has the broadest reach of any medium. True or false?

Review Questions

1. What are two good, but often overlooked, types of advertising that can provide real value for a marketer?
2. Name two popular fonts that are generally regarded as highly readable.
3. What's a very common problem with brochures that causes them to be a possible waste of money?
4. What are some ways to reduce your risk when advertising?

Applying This Chapter

1. You are a marketer with a small budget for a start-up cable company. The market has recently been deregulated, and you are going up against a giant. What kind of ads would you use? What information do you need to know about your market?

2. Imagine you work for a national car dealership that's introducing a car aimed at young adults. You are using television and radio ads to get the word out. Should you pick the shows or stations with the highest ratings? What information do you need to get the best reach for your advertising?

3. Your small company is growing rapidly and your marketing budget is $12,000 for the year. You want to buy some print ads in a magazine, or at least a newspaper ad. Which is the best choice, if the local newspaper charges $400 for a half-page ad, $600 for a full-page ad, and a regional magazine will charge you $550 for a display ad?

Billboard Advertising

Try to remember the billboards on your commute to work or school. How many do you think there are? Explain why you remembered any of them. Next time you are on that route, note how many billboards there actually are. Are they effective?

Radio Script

What if an electronics store is targeting young adult males for a new car radio speaker technology? What sort of images in a radio script do you think would encourage a sale? What kind of characters would you prefer and where would the action take place? How would you include the new technology? What sound effects might get attention?

12

PUBLICITY, PUBLIC RELATIONS, AND SALES PROMOTIONS
Drawing Attention to Your Product

Starting Point

Go to www.wiley.com/college/Hiam to assess your knowledge of the basics of publicity and promotion.
Determine where you need to concentrate your effort.

What You'll Learn in This Chapter

▲ Types of sales promotions and premiums
▲ The role of publicity
▲ The elements of a good hook
▲ What journalists want you to know

After Studying This Chapter, You'll Be Able To

▲ Handle public-relations tasks
▲ Prepare reasonable impact scenarios
▲ Use press releases to tell a story

Goals and Outcomes

▲ Evaluate promotions to increase sales
▲ Manage word of mouth to your advantage
▲ Develop mutually beneficial relationships with the press

INTRODUCTION

You'll pay for advertising, yet you can get your company in the news and talked about by the average person inexpensively with skillful public relations and through compelling sales promotions. Sales promotions draw attention to your product and get people to buy quickly.

12.1 The Role of Publicity

When people bump into reminders of your company name, brand name, product, or service, they are more likely to buy. If those exposures to your identity can be good ones that create a strongly positive impression, those exposures can have a big impact on sales.

There are many ways to do this, but few ways that avoid looking like out-and-out advertising. If you can work your way into the environment of prospective customers in positive ways that do not have the costs and stridency of advertising, you can make a positive impact in a low-key, and low-cost, manner.

Public relations is the active pursuit of publicity for marketing purposes. You use PR to generate good publicity and to minimize bad publicity. Generally, marketers have the responsibility of generating good publicity. If they create good stories and communicate them to the media effectively, the media pick up the stories and turn those stories into news or entertainment content.

You get good publicity and it doesn't cost you anything. Marketers or general managers wear the PR hat in smaller organizations, but large companies generally have a PR person or department whose sole job is to generate positive publicity.

FOR EXAMPLE

Tylenol's Effective PR

When cyanide-laced Tylenol capsules killed seven people in Chicago in 1982, Johnson & Johnson reacted by putting customer safety first. The company pulled ads for the capsules, alerted the media, recalled 31 million bottles, and offered to trade capsules for tablets, at great expense to itself. J&J also cooperated with the Chicago police, the FDA, and the FBI in investigating the deaths. The event got the company good publicity for acting in the public trust. When it introduced tamper-resistant packaging soon after, along with new ads, discounts, and sales presentations to medical providers, Tylenol was able to quickly regain its position and go on to become the number-one pain reliever in the United States.

Also, many businesses hire publicists or PR firms to do PR on a freelance or consulting basis. A regional or smaller PR firm can often do a decent job for you on a retainer of 1,000 to 2,000 dollars a month. You'll need assistance writing a good press release and placing the story. If this is done badly, you will not get any coverage.

12.1.1 Finding the Story

To a journalist, a good story is anything that has enough public interest to attract readers, viewers, or listeners and hold their attention. But most of what you want to communicate to your market, unfortunately, doesn't fall into the category of a good story. You need to develop your story to a level that may qualify as good editorial content. Journalists and editors do *not* want stories about

▲ Your new product or service and how it differs from competitors' or your previous models (unless that's their coverage specialty).

▲ Why you or your company's senior executives think your products are really great.

▲ Your version of an *old story* — one that they've covered in the same way before.

▲ Anything that seems boring or self-serving to anyone who doesn't work for your firm.

Yet reporters often get those kinds of stories because the people handling PR generally aren't putting enough thought into the needs of their publications. You have to give the reporters what they want. Sniff out a story, put together sufficient information to back up the story, and script a version of the story that reporters can run with minimal work. To generate good positive publicity, you need to think like a journalist!

▲ Journalists look for **hooks** — the things that make a story newsworthy.

Hooks differ. The hook can be a new trend, a new survey about your industry (preferably by an independent entity) — anything that readers may want to know about. Certain elements are common:

▲ Hooks often give you new information (information you didn't know or weren't sure of).

▲ Hooks make that new information relevant to your activities or interests.

▲ Hooks catch your attention, often by surprising you with something you hadn't expected.

▲ Hooks promise some benefit to you — although the benefit may be indirect — by helping you understand your world better, avoid something undesirable, or simply enjoy yourself as you read the paper.

You need to design hooks to turn your marketing message into stories that appeal to journalists. At least a thin line should connect the hook to your brand identity, the news that you've just introduced a new product, or whatever else you want the public to know.

That way, when journalists use your hook in their own work, they end up including some of your marketing information in their stories as an almost accidental side effect. Journalists do not care about helping you communicate with your target market (in fact, they'll resist too-blatant attempts to do so, when they do not think your story has any news value). But journalists happily use any good stories that you are willing to tip them off about, and if your product gets mentioned or you get quoted as a result, they do not have a problem giving you the reference.

So what's the key to getting good publicity? Develop stories with effective hooks and give those stories away to overworked journalists.

12.1.2 Cultivating Media Contacts

You want to pitch your stories to media outlets, but you also want them to call you when something is happening in your industry. This requires establishing yourself as a trustworthy, accurate, pleasant, and helpful source who reporters enjoy dealing with. Journalists often develop friendly relationships with those they cover.

This is true even though you and they are actually adversaries with goals that may conflict (they want to publish everything that's going on in your company, but you want to portray your company in the best possible light). Friendly relationships are possible if you realize that they are just doing their jobs, as you are doing yours. Developing courteous and mutually respectful relationships with the people covering your industry or your company will not only help get you fair coverage, it will put you ahead of the game if trouble hits.

For instance, say you work for a company that is trying to differentiate its product from the market leader on the basis of safety. There's an accident involving your competitor's product, which you know is not as safe as yours, and politicians are suddenly calling for legislation that would restrict your industry.

Journalists may incorrectly assume that your products, because you are in the same industry, are also dangerous — *unless* you have already gotten to know them and they know your product is different. If they know you have safety features, they are likely to call you, as well as your competitor, for a quote about any proposed legislation.

How will they know this? Because you have already established yourself as an authority on safety issues in your field and the issue is already on their radar. You took them out to lunch last month and mentioned it. Maybe they didn't write about it then, but now they know you and can call you when they are scrambling to get the story done for a deadline.

Some tips for cultivating journalists:

▲ **Remember that they do not work for you.** Journalists may work for news organizations, but many view the public as their ultimate employer. They see themselves as on a mission to find the truth for the public good. Even if they like you personally, they will not care about protecting your company if they think it may be breaking the law or deceiving the public in any way.

▲ **Do not say too much.** If you are a public company, you can be seen as trying to inflate the stock price, especially before earnings reports are announced. Be careful or you can find yourself in trouble with the SEC. Even if you are not public, do not tell a reporter anything that can be mis-construed negatively. Consider whether any information you give is useful before you give it.

▲ **Get to know them and their beats.** PR departments at large companies have expense accounts for taking reporters out to lunch, for coffee, or for other types of business socializing. You can also get to know them informally at industry events or by chatting on the phone (though they do not always have time for chitchat, reporters love to talk about their beats, or what they cover). Just remember you are always **on the record** and what you say is fair game for publication, unless you both verbally agree *before* you say something that it's **off the record**, or not for publica-tion. Journalistic ethics require journalists to identify themselves and their organizations when they speak to you, but not to remind you that you are on the record after you know they are journalists. Journalists assume you understand these ground rules.

▲ **Speak on background or off the record only if you know you can trust the reporter.** Sometimes giving **background** information (not for attribution) or explaining something off the record can help a journalist understand a story better. But be judicious about who you use these tools with. Most reporters will not "burn" their sources, but some are inexperienced or overly ambitious and that can make them untrustworthy. Get to know them before speaking off the record.

SELF-CHECK

- Define **hook, on the record,** and **off the record.**
- What do hooks do?
- Name four ways to cultivate relationships with journalists.

12.2 Tools for Getting Talked About

After you know what's a good story and how to talk to reporters, you are still not ready. You need some more tools for getting the word out. We'll explain how to write a news release, get creative about publicity, and generate positive word of mouth about your product and your company.

12.2.1 Writing Press Releases

The most important and basic format for communicating a story is the press release. A **press release** (or news release) is a short document with a clear headline, sufficient facts and quotes to support a short news story; brief supporting background on the company/product involved; a date; and contact information for journalists who want to call to get more information or to arrange an interview.

The good news is that an effective press release with a good hook will get you onto a journalist's desk. A follow-up call to the editor a week after a press release is sent is a good strategy, just to double-check that he or she got the press release and to gauge interest and give additional information. If the media outlet is interested in your story, the press release can set the ball rolling.

The bad news is that the odds of your release getting picked up by media and receiving any coverage are terribly low. Journalists and editors throw away more than 90 percent of the releases they receive. Your release must stand out from the junk in a journalist's inbox. To beat the odds, pay attention to content and avoid these common errors that journalists complain about:

▲ **Do not send inappropriate or late releases.** Target the right media and contacts. The food critic doesn't need a release about a new robotics manufacturing facility. And the business correspondent doesn't either, if the facility opened two months ago, because now it's old news. Build up an accurate database of media contacts and mail your release first class on occasion to validate it (with first class mail, you get envelopes back if addresses aren't valid). Faxing or e-mailing your release can be sensible because journalists work on tight deadlines, so include fields for fax and e-mail numbers in your database. Develop a list identifying authors of stories you like that may be similar to stories related to your business. Now you have a smaller list that's a much tighter match with your content and target audience.

▲ **Do not make any errors.** Typos throw the facts into question. And do not include any inaccurate claims. You want the journalist to trust you to do his research for him, which means he really has to trust you. Be worthy of his trust. Even better, include contact info for independent sources so that he can verify the information.

▲ **Do not give incomplete contact information.** Be sure that you include up-to-date names, addresses, and phone numbers. Let the contacts know when they should be available and what they should say so that the journalist finds them helpful and cooperative.

▲ **Do not ignore the journalists' research needs.** The more support you give them, the easier it is for them to cover your story. You can include photographs of the expert you quote in a mailed release (include the date, name of the person, and information about the supplier of the photo on the back or the margin of the photo). Also consider offering plant tours, interview times, sample products, or whatever else may help journalists cover your story.

▲ **Do not bug the reporters.** Journalists do not have time to send you clippings of the articles they write. Nor do they care to discuss with you why they didn't run a story, or why they cut off part of a quote when they did run a story. They're too busy, and their readers' and editors' needs come first, yours last.

▲ **Do not forget that journalists work on a faster clock than you do.** When a journalist calls about your release, return the call (or make sure that somebody returns it) in hours, not days. If you handle her requests slowly, she just finds another source or writes another story by the time you get back to her.

These don'ts can be balanced by a few good do's that help you get pickup (coverage) in the media:

▲ **Do include a list of five tips, rules, or principles.** Include something helpful that the media can quote. (A chiropractor's practice may send out a release that includes five ways to have a healthier back. A management consultant may offer five tips for avoiding cash-flow crises. A home inspection firm may offer five tips to avoid costly surprises when buying a home.)

▲ **Do offer yourself as an expert commentator on industry-related matters, in case they need a quote for another article.** They may just include one sentence from you, but if they mention your company name, you just got some good publicity. For example, an article on how to shop for a used car in the Sunday magazine of a newspaper may quote the owner of a large auto dealership as saying, "If you do not have an independent mechanic evaluate a used car before buying it, I guarantee you will be in for some unpleasant surprises." The article may also mention that this dealership's repair department does free evaluations for car buyers. The combination of a quote and a bit of information about the free service is going to attract many new customers for the dealership's repair service, some of whom will buy cars there.

▲ **Do keep it brief.** Journalists are quick on the uptake and work fast, so let them call or e-mail if they need more information.

▲ **Do post your press releases on your Web site.** Your press releases can do double duty on the Web, providing information for both curious journalists and potential consumers.

▲ **Do send releases to every local editor in your area, no matter how small their publication or station.** You can get local coverage more easily than regional or national coverage, and that local coverage can be surprisingly helpful.

▲ **Do collect examples of good coverage of your type of product or service and build a mailing list of journalists and media that cover your type of business.** Sending your releases to these people makes sense because they've already proven they give similar stories coverage.

You can get a story out to the media in ways other than press releases. You can generate a video release, with useful footage that a television producer may decide to run as part of a news story.

You can also put a written press release on the PR Newswire or any other such service that distributes hard copy or electronic releases to its media clients — for a fee to the source of the release, of course. You can also pitch your stories to the Associated Press and other newswires (but it's best to use a major PR firm to contact a newswire).

12.2.2 Creating Exciting Publicity

Marketing is more an art than a science, and it's limited only by your imagination. Here are some ways to get the media to notice you:

▲ **Think big.** Sponsor a crazy contest for baking the largest cookie, or growing the largest tomato, or something that relates to your business. Invite the media to cover your event.

▲ **Brainstorm at least 10 ways to get a famous person to use your product.** Give it a try. Maybe you can come up with an idea good enough to actually pitch to the celebrity. Then let the media find out.

▲ **Throw a party.** Treat your customers and employees to a party at least once a quarter. Invite journalists. How about a customer appreciation party? Parties bring people together in a fun way, building goodwill and strengthening relationships that turn into future business.

▲ **Offer a community service award.** Accept nominations for it throughout the year and announce your winner at an award ceremony. Use PSAs (public-service announcements) and press releases to publicize your event in advance. Send special VIP invitations to your best customers. But be sure to take this project seriously and do it with sincerity or it will be seen as a cynical publicity stunt.

▲ **Conduct a survey and publicize the results.** What's the latest trend in your industry? If you knew the answer to this question before others did, you could get attention and publicity by sending out releases and sharing your findings. You can conduct it yourself or do an omnibus survey, in which you buy a few question slots in a large consumer survey.

12.2.3 Making the Most of Word of Mouth

Word of mouth, or what consumers tell each other about your products or services, gives a consumer (or a marketer) the most credible source of information about products, aside from actual personal experience.

Word of mouth has a huge impact on your efforts to recruit new customers, and it also has a secondary, but still significant, impact on your efforts to retain old customers. If you make an effort to track and manage word of mouth, it can be your most powerful form of marketing communication, because it holds more sway over purchase decisions than advertising or any other form of marketing.

Yet most marketers simply ignore word of mouth on the assumption that they cannot affect what customers say. Not true. Some marketers combine excellent service and a friendly approach with incentives and encouragement to get those customers to give them referrals, for example. When this is done right, it can be the best and cheapest source of new customers. Word of mouth needs to be an integral part of your marketing program.

So how to get positive WOM? In general, you should focus on doing what you do best. If you are the best at something, you are automatically newsworthy. The media wants to talk about and to you. And your customers are wowed by your excellence and want to tell others about you. So do not spread yourself too thin. Know what you do best and keep improving how you do it. Good referrals and publicity come naturally over time if you keep some aspect of your business head and shoulders above the rest.

If you survey customers to identify the source of positive attitudes toward new products, you generally find that answers like "my friend told me about it" outnumber answers like "I saw an ad" by 10 to 1. Word-of-mouth communications about your product do not actually outnumber advertising messages; but when customers talk, other customers listen.

How can you control what people say about your product? You cannot very effectively encourage customers to say nice things about or prevent them from slamming your product — many marketers assume that no one can do it. But you can influence word of mouth to some degree, and you must try. Here are some ideas:

▲ **Make your product special.** A product that surprises people because of its unexpectedly good quality or service is special enough to talk about. A good product or a well-delivered service turns your customers into your sales force.

> **FOR EXAMPLE**
>
> ### Toyota Takes on Texas
>
> Toyota's Tundra light pickup truck, though popular, is still being outsold by Ford's trucks. So when Toyota built a new plant in San Antonio, Texas, they donated $25,000 to a nonprofit corporation being backed by business and political leaders there. Toyota also promoted the Tundra at home-improvement shows, country-western concerts, rodeos, and monster truck jams. This effort, coupled with becoming the largest single contributor for "the Fund," generated positive word of mouth for the company, and business coverage in the *Wall Street Journal*.

▲ **Do something noteworthy in the name of your product or company.** If no aspect of your product itself is incredibly wonderful and surprising, get creative. Support a neat not-for-profit organization in your neighborhood. Stage a fun event for kids. Let your employees take short sabbaticals to volunteer in community services. All these strategies have worked well to generate positive publicity and word of mouth. You can think of something worthwhile, some way of helping improve your world that surprises people and makes them take notice of the good you are doing in the name of your product.

▲ **Use exciting sales promotions and premiums, not boring ones.** A 24-cent coupon isn't worth talking about. But a sweepstakes in which the winners get to spend a day with a celebrity can get consumers excited. A premium like this sweepstakes generates positive PR and a lot of WOM. (The next section deals with sales promotions.)

▲ **Identify and cultivate decision influencers.** In many markets, some people's opinions matter a lot more than others. These people are **decision influencers,** people who exert strong influence over other people's opinions, and if you (hypothetically) diagram the flow of opinions, you find that many of them originate with these people. In business-to-business marketing, the decision influencers are often obvious.

A handful of prominent executives, a few editors working for trade magazines, and some of the staff at trade associations probably affect many people's perceptions of your product. You can find identifiable decision influencers in consumer markets, as well. In the market for soccer equipment, youth coaches, league managers, and the owners of independent sporting goods stores are important decision influencers.

To take advantage of decision influencers, develop a list of them and then make a plan for cultivating them. Match them with appropriate managers or salespeople who can take them to events or out to lunch, just for fun. You just need to make sure that people associated with your business are in the personal networks of these decision influencers.

Consider developing a series of giveaways and informational mailings to send to these decision influencers. To sell the shoe to youth players, send free samples of a new soccer cleat to youth coaches. When you know who's talking and who's listening, you can easily focus your efforts on influencing the talkers.

SELF-CHECK

- Define **press release, word of mouth,** and **decision influencers.**
- List the components of a press release.
- List some do's and don'ts for dealing with journalists.
- Name four ways to *influence* word of mouth.

12.3 Sales Promotions

A **sales promotion** is a marketing initiative that's designed to boost sales. There are different types of sales promotions, including coupons, discounts, premiums, competitions, frequent user/loyalty incentives, and point-of-sale displays.

12.3.1 Price Promotions and Coupons

Discounts and special offers are temporary inducements to stimulate purchases based on price. (Pricing itself is the subject of Chapter 9 .) A price cut is easy to do, but hard to undo. Your customers may come to expect and demand it.

Some reasons for using price-based promotions are as follows:

▲ When you want to get consumers to try a new product
▲ When you want to experiment with price to see how sensitive your customers are to pricing
▲ To counter a competitor's special offer
▲ When your competitors are all offering lower prices and you think you have no choice to stay competitive

The problem with the last reason is that every marketer loses in this scenario. You end up training your customers to expect lower prices and you focus attention on price at the expense of brand and benefit considerations. Special promotions attract price switchers, people who aren't loyal to any brand but just shop on the basis of price.

FOR EXAMPLE

When Coupons Backfire

Sometimes too many coupon promotions can cause customers to buy only based on price, not brand loyalty. Upon realizing this was happening, Proctor and Gamble once unsuccessfully tried to stop what it called "coupon fever." Retailers resisted. Then the U.S. government got involved and raised alarms about "price fixing." P&G now allows discounts again.

Special offers have the potential to erode brand equity, reduce customer loyalty, and cut your profits. That's why Proctor & Gamble tried to stop them. But there may be legitimate reasons for using them. Or you may have to go with the flow in your market.

A common form of discounting is the coupon — more common than the refund, which consumers often view as too much trouble. In consumer nondurables, whether toothpaste or canned soup, research shows you have to offer at least 50 cents off your list price to attract much attention. When offers get over the 50-cent level, attractiveness grows rapidly, sometimes reaching 80 percent!

Some marketers take a broader approach, offering many smaller coupons rather than fewer bigger offers. We think this approach is misguided. Why add to the clutter of messages? In North America, only a little over 3 percent of coupons are redeemed. You need to study your response rates compared to your past efforts, and what you are offering compared to your competitors.

To forecast how much your offer will cost you, you have to take your estimate of the redemption rate and multiply it by how much of the product you think will be bought at the reduced price, to figure out the cost of the promotion. Compare the increase in sales to the cost of the promotion. Will it be worth it? That's a judgment call. Discounts are risky, and marketers debate their benefits. The important thing is to keep track of the effects of what you are doing and not cut into your profits unnecessarily.

Other types of promotions that have been used successfully:

▲ **Competitions and prizes:** These are good for creating excitement around the brand, and work well on the Web, where they can be changed often. Most of these are subject to legal restrictions, so make sure you research this carefully in the state or states in which you want to offer the competition.

▲ **Frequent user/loyalty incentives:** Frequent-buyer programs are used by airlines, hotel chains, stores, and restaurants. Many supermarkets are getting into this game too, by giving out cards that can be run through a scanner at checkout for special discounts.

▲ **Point-of-sale displays:** In retail stores these can be very effective. Displays need to be attractive and well-positioned. See the Swiss Army Knife For Example in Section 2.1 for how a POS display can work as a marketing strategy.

12.3.2 Premiums: Used and Abused

▲ A **premium** is any product with a marketing message somewhere on it that you give away or include with a purchase.

▲ A **premium promotion** is when you give the customer something extra for buying something.

Magazines are often sold this way, and so are consumer luxuries such as perfumes and high-end cosmetics. This "gift with purchase" is a frequent promotional strategy. The customer feels like he's getting more than he paid for, and sales rise, at least temporarily.

Classic premium giveaways include T-shirts, coffee mugs, pens, wall calendars, and baseball caps with your company name or logo on them. You may want to consider something more innovative, too. Old standards include pens, pencils, calendars, and key chains, and new classics are mouse pads, calculators, Frisbees, tote bags, water bottles, and even kaleidoscopes. See Table 12-1. The premium industry offers such a wide variety of choices to advertisers that you should think of premiums as a group of specialized media instead of thinking of them as a single medium.

Premiums, like anything, can be overdone. How many pens with some company's name on them have made their way into your possession over the last five years? One more doesn't get noticed and used unless it's a nice pen that people like the look and feel of. A good rule is to select products that people will truly enjoy, even if they cost more than cheap ones. You want your premium to be saved and used, not thrown out.

▲ As with any marketing initiative, you want a premium to change behavior. To do this, you have to build an impact scenario to make a premium work. An **impact scenario** is a realistic story about the premium and its user in which the premium somehow affects that user's purchase behavior.

Say that you are marketing banking services for small businesses, and you want to spread the word to business owners who currently have checking accounts with your bank. Specifically, you want to let these businesses know that you have many helpful new services, and you want the business owners to call or visit their branch offices to find out more.

Table 12-1: Finding the Premium Options

Old Classics	New Classics
Pens, pencils	Clocks, watches
Calendars	Mouse pads
Key chains	Imprinted computer discs
Notepads	Pocket knives
Rulers	Flashlights
Mugs	Calculators
Caps	Stress-ease balls
T-shirts	Frisbees
Thermometers	Leather pad holders and portfolios
Coasters	Children's toys
Balloons	Canvas or nylon tote bags
Umbrellas	Magnetic calendars
Golf balls	Packaged snacks (popcorn, candy, healthy protein bars)
Lapel pins	Sports/water bottles
Watches	Books with customized covers, globe paper-weights, kaleidoscopes

An impact scenario starts with this wish list of what the target customer should understand and do. You finish the scenario by thinking of ways that premium items can accomplish your wish-list goals. What if you have the bank's name and the slogan, "Servicing small businesses better" printed on pens, which you then distribute in the next mailing of checking account statements?

Try to imagine it. The small business owner opens his bank statement, and a pen falls out. He grabs the pen and eagerly reads the slogan. Then, curious about what the slogan means, he immediately dials his local branch and waits patiently on hold for a couple of minutes. When he finally gets someone on the phone, he says, "Hey, I got your pen! Please tell me all about your services for small businesses!" Not too likely, is it? If you really look at most premiums, you see that they're a part of equally unlikely scenarios. They often cost little, and so marketers use them. But they usually do not work too well, so that money is wasted.

But do not give up hope. You can find some impact scenario that works — some way to use a premium so that people actually take some action. A coffee mug may work better than a pen. A mug gives you enough room to print more information. You can print a "Did You Know?" headline on the mug, followed by short, bulleted facts about the problems the bank can solve for a small business owner ("Miser National Bank offers automatic bill paying," and so on).

A customer, drinking coffee at the office, sees the information often and may become curious enough about one of the services listed to ask for details while at the bank. But why will he keep it at the office and use it? Because it's an attractive mug, and perhaps because it has something attractive (a nice picture, for example) on the opposite side of your marketing message.

Can this premium work? Maybe — at least the scenario is plausible. You need to run the numbers to be sure, of course. If you estimate that 1 in 20 customers receiving the mug will end up trying a new service, does this number give you a big enough return to justify the cost of producing and mailing them? That's the question you must ask.

12.3.3 Using the Quality Strategy

Most marketers think more about the message (the copy and/or artwork) that they put on the premium. But this focus can lead you to forget that the premium itself communicates a strong message. The premium is a gift from you to your customer.

Therefore, the premium tells your customers a great deal about you and what you think of them. A cheap, tacky gift may look good when you run the numbers, but it doesn't look good to the customer who receives it. Yet most premiums are of low or medium quality. Few are as good as, or better than, what we'd buy for ourselves.

You can make your premium stand out by simply selecting an item of higher-than-usual quality. One health spa, for example, orders the nicest terry-cloth robes money can buy, with an elegant embroidered version of its logo on the chest, and sells them at cost to customers, who view them as prized possessions.

A customer remembers a better gift more easily, and that gift creates a stronger and more positive image of the marketer. And more customers keep and use the item for a lengthy period of time. Of course, a better gift usually costs more. But you can justify this cost by selecting a gift that makes a greater impact — and reduce the cost by distributing the gift to a better-quality, more selective list. Consider the following table:

Premium A (Cheap gift with direct mail solicitation)
Cost of Premium A = $5 each, or $5,000 for a distribution of 1,000.
Response rate (customer orders within 1 month) = 1.5 percent, or 15 per thousand.
If profit from each order is $1,000, premium gross = $15,000.
Return = gross of $15,000 per thousand minus cost of $5,000 per thousand = $10,000 per thousand.

Premium B (Expensive gift with direct mail solicitation)

Cost of Premium B = $25 each, or $25,000 for a distribution of 1,000.

Response rate (customer orders within 1 month) = 12 percent, or 120 per thousand.

If profit from each order is $1,000, *premium gross* = $120,000.

Return = gross of $120,000 per thousand minus cost of $25,000 per thousand = $95,000 per thousand.

And if the $25 gift item is of significantly higher quality, you can expect a more positive impact on your customers — and higher response rates in any direct response program. Thus, the return is often considerably higher on a high-quality premium — provided you target the premium to the right customers (those likely to respond according to your scenario) and do not just blast it out to a poor-quality list.

Most marketers have difficulty bringing themselves to give away an expensive gift. They waver, lose their nerve, and go for a $5 item over a $25 item. Do not assume the cheaper one is more cost-efficient! Run the numbers first.

Very often, the quality strategy wins, giving you much higher returns, as well as the far more favorable intangible benefit of improved brand image and customer loyalty. If you aren't sure about response rates, experiment on a small scale before making your final decision.

SELF-CHECK

- Define **sales promotion, premium, premium promotion,** and **impact scenario.**
- List four types of sales promotions.
- Explain the quality strategy.

SUMMARY

Public relations involves developing relationships with journalists, packaging a story so they can use it, creating exciting publicity, and cultivating decision influencers. Word of mouth is used to get the kind of attention you cannot get through advertising. Sales promotions and premiums remind people to buy your product.

KEY TERMS

Background	Explanatory communication that a journalist agrees will not be attributed to the source.
Decision influencers	People who exert strong influence over other people's opinions.
Hook	The thing that makes a story newsworthy.
Impact scenario	A realistic story about the premium and its user in which the premium somehow affects that user's purchase behavior.
Off the record	Communication with a reporter that is not for publication.
On the record	Communication with a journalist that you agree may appear in the media, with direct attribution to that source.
Premium	Any product with a marketing message somewhere on it that you give away or include with a purchase.
Premium promotion	When you give the customer something extra for buying something.
Press release	A short document designed for journalists who want to call to get more information or to arrange an interview about a story.
Public relations	The active pursuit of publicity for marketing purposes.
Sales promotion	A marketing initiative that's designed to boost sales.
Word of mouth (WOM)	What consumers tell each other about your products or services.

ASSESS YOUR UNDERSTANDING

Go to www.wiley.com/college/Hiam to evaluate your knowledge of the basics of publicity and promotion.
Measure your learning by comparing pre-test and post-test results.

Summary Questions

1. Which is a feature of a good news story?
   (a) It makes your company look good.
   (b) It has news value.
   (c) It repeats stories already in the news.
   (d) It is of interest to all your customers.

2. Reporters are not interested in talking to you unless you have a new product on the market. True or false?

3. Press releases are effective for influencing word of mouth. True or false?

4. If you tell a reporter something and then ask her not to use it, she can claim that you were on the record when you said it. True or false?

5. For premiums, investing more money is always a better strategy. True or false?

6. A premium promotion is when you give the customer something extra for buying something. True or false?

7. What customers say to each other may not be very important in the long run. True or false?

8. Keep following up if your press release doesn't get picked up immediately. True or false?

9. How much does a coupon have to discount a product, in general, to get consumers' attention?
   (a) 25 cents
   (b) 50 cents
   (c) 75 cents
   (d) one dollar

Review Questions

1. What steps can you take to maximize the chance of your press release being picked up by the media?

2. What are the pros and cons of using discount promotions for boosting sales?

3. Explain what is meant by a reasonable impact scenario and why it is needed.

Applying This Chapter

1. Assume your retail corporation has an enormous surplus of bath towels. Design and explain a sales promotion you'd use. Which strategy — discount, point-of-sale display, customer-loyalty incentive, premium promotion — would you pursue and why? What data might you need to collect before making your decision?

2. You are marketing a new fruit juice beverage that is mainly sold in health food stores and juice bars. How might you broaden your audience with a premium promotion? Can you think of a reasonable impact scenario for this premium?

3. Explain how to determine whether a price promotion will pay off. What are the figures you need to estimate to plan your promotion?

YOU TRY IT

Copy This

What if your product, office copier equipment, is suffering from a negative association with another manufacturer's unreliable product? How could you get customers to talk about you in a good way? How would you determine the decision influencers in your business, and what could you do to change their minds?

In the News

Scan today's business section and rank the top three stories based on your interest in them. Now analyze each one in turn to identify the one thing that made that story interesting. What was the hook the writer used to catch your interest? Would that story indirectly generate positive publicity for a business?

Safe Spots for Tots

Your company has developed a new auto restraint system for children. What kind of research might you hope to find that would provide a hook for selling your product? Write a press release to a business reporter in which you include a hook that will interest his or her readers.

13

INTERNET MARKETING
Selling on the World Wide Web

Starting Point

Go to www.wiley.com/college/Hiam to assess your knowledge of the basics of internet marketing.
Determine where you need to concentrate your effort.

What You'll Learn in This Chapter

▲ The four marketing domains of Internet commerce
▲ How to design an effective Web site and drive traffic to it
▲ Online tools in addition to your site for enhancing your marketing

After Studying This Chapter, You'll Be Able To

▲ Analyze Web content for *stickiness*
▲ Investigate search-engine resources
▲ Be a good "**netizen**"
▲ Evaluate e-mail and banner advertising

Goals and Outcomes

▲ Assess how the Internet is changing marketing practices
▲ Practice ways to drive traffic to your home page
▲ Use banner ads and e-mail to get sales
▲ Budget your Web marketing

INTRODUCTION

The World Wide Web creates a wonderfully versatile — and often misused — medium for direct marketing. Four marketing domains are available. Chats, **Webcasts, e-zines,** and search engines can help you focus your marketing. In this chapter, you'll find tips and techniques for making the Web a major component of your sales and marketing efforts.

13.1 The Digital Explosion

You can use the Web to build sales in a lot of exciting ways, regardless of the size of your budget or your company. You can do much more than just host a Web site. online marketing is creating new possibilities every day for finding and serving customers, opening up new channels of communication, and increasing your sales. You do not need to be a Web-based business or sell products online to take advantage of it.

Direct marketers have never had so many cost-effective ways to access prospective customers. The Internet has also helped to put businesses on an equal footing with one another, so that online, a small business can compete against a giant with far larger resources.

Some of the possibilities are as follows:

▲ Create a Web newsletter.
▲ Put together a mailing list of e-mail addresses for your customers.
▲ Track your visibility on search engines.
▲ Do live Webcasts of marketing or sales events to reach a broader audience.

The single most important point to remember is to invest routinely so that you are always changing and improving your Web presence. Whether you are a do-it-yourself Web marketer or are willing to hire a professional firm (which can be as inexpensive as $200 a month), your Web marketing needs to be a living thing. Do not let parts of your site get old and stale.

Do not continue to run a *banner ad* or bid on a *key term* if you aren't getting results in clicks and sales.

▲ **Banner ad:** An ad that appears on a major Web site or service.
▲ **Key term:** A word people use in searching for Web sites, which you can pay to have your message linked to.

Do adapt and change every month. The Web is a dynamic marketing medium. Be dynamic!

The wonderful thing about the Internet is that it has multiplied the ways that consumers and businesses can talk to one another. Information on almost any topic is easy to find, which is why so many people use it to research products before they buy. With the sea of information, though, it's getting harder to organize and evaluate what's out there.

A good Web marketer will know how to maintain credibility, stay within the law, and not drive away potential customers with **spam** or too much information. Your job is to help customers navigate successfully. A good Web site is usually promoted by off-line marketing, too. An online catalog should have a paper one, also.

13.1.1 Budgeting Your Web Marketing

Many marketers hold Web spending down to a small minority of their budget for no good reason other than tradition and fear of all things new. Successful marketers break tradition and keep innovating. If you find that your Web ads, search-engine listings, or e-mails (all explained in this chapter) are pulling well for you and making a profit, try doubling your effort and spending on them for a month and see what happens. Still working well? Double again. You may find that the Web can do a lot more of your basic marketing work than you think.

If you are in a business-to-business marketing situation, it's a good idea to put at least 10 percent of your marketing budget into the Web, both for maintaining a strong Web site and for doing some Web advertising and search-engine placement purchases. If you add an e-newsletter, Web distribution of press releases, and occasional announcements to your e-mail list, you may need to make the percentage significantly higher.

As mentioned above, business-to-business marketers typically put about 5 percent of their advertising budget into Web ads. (Remember that the ad budget is just one section of your overall marketing budget.) Five percent of ad spending on the Web is significant, but it's by no means dominant.

Although ads in business publications make up the biggest part of the typical ad budget, you can find exceptions to every rule, and being the exception often gives you the most profitable and powerful strategy in marketing.

If you are a consumer-oriented marketer, you may find that your Web site is even more important (although you cannot as easily generalize about the share of budget to give it — that depends on your unique situation and what you find works best). Be sure your site does the following:

▲ Engages existing customers, giving them reasons to feel good about their past purchases and connect with your company and other consumers (at least to connect emotionally, if not in actual fact).
▲ Shares interesting and frequently updated information about your products or services and organization on the site, so the consumer can gain useful knowledge by visiting it.

▲ Maintains a section of the site or a dedicated site for business-to-business relationships that matter to your marketing (such as distributors, stores, and sales reps). Almost all consumer marketers also work as business-to-business marketers, and most B-to-B principles also apply to this aspect of consumer marketing, too.

13.2 Marketing Domains

The Internet has created opportunities for marketing communication that have enabled businesses to speak not only to consumers and to other businesses, but for consumers to talk to each other to compare prices and to share information about products. Savvy marketers will take advantage of as many online marketing domains as they can.

13.2.1 Business to Consumer

A whole new world of faster, more convenient options has made shopping online a phenomenal success. Yet pitfalls await the inexperienced marketer. Just having a Web site isn't enough, because even if your site is beautiful it will be useless if you cannot get customers, or traffic, to visit and keep visiting. (We talk about this more fully in Section 13.3.) Make your site welcoming.

Ways to drive traffic to your site, to reach out to customers, and to build a credible e-presence are all important to know for success. E-mail is only a good thing if your prospect wants to receive it; if they do not, it's called spam.

13.2.2 Business to Business

Many of the techniques explained here apply equally to the B-to-B domain. If you are marketing to other businesses, learn how to use the Web and you are likely to prosper. *B2B Magazine* reports from its extensive company surveys that business-to-business marketers put about 5 percent of their advertising budget into Web ads.

13.2.3 Consumer to Consumer

C-to-C commerce is where consumers can buy or exchange goods directly with one another. The old-fashioned garage sale has gone online with eBay, enabling people to sell to the other side of the world, not just to their neighbors. eBay (followed by Amazon.com Auctions) has set the standard for this kind of interaction by creating online auctions where people can bid on each other's products. Even big-ticket items like cars and computers are being sold online. Many people have successfully gone into business (creating B-to-C businesses) from their computers by opening eBay "stores."

FOR EXAMPLE

Do-It-Yourself Travel

Travel agents used to book most airline tickets, along with reserving hotel rooms and rental cars, before the Internet simplified shopping around. Marketers jumped in with sites like Expedia, Travelocity, Orbitz, and Priceline, the "name your own price" site hawked by William Shatner of *Star Trek* fame. Most American business travelers now use the Internet to arrange travel, the *International Herald Tribune* reported (June 3, 2005). Yet many of these highly desirable customers complain about agencies: not knowing what they're paying or what they're getting until it's too late. Some prefer to go directly to an airline or hotel site so they have more options. These vendors, wanting to keep control of their own markets, have had to improve their own sites and services.

Corporate-sponsored **blogs** (online journals or Web logs) and chat rooms (we revisit both of these in Section 13.3) also enable people to buy and sell information about products and services. You can set up a commercial blog linked to your site that will promote something you are doing and get people talking. Consumer review sites, such as eComplaints.com and ConsumerReview.com, where people can share information about products and services, are popular.

13.2.4 Consumer to Business

Another wonderful aspect of the Web is the power it gives to consumers to become actively involved in driving transactions with businesses. Those people can be your best customers.

If you invite your prospects and customers to send in suggestions and questions on your Web site, you get useful information about what they're thinking and help them feel that they have some input into your business decisions. Priceline.com has become a household name by allowing customers to name the prices they would like to pay.

SELF-CHECK

- Define **banner ad, key term,** and **blog.**
- Name the four marketing domains on the Internet.

13.3 Designing an Effective Web Page

Most Web sites are really just huge, interactive advertisements or sales promotions. After a while, even the most cleverly designed ad gets boring. To increase the length of time users spend with your materials, and to ensure high involvement and return visits, you need to think like a publisher, not just an advertiser. Your online marketing goals are to:

▲ Design a good Web site that's user friendly and engaging.
▲ Bring traffic to your site by making it easy to find and current.

Designing good Web pages is a key marketing skill, because your Web site is at the center of all you do to market on the Web. Also, increasingly, Web sites are at the heart of marketing programs — businesses put their Web addresses on every marketing communication, from premium items (like company pens) to letterheads and business cards, and also in ads, brochures, and catalogs.

Serious shoppers will visit your Web site to find out more about what you offer, so make sure your site is ready to close the sale. Include excellent, clear design, along with plenty of information to answer likely questions and move visitors toward a purchase. Web sites have earned their place in the core of any marketing program.

13.3.1 Finding Resources to Help with Design

Start by determining your goals and budget for your Web site. A site can serve as a simple online brochure, storefront, or dynamic application using a company database. The cost can range from $600 to $20,000 or more, depending on your needs.

Good Web-site design is harder than it looks and you should probably use a reputable design firm to do it for you. Contract a business relationship (spelled out on paper in advance) that specifies the following:

▲ You, not they, own the copyright to the content so that you can switch to another vendor if it doesn't work out.
▲ An hourly bill rate and an estimate of the site's size and complexity, with a cap on the number of billable hours needed to design it.

If you know how to use authoring languages or do any of the programming, you may want to do it yourself. If you like tinkering, you can certainly build your own Web pages and contract with an Internet service provider (ISP) to put them up on the Web. Entire books go into all the details, but like creating advertising materials, it is a complicated skill that takes a long time to master.

You can find an Internet service provider to host your site quite easily. Dozens of them may be trying to find you to make a sale. Just pick one that offers the fee structure, services, and flexibility you want — and change providers if they do not satisfy.

Consider using your domain name and ISP to provide your own e-mail addresses, too. Having your e-mail done through your own domain looks so much more professional and gives you more control over the parameters than going through Yahoo!, AOL, or some other public domain does.

When shopping for a designer, here are some guidelines:

▲ For a basic site (around 5–10 pages), where you provide a company logo, images, and copy, plan to spend at least $1000 for a custom-designed site. This price would include domain-name registration and hosting setup. A basic hosting plan costs approximately $200 to $300 per year.

▲ For a lower budget, you can find many Web-site templates available from Web authoring programs. Some are quite good, but people often recognize these cookie-cutter designs, which lower viewers' opinions of the site design.

13.3.2 Creating Engaging Content

Consider Web content to be the hidden factor for increasing site traffic. Unless you have valuable and appealing content, you may have difficulty building up traffic on your site. **Stickiness** is the term Web marketers use to describe a site that keeps people coming back. When putting up the site itself, whether you do it yourself or hire somebody else, keep these points in mind:

▲ Include stock photography in the budget because sites with relevant images — especially of real people — are graphically more appealing and hold the visitor's attention longer. We highly recommend using photographs in most sites.

▲ Although customized graphics and stock photography can drive up your costs, your online presence needs a unique, professional Web site that can set you apart from your competitors.

▲ Consider an online **shopping cart**. Many basic hosting plans include a shopping cart (also called a *shopcart*), so you can implement this feature fairly easily by using theirs. Assume that you will be adding products over time, so select a shopping cart that gives you room to grow.

▲ If you use high-resolution files of the photos, they may be slow to load, which means you could lose some impatient viewers or the few who are still on low-speed phone lines. But stock photography houses sell (at a lower price) low-resolution images that are optimal for the Web and load quickly. These won't slow your site down.

▲ Consider streaming video, animation, and database management. You can use these technologies as important delivery methods, like showing a speaker in action, demonstrating a new product or providing services, and supporting the consumer online. Make the video an option that visitors can click on if interested (rather than something they have to watch before the site finishes loading). Use the video to entertain or inform if you are in a consumer business, but stick to good solid information if you are in business-to-business sales. A short talk by an expert is a simple and appropriate way to jazz up your site.

▲ Offer a links page as a service to your customers. Cue up good links to useful services, vendors, and sources of information, and maintain these links so that they all work. This simple service for your target customers earns you their regular traffic. Then when they want to buy, they probably begin their search on your site.

▲ The Web-site address, which appears above the page in the address bar, should be the same. The Web-site developer should make sure it looks its best by not showing the individual page names.

▲ Put promotional offers on your home page. Offer a special discount, a free sample of a new product, or a nice premium item (gift for customers) if people make a purchase through your site before the end of the next month. Put this offer up in a prominent place on your main (home) page and see what happens. A simple offer like this may increase sales and inquiries.

▲ Solicit customer feedback (C-to-B). Let users tell you which parts of your site to expand and contract. Your ISP can provide you with information on the usage of your site, breaking it down right to the page level. Study this information to figure out where people are going. Which parts of your site are most popular? Use this feedback to make your site even more useful. You can also use a rating system for your products (if you sell a variety of retail products) and let customers do the rating.

▲ Put your Web address on all your other marketing materials. Most marketers overlook this no-brainer: Use your own communications to promote your Web site! Every e-mail that your firm sends out should have an attractive, clickable logo linking to your site, as well as your address and phone number(s) for follow-up. Also, put your Web address on everything you print, including business cards, envelopes, brochures, bills, packaging, and letters.

Create and deliver fascinating content and refresh it regularly. Strong content gives your site real appeal, and it can lead to good referrals and word-of-mouth marketing. On the Web, people can easily send each other good links. They can do this word-of-mouth marketing for your site if they like what they see.

To keep your content fresh and appealing:

▲ **Keep changing content.** Have your contractor update your site monthly because these updates give customers good reasons to keep coming back to the site. Use special promotions or some other monthly feature to add to this evolving appeal. Offer a weekly tip or showcase a different featured product each month. Put up a quote of the day. Ideas like these help avoid boredom and reward frequent visitors with fresh content. See the For Example later in this section for how Crayola did this.

▲ **Put useful, noncommercial information on your site.** Even if you just collect and cue up surveys, technical specifications, links, or other information they want, do it! When people find a site useful, they bookmark it and go there regularly. Guess which site gets the most business? Right. The one people go to regularly.

▲ **Offer white papers (research-oriented or factual reports on a technical topic) or newsletters.** People like to use the Web for research. Often, that research relates to a purchase decision. The white paper gives you the easiest and best way to present this noncommercial information for business-to-business marketing or for consumer durables (because research is important in both types of purchases).

13.3.3 Chats and Webcasts: Adding Human Contact and Support

A growing number of companies can set up a live chat center for your Web-site visitors to use if they need sales or service support. But if you decide to go this route, you do need to have someone online to monitor the chat area and answer customer questions. You'll find this option worthwhile only if you build up your Web site's traffic to the point that you almost always have at least one customer in the chat area.

Explore the chat-room option after you've built up good basic traffic on your site (as measured by a high number of visitors and clicks). See Section 13.4.3 for information on measuring traffic. It may require having thousands of clicks a day to pay off, unless you have a business in which a small number of customers tend to do high-value orders. In that case, you may be able to financially justify the chat room addition with fewer site visits per day.

You can go even further, if you want, by creating live events on the Web. You can do Web conferencing, virtual sales presentations, and Webcasts of conferences or presentations, with potentially thousands of people watching and listening from the comfort of their office or home computers. These events are becoming an important business-to-business marketing medium.

If you Webcast a live event to effectively reach viewers, you must face the challenge of lining up an interested audience. Try starting with your own in-house list of good customers and offering some kind of seminar or event that they may find interesting.

FOR EXAMPLE

Color Me Gold and Silver

As a regular feature, try having some kind of interactive event or contest on your site. Crayola brand crayons used this technique effectively. It staged an interactive event targeting households with young children — a coloring contest in which parents entered their work and kids were the judges. In fact, a contest was held for the judges, too, with kids filling out a written application. The winner of this Big Kid Challenge, as the company called the contest, received $25,000 worth of gold and silver. Not bad! Because the contest was such a big draw, Crayola had great traffic. The site also has a section on how they make crayons and, for the practical parent, advice on how to remove stains.

Keep it fairly simple by focusing your event on education about your product or service and how to use it. This approach may not attract as big an audience as something exciting like, say, a sleight-of-hand demonstration by a magician — but the audience you attract for a product demonstration is more likely to buy that product.

13.3.4 Developing a Registration-Based Site

Many companies have a pop-up box that appears as the main site is loading or later as you surf the site. You are told to register now to gain access to the entire site. Registering costs you nothing, and you have much to gain, but of course, some people may not take the time.

Why would marketers want to do this — give extra content to registered users, and give away this valuable content? To find out who their customers are. The registered users stay in touch and may choose to purchase directly over the site. Crayola, among others, uses its Web site to develop direct marketing relationships with registered users. It's a very savvy way to use the Web site as a major marketing tool.

SELF-CHECK

- What should be your two online marketing goals?
- What is **stickiness**?
- List three ways to keep your content engaging.

13.4 Drawing Traffic to Your Site

Even if you have been able to build a stunning, outstanding Web site, it won't do you much good unless you can get people to visit. This involves the right address, working with search engines, and encouraging visitors to come there.

13.4.1 Selecting a Web Address

To test the availability of a possible Web address (also called a **domain name** or a **URL**), go to www.register.com. You'll get a detailed analysis of any relevant registrations. For example, you may find out that someone has registered the name you want with the .com extension, but not with a .org or .net extension.

If someone has already gotten there first, seek a unique name because someone could forget your extension and go to the competing site, instead. You can best maintain uniqueness by owning most or all of the possible extensions and versions of your Web address.

If consumers may get confused by alternate spellings or misspellings of your domain name, register them, too. Registering a name is cheap, so you shouldn't lose a prospective customer just because they cannot spell your name. How would consumers be most likely to misspell your business name? Make sure you register those misspellings.

If you register more than one domain name, all of them should take you to the main business site. It's easy to redirect traffic in this way, so make sure you register any obvious domain names where people may expect to find you, even if you do not want to create separate Web sites for each.

If you find that some firm has bought your desired address for the purpose of selling domain names and wants you to bid on it, do not. Just go back to the drawing board and find another name that isn't being held hostage. Most of these domain-hoarding companies process a large fee on your credit card before you can say "marketing mistake."

As you search for potential names, keep the following three criteria in mind to make sure you obtain a good address for your site:

▲ **A good address relates to your business or brand.** You can register catchy, amusing addresses, but should you use them, necessarily? No. It doesn't relate to your business or brand. Use a Web address that is clearly relevant to your business.

▲ **A good domain name is memorable.** Someone who wants to remember it can. It doesn't mean that you have to register something stunningly cool or clever — besides, by now, someone else has already registered most of the extremely clever addresses.

▲ **Your Web address should be unique.** It needs to be unique to avoid two problems. If consumers can easily confuse your site with similar addresses, some people go to the wrong site by accident. If your company name is similar to others, add a unique term or word in your Web address to make it unique. Also be careful about trademark violations. Check any Web address against a database of trademarks. Or ask a lawyer to do a more detailed analysis if you think you may run into an issue.

13.4.2 Buying Visibility on Search Engines

Search engines locate (or index) billions of sites from user queries each day. A lot of prospective customers are in that statistic somewhere. Google alone indexes more than 3.3 billion Web-site pages. So how can relevant queries find their way to your pages rather than to all the others? You are a needle in an immense haystack.

Because the search engines look at traffic when ranking pages, anything you do through direct communication with your customers to build traffic can help. Also, you should use a link to related sites to improve your ranking. You can use the simple but powerful strategy of doing a search, like one your customers may do, and see what sites appear in the top 10 listings. Then visit each of them and see if you can find appropriate places and ways to link to their sites.

For example, a company that distributes products for you or vice versa is a natural to link to your site. Also, a professional association in your industry may be a good fit, although it may be harder to convince them to link back to your site. Build such links and the higher-ranked sites tend to draw yours up toward them. Make sure your content is good enough to justify those links!

Next, to make your site visible to anyone searching for it, you will have to spend some money on your listing. Sorry, but there's no such thing as a free lunch on the Internet anymore! Google AdWords is a program allowing you to pay per click when people click through to your site. You are paying for customers to visit your site, which is a good investment, especially if they buy something. To use this option, do the following:

1. Designate a short list of highly specific and appropriate key terms that customers may use to search for you.
2. Bid by saying how much you'd pay for a click. Starting at $0.10 to $0.15 a click usually gets you into the game. Web advertisers call this offer your per-click bid. Google allows you to track your results day by day, see your ranking, and see what results (clicks and costs) you get.
3. If you want more clicks, raise your bid for a higher listing or improve your use of terms or descriptive sentences, and watch to see if your results improve.

FOR EXAMPLE

Names That Get Remembered

Using your company or brand name makes the Web site memorable to any-one who knows the name of your business. You can easily remember that e-Bay's site is at www.ebay.com. Or you can simply combine two or three easy words and make the string into a memorable Web address. A firm selling UV filtering glass and Plexiglas for framing valuable art could choose a sufficiently relevant and memorable Web address like www.uvprotectionglass.com.

You do not need to make a long-term commitment; you can experiment with pro-grams at low cost until you find a mix that works. Be aware, however, that click fraud is common, and Google actually refunds marketers who have been scammed by clicks that are not from potential customers. Sometimes the phony clicks come from rival marketers trying to drive up your costs, and sometimes they come from advertising partners who are supposed to be driving traffic to your site.

Yahoo! also has a service for buying search engine visibility. It uses a bidding system based on the number of clicks your site gets, much like Google's AdWords. A Nielsen audit found that Yahoo! search engine listings reached more than 80 percent of active Internet users. You may want to buy some visibility in Yahoo! searches, as well as Google.

Often, you can use the same key terms in both, which simplifies your work as a marketer. However, you may need to adjust your per-click bids differently to get good visibility on Yahoo!. Depending on your industry, one or the other search engine may tend to be more expensive.

Web-based promotions have the advantage of being changeable, and you can change them as often as you like. The development time and cost is low compared to other sorts of events.

13.4.3 Keeping Track of Visitors

You probably do not have as much traffic as you may want. Sure, millions of peo-ple use Google to do searches or go to eBay to bid on auctioned products. But the average Web site only has a few dozen visitors a day. For an effective site, you need to build up this traffic at least into the thousands of visitors per day.

Much of what Internet firms do involves optimizing the site to make it more visible in search engines so that traffic goes up. Even if you hire someone to do the technical work, you ought to be involved in the strategizing.

Each time someone visits your Web site, he is exhibiting interest in you and your products (or he's lost — which is less likely if your site is aptly named and clearly designed so that no one can confuse it with unrelated types of businesses).

However you go about setting up a site, make sure that you capture information about your visitors in a useful form that gets sent to you regularly. Ask your ISP what kinds of reports they can offer you — probably more than you imagined possible. With these reports in hand, you can track traffic to your site.

13.4.4 Using Header and META Tags

Make your site easy to find by tagging it with appropriate terms or words describing its contents for the search engines to pick up. The first thing you need is a **header block,** similar to a headline in an ad, that encodes (in HTML, the language of Web programming) some words to describe your site.

It needs to be clean, focused, and simple (search engines do not appreciate creativity). You can incorporate a header tag in this block, which search engines read and pick up for display when someone does a relevant search.

Next, your Web site developer should think about what META tags your site has. **META tags** are simply some additional instructions to Web browsers that include keywords that some search engines, not including Google, pick up. You may find *description* and *key word* META NAME tags the most important for what you are trying to do. Both permit you to list information about your content (in the form of terms, and in the form of a short descriptive sentence).

They can sometimes include additional words to signal what you offer and help the Web surfer find your site. These META tags control when and how (some) search engines describe your site. You can cue the site up for display when someone searches for one of your terms, and then you can determine what sentence that search engine displays to describe the site — essentially, a small, free advertisement for your site. Draft this ad carefully to attract the right prospects with appropriate, accurate information on your content.

Developers do not put as much care into most sites' META tags as they should, and the site loses traffic as a result. This field of marketing research is known as search engine optimization, and some overly aggressive marketers are engaging in what some search engines consider to be unfair marketing practices.

Do not try to cover every base by using a laundry list of tags. Search engines are pretty good at noticing and avoiding such ploys, and you do not want everyone coming to your site, anyway. You should make your tags clear and narrowly focused to attract only the best prospects. A recent practice called keyword stuffing has caused some search engines to penalize sites by lowering their rankings if they repeat their keywords too many times. So don't try to cheat the system!

Your META tags cannot guarantee that people using any of the common search engines get there. Numerous sites are competing for attention, and yours may be listed on the 15th page, after 140 other listings, where nobody will see it. META tags can help put you in the running, but they cannot ensure a prominent page-one placement in a search engine's results.

13.4.5 Interpreting Click Statistics

You may find click-through statistics a useful and easy-to-get indicator of how well an ad or search-engine placement is performing. If many people are clicking through to your site from an ad or placement, that ad is clearly doing its job of attracting traffic for you. So, all else being equal, more clicks are better.

However, all else isn't equal all the time. Here are a few wrinkles to keep in mind when interpreting click rates:

▲ When a pop-up ad pops up, the companies you buy the ad space through usually report it as a click. But do not believe the numbers because you have no indication that someone actually read or acted on that pop-up. They may have just closed it without looking. Dig deeper into the statistics from whoever sold you that pop-up ad to find out how it actually performed. You can probably get some more detailed data if you ask, but you need more than the simple click count.

▲ Some ads have multiple elements that load in sequence, creating a countable click with each loading so that one ad may generate several click-through counts. This counting method may lead you to think that the more complex ad is better, but the higher number can be an artifact of the way those who sell ad space on the Web count the clicks. (Ask your ISP if it can sell Web ad space to you, or visit any really popular site and look for the section in it that's for advertisers if you want to buy ad space.)

▲ Quality is more important than quantity. Who are these people who clicked to your site? That information is harder to access, but more important. You need to evaluate the quality of those clicks.

▲ If you are getting poor quality of traffic clicking through, you need to experiment with putting ads in other places or you need to redesign your ads to specifically focus on your desired target. Keep working on it until you have not the most click-throughs, but the best.

You can evaluate performance of Web advertising every day or week, and you can get statistics on each and every ad that you run. So use this data intelligently to experiment and adjust your approach. Aim to increase both the quantity and the quality of clicks week by week throughout your marketing campaign and track the impact on inquiries and sales.

SELF-CHECK

- Define **domain name, header block,** and **META tag.**
- What are the three criteria for a good domain name?
- Name the four ways to interpret click-rate statistics.

13.5 Utilizing E-Mail, E-Zines, and Web Advertising

What other ways can you reach out to prospects and bring in sales? You can send out e-mails, do Web advertising, even become a Web publisher. Many companies and individuals have used the Internet to self-publish.

You can get attention for your ideas by selling e-books, publishing an **e-zine** on a regular basis, or putting together other interactive content that you give away or sell. Make sure, though, that you understand **netiquette**, or e-mail etiquette. Nobody likes a spammer.

13.5.1 Understanding E-Mail Etiquette

You can create, or hire your Web site designer to create, an e-mail that looks like a well-designed Web page, with animation and clickable buttons linking to your site. Now, all you have to do is blast it out to millions of e-mail addresses and surely sales will go through the roof.

Not so fast! Okay, so you have this great marketing message or sales pitch, and you want to send it to everyone in the world who has an e-mail address. You can actually do that, but it's a very bad idea.

The more specific and narrow your use of e-mail for marketing, the better. And since Congress passed the Can Spam Act, U.S. marketers must be careful to avoid violating federal restrictions on junk e-mails. Stay on the sunny side of this law.

The best e-mail is a personal communication with a customer you know, sent individually from you with an accurate e-mail return address as well as your name, title, company name, full mailing address, and phone number. It may read as follows:

Dear so-and-so,

I wanted to follow up after your purchase of (your product) on (date) to see how it's working out for you and to thank you for your continuing business. If you have any concerns or questions, please let me know by return e-mail, or feel free to call my private cell phone number, (xxx) yyy-zzzz. Thanks!

Best,

Your Name

Your customer is going to receive, open, read, and appreciate an e-mail like this one. She may even respond to it, especially if the customer has any current concerns or questions or has another order on its way. Even if she doesn't reply to it, however, she appreciates that e-mail. And that message doesn't bug anyone or look like spam.

Use e-mail as much as you can for legitimate, helpful one-on-one contact and support of customers or prospects. Sometimes, you can also send out an e-mail to a list rather than an individual, but have a clear purpose that benefits those people on the list. Make your list as focused as possible to avoid angering people. Goodwill is a valuable asset, so do not destroy it!

Learn these additional rules of good mass e-mailing that all marketers should follow, inspired by the Association for Interactive Marketing and the Direct Marketing Association, where they have guidelines for responsible use of e-mail. The restrictions in U.S. federal regulations also provide some guidelines for your bulk e-mailings:

▲ **Send e-mails only to those people who ask for them.** Your bulk e-mails should ideally go only to those people who have given you permission. If you are not sure about a particular contact, ask the people who receive the mailing if they mind and give them an option to reply and be taken off the list. It's not (yet) illegal to send e-mails without permission (providing your list is legitimate and not random), but it's not very polite.

▲ **You get the most solid form of consent when someone asks you to include him in your mailing.** You can get these requests by creating a useful e-newsletter and advertising it on the Web as a free subscription. Those people who sign up really want it, and they're happy to see the next issue arrive.

▲ **Remove addresses from your list immediately when they ask to be removed.** Refusing to allow people to opt out is illegal. Also, people have such widespread distrust of Web marketers that you may consider writing the person a brief, individual e-mail from you (identify yourself and your title for credibility), letting them know that you have eliminated them from the list and are sorry if you've inconvenienced them. You shouldn't say any more. Do not try to make a sale — you just make them even madder. You generally make a positive impression by being so responsive to their complaint, so do not be surprised if your special attention to their request leads them to initiate a sale later on.

▲ **If you insist on buying e-mail lists, test them before using them.** Try a very simple, short, nonirritating message to the list, like an offer to send them a catalog or free sample, and ask for a few pieces of qualifying information in return. See what happens. Cull all the many bounce-backs and irritated people from the list. Now your list is a bit better in quality than the raw list was. Save those replies in a separate list — they're significantly better and more qualified and deserve a more elaborate e-mail, mailing, or (if the numbers aren't too high) a personal contact.

▲ **Respect privacy.** People do not want to feel like someone's spying on them. Never send to a list if you'd be embarrassed to admit where you got the names. You can develop an e-mail list in plenty of legitimate ways (from customer data, from Web ads, from inquiries at trade shows, from return postcards included in mailings, and so on), so do not do anything that your neighbors would consider irritating or sleazy.

▲ **Send out your bulk e-mails just like you send an individual one.** Use a real, live, reply-able e-mail address. It's annoying when you cannot reply to an e-mail. A good rule of marketing is to try not to irritate customers and prospects.

▲ **Include your company name and a real mailing address.** If you are in the United States, federal law now requires that you include this contact information and that you give recipients an easy way to opt out of future mailings.

▲ **Make sure that the subject line isn't deceptive.** U.S. law now requires that you make the subject line straightforward, and it's just good sense, anyway. In marketing, you want to know right away if someone isn't a good prospect, instead of wasting your time or theirs when they have no interest in your offer.

▲ **Keep your e-mail address lists current.** When you get a *hard bounce-back* from an address, remove it and update your e-mail list.

- **Hard bounce-back.** A notice that a message was undeliverable
- **Soft bounce-back.** An undeliverable message resulting from some kind of temporary problem. Track it to see if the e-mail eventually goes through. If not, eliminate this address, too. People change their addresses and switch servers. You can have bounce-backs on your list who may still be good customers or prospects. At least once a year, check these inactive names and try to contact them by phone or mail to update their addresses. Some of them are still interested and do not need to be cut from your list; you just need their new information.

If you are e-mailing to an in-house list of people who have bought from you, gone to your seminar, or asked for information in the past, remind them of your relationship in the e-mail. They may have forgotten.

People hate **spam**, or junk e-mails that clog up their mailboxes. In fact, many change their e-mail addresses whenever the spam begins to find them. You probably feel the same way. So do not let your Web marketing make you part of this problem. Real people live at the end of those e-mail addresses. Treat them as such!

online privacy is being hotly debated on the Internet and in state and federal legislatures, as marketers try to develop more tools to get information from the Internet, some of which are less invasive and objectionable to consumers than others.

Many states, including California and Alaska, are passing laws to regulate the use of these technologies.

▲ **Adware or spyware:** Computer code that goes into personal computers and collects information about their users, mainly for marketing purposes.

▲ **Pop-ups:** Promotional windows that open, especially while you are leaving a site.

FOR EXAMPLE

Technology to Help Market Research

Programmers are in demand by marketers these days. Automated software called *bots* or *spiders* crawl the Internet and gather information about what people think about products. Business 2.0 reports (Sept. 2005) that one marketing company has devised software to go through blogs, and find out what people think of products or trends. Another kind of software attempts to *upsell,* or recommend additional products to past customers based on their purchase histories. Amazon.com and other major e-tailers do this with limited success (in the single digits), so demand is growing for software that can make better recommendations.

Pop-up blockers are popular, as is **anti-spyware,** which are programs to detect and remove tracking cookies.

Tracking cookies are small text files that Web-site operators and third-party companies that do Web advertising place on a user's computer.

As a marketer, you can be a good netizen, or Net citizen, by doing the following:

▲ Use good-quality lists to send e-mails only to people who want to hear from you.

▲ Be polite and respectful in your communications.

▲ Integrate e-mail into your broader Web strategy so that you do not have to rely too heavily on it.

▲ Limit pop-ups because many people find them annoying and are actively trying to block them. You can set up pop-ups to show up only when a first time visitor leaves your site, but not on return visits.

▲ Most of all, keep up to date with and stay within the laws.

13.5.2 E-Publishing

You can create an electronic magazine, or e-zine, either by hosting it on your Web site or e-mailing it to customers. Or you can just buy advertising space in somebody else's newsletter. Having your own publication, however, is a marketing tool that can establish you as an expert in a topic. E-zines are a kind of *viral marketing.* **Viral marketing** uses social networks to create awareness of a brand or product; it's an inexpensive form of word-of-mouth advertising. (See more on word of mouth in Section 12.2.3.)

Reasons to publish online include the following:

▲ It increases sales of your product or service.

▲ It establishes you or our company as an expert in your industry.

▲ It is an effective promotional vehicle for your business with minimal overhead costs.

▲ It gives you a list of people you can sell to or test promotions with.

▲ It can help you gain advertising revenue by selling ads to other companies.

13.5.3 Designing and Placing a Banner Ad

A banner ad, those brightly colored rectangles at the top of popular Web pages, are the Web's answer to display advertising in a print medium or outdoor advertising on a billboard.

Viewers do not want to read as much copy as they may in a print ad, so use banners the same way you use a billboard (check out Section 11.2 for a discussion of billboards). Banners are effective to get across a very simple, clear, and engaging message.

Use only a single, brief headline, perhaps supported by a logo and a couple of lines of body copy. Or maybe you can use a brand name and an illustration. In either case, the ad must be simple and bold — able to attract the viewer's attention from desired information elsewhere on the screen for long enough to make a simple point. Do not expect too much from a banner ad.

If you decide to use the Web for direct-action advertising, be sure to include a clear call to action in the ad. Typical Web banner ads do not give enough information about the product to stimulate an urge for immediate action. Nor do they make taking action easy. They simply build awareness, at best.

Companies that provide Web-page design can also design and place banner ads and pop-up ads for you. You can also find plenty of factory-oriented banner ad designers that can make you an ad quickly and economically or sell you a template. Any competent Web designer or programmer can create custom banners to your specification quite easily because it's such a small ad format.

The best design for starters is a banner that flashes a simple one-line offer or headline statement, shows an image of your logo or product, and then switches to a couple more lines of text explaining what to do and why to do it ("Click here to take advantage of our introductory offer for small business owners and get 20% off your first order of. . . .").

This ad style delivers a clear marketing message using both print and illustration. Make sure that prospects go directly to a page on your Web site if they click on the banner that supports the product or service with more information and with several easy purchase options.

Then you have to buy space to display the banner. You can use large sites like Yahoo!, or you can go to a specialty firm, and hire them to do the placement. They take a small commission but probably more than make up for this loss by negotiating better rates and avoiding some of the inflation of exposure numbers that can happen when you have to rely on the publisher's accounting.

Watch the banner ad closely and pull or modify it, or try running it elsewhere, if the click rate is too low to justify the cost. You may have to make a few tries to get it right, but with the rapid feedback possible on the Web, this experimentation can take place fairly quickly and inexpensively.

SELF-CHECK

- List several ways to be a good netizen.
- What are **adware** and **spyware**?
- What's the difference between **hard** and **soft bounce-backs**?
- What are **pop-ups**?
- What's a **banner ad**?
- What's a **tracking cookie**?

SUMMARY

Internet marketing can help the non-Web-based marketer, as well as the dot-com. The four marketing domains define Internet marketing activity. Create a user-friendly site and a good address for your home page. Steer clear of anti-spam and anti-spyware laws, and you'll keep your customers coming back.

KEY TERMS

Banner ad	An ad that appears on a major Web site or service.
Blog	An online journal.
E-zine or Webzine	An Internet publication, similar to a magazine.
Hard bounce-back	A notice that a message was undeliverable.
Header block	Block of text, preceding data that is sent across a network, that contains source and destination addresses, as well as data that describes the content of the message.
Key term	A word people use in searching for Web sites, which you can pay to have your message linked to.
META tag	Instructions to Web browsers.
Netiquette	Internet etiquette.
Netizen	Internet citizen.
Pop-up blocker	Programs to detect and remove tracking cookies.
Pop-ups	Promotional windows that open, especially while you are leaving a site.

Shopping cart	An online shopping cart.
Soft bounce-back	An undeliverable message resulting from some kind of temporary problem.
Spam	Junk e-mails.
Spyware and adware	Computer code that goes into personal computers and collects information about their users, mainly for marketing purposes.
Stickiness	The term Web marketers use to describe a site that keeps people coming back.
Tracking cookies	Small text files that Web-site operators and third-party companies that do Web advertising place on a user's computer.
URL	A Web address.
Viral marketing	An inexpensive way of getting word-of-mouth advertising.
Webcast	Similar to a broadcast, but on the Internet rather than television or radio.

ASSESS YOUR UNDERSTANDING

Go to www.wiley.com/college/Hiam to evaluate your knowledge of the basics of internet marketing.

Measure your learning by comparing pre-test and post-test results.

Summary Questions

1. eBay is an example of which marketing domain?
   (a) B to C
   (b) C to B
   (c) B to B
   (d) C to C

2. High-resolution photo files are the best choice for Web sites. True or false?

3. Which is probably **not** a good idea for your Web site?
   (a) Changing the content often
   (b) An online shopping cart
   (c) Using streaming video for sales promotions
   (d) Stock photography of people

4. Using your own domain and ISP will make your site seem more professional. True or false?

5. How many clicks a day, in general, do you need for an effective Web presence?
   (a) 100
   (b) 500
   (c) 1000
   (d) 5000

6. All click rates are not created equal. True or false?

7. What is viral marketing?
   (a) Spreading viruses through e-mails
   (b) An online form of word-of-mouth
   (c) Using bots and spiders to track your customer's purchases

8. Your banner ads should include a call to action. True or false?

9. The best e-mail is a personal communication with a customer you know. True or false?

10. What are the essentials of a good Web address?

    (a) Relates to your business or brand

    (b) Memorable

    (c) Clever

    (d) Not trademarked by somebody else

Review Questions

1. What distinguishes spam from e-mails consumers want to receive? What U.S. law regulates spam?

2. Name three things that will give your Web site low stickiness.

3. How much do business-to-business marketers typically budget for Web advertising?

Applying This Chapter

1. Explain how to give your Web site high visibility in search engines.

2. How is the Internet helping marketers to improve their contacts with customers?

3. You own a small business that sells flooring and tile. What are some specific ways you could take advantage of the Internet to improve sales and customer relationships?

Purebred Pupdates

If you breed dogs for a living and you hire one of your customers to create a blog with daily updates about her experiences with raising purebred puppies, what marketing domain does this fall under? Which domain is being used if you link this blog to your own site and people write in, asking for more information about the dogs you have available?

A Better Banner

Which do you think sounds like a better banner advertisement for your speakers' bureau: "Click here to find out the 10 most frequent mistakes public speakers make" or "Our highly trained speakers get the most repeat bookings!" Explain why you preferred one over the other.

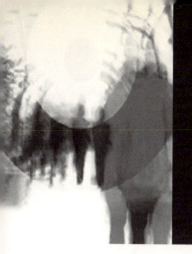

GLOSSARY

Aftermarket customer   Those who purchase spare parts for a piece of machinery.

Attitudes   Predispositions to behave in certain ways in response to a given stimulus.

Background   Explanatory communication that a journalist agrees will not be attributed to the source.

Backward integration   When a retailer takes over the wholesaling and manufacturing tasks.

Balanced mix approach   A marketing approach that uses a combination of informational and emotional appeals.

Banner ad   An ad that appears on a major Web site or service.

Base sales   What you can reasonably count on if you maintain the status quo in your marketing.

Blog   An online journal or web log.

Brand   Any brand name, term, sign, symbol, design, or a combination of these that is intended to identify the goods or services of one seller or group of sellers and to differentiate them from competitors.

Brand equity   Building the value of your brand.

Brand mark   That part of the brand that is recognized but is not utterable, such as a symbol, design, or distinctive coloring or lettering.

Brand names   The part of the brand that can be vocalized.

Breadth   Alternatives you give the customer across categories.

Buildup forecasts   These predictions go from the specific to the general, or from the bottom up.

Call centers   Central collections of equipment and staff for handling incoming and/or outgoing calls more efficiently.

Caption   Copy attached to the visual to explain or discuss that visual.

Category appraisal   A research technique that seeks new product opportunities within an existing category by finding out what makes the category "tick."

Champions   Customers who love a product and will champion it to people they know.

Channel manager   The driving force of the channel.

Claims table   A way to compare yourself to your competitors, through the eyes of your customers.

Coattails strategy   A promotional device for replacing an old product with a new one.

Competitive pricing   Pricing relative to an important competitor or set of competitors.

Competitive strategy   Used when the majority of prospects have tried at least one competitor's product.

Comps   The design stage preceding a final version of the design.

Concentration strategy   Targeting only one segment of the market.

Concept   A creative mix of merchandising strategy and atmosphere that you can use to give your store higher-than-average drawing power.

Consumer socialization   How people learn about products and services by taking part in social interactions with other people.

Conventional channels   Channel members who are working independently without a central leader.

Copy or body copy   The main text, set in a readable size, like what printers use in the main text of a book or magazine.

Copyright   Legal protection for writing, artwork, performances, and software.

Cost-based pricing   Using your costs as the only basis for your pricing without taking other factors into consideration.

Cost per thousand readers   The cost of buying an ad divided by the number of readers who read the publication, then multiplied by 1000.

Coupon   Any certificate entitling the holder to a reduced price.

Customer perception   How the customer sees the category, and what matters when determining a market share strategy.

Customer turnover rate   The percent of customers who leave each year

Decision influencers   People who exert strong influence over other people's opinions.

Demographics   Statistics — such as age, gender, or income — that give information about a population.

Demonstration strategy   Leverages the fundamental appeal of the product itself by simply making that product available to prospects.

Depth   Alternatives you give the customer within any single category.

Direct mail   The use of personalized sales letters.

Direct marketing   When the consumer purchases directly from the manufacturer.

Direct-response ad   Asks readers to take a measurable action like call, fax, or go to a store.

Dummy   A form of comp that simulates the look and feel of the final design.

Dumping   Buying your way into a market by dumping a lot of product into that market at artificially low prices.

Emotional approach   A marketing approach that pushes emotional instead of rational buttons.

End user   Those who purchase products produced by OEMs.

Exclusive distribution   When you cherry pick to find the best intermediaries and customers.

Experimental research   Finding information about a basic problem through the use of a small-scale simulated program designed to test a specific research hypothesis.

E-zine or Webzine   An Internet publication, similar to a magazine.

Fact base   The information you need to accomplish your purposes.

Five P's or Marketing Mix   Where marketers focus their attention.

Focus groups   Potential or actual customers who discuss your product while a trained moderator guides their conversation.

Font   A particular size and style of a typeface design (such as 10-point, bold, Times New Roman).

Forward integration   When a manufacturer owns the various members of its channel network.

Frequency   How many times viewers see your ad.

Gross rating point (GRP)   The total rating points achieved by your media schedule.

Hard bounce-back   Notice that a message was undeliverable.

Header block   Block of text, preceding data that is sent across a network, which contains source and destination addresses, as well as data that describes the content of the message.

Headline   The large-print words that first attract the eye, usually at the top of the page.

High-involvement decision   A high-involvement decision is very important to you. It's tied up with your ego and self-image, and has either financial, social, or psychological risk.

Hook   The thing that makes a story newsworthy.

Horizontal channel system   When two companies get together and establish a relationship to work with each other, usually because they do not have the capital or the technical or production know-how to market their products themselves.

Image strategy   A strategy that presents a good image of your brand, product, service, or business.

Impact scenario   A realistic story about the premium and its user in which the premium somehow affects that user's purchase behavior.

Inbound telemarketing   Customers call you in response to direct-response advertising.

Indicator forecasts   This forecasting method links your forecast to economic indicators that ought to vary with sales.

Indifference zone   The difference between the customer's desired price and a noticeably higher price.

Influence point   Each customer interaction, exposure, or contact.

Information advantage   Insight into the market that your competitors do not have.

Informational approach   Used if your customers buy in a rational manner.

Information parity   When you know as much as your leading competitors know.

Information strategy   Communicates facts that make you appealing.

Intensity   The extent of your geographic coverage of the market.

Intensive distribution strategy   This attempts to put every customer within reach of your products by using as many intermediaries and layers as needed to create maximum coverage.

Key term   A word people use in searching for Web sites, which you can pay to have your message linked to.

Lifestyle   A pattern of attitudes, interests, and opinions held by a person.

Lifestyle   A set of attitudes, interests, and opinions of the potential customer.

Lift   The increase in sales of a product attributable to POP marketing.

Limited-line retailing   A strategy emphasizing depth over variety.

Limit pricing   Pricing so agressively that it locks other competitors out of a market.

Local advertising   Advertising that is focused on a specific city or county.

Low-involvement decision   A routine purchase — the opposite of a high-involvement decision.

Market   A group of potential buyers with needs and wants and the purchasing power to satisfy them.

Market expansion   Increasing the overall market for whatever it is you do.

Market expansion strategy   The most common marketing strategy, with two variants: You can expand your market by finding new customers for your current products or you can try to sell new products to your existing customers and market.

Marketing program   Based on a marketing strategy, and shows all the coordinated activities that together make up the tactics.

Marketing strategy   The big-picture idea driving your success.

Market offerings   The selection of goods and services available for purchase in the marketplace.

Market segmentation strategy   A specialization strategy in which you target and cater to (specialize in) just one narrow type or group of customer.

Market share   Your sales as a percentage of total sales for your product category in your market (or in your market segment if you use a segmentation strategy too).

Market share strategy   A strategy that relies on market share as your competitive advantage.

Media schedule   All the times you run an ad over a specific period.

Merchandising strategy   The selection and assortment of products offered.

Meta-tag   Instructions to Web browsers.

Morphemes   Meaningful components for a made-up name.

Motivational strategy   Builds a compelling argument or feeling that should lead prospects to take action and make a purchase.

Motives   A reason for behavior that triggers purchasing activity.

Multibase segmentation   Segmenting your market, using more than one basis.

Multiple-scenario forecasts   You base these forecasts on what-if stories. They start with a straight-line forecast in which you assume that your sales will grow by the same percentage next year as they did last year. Then you make up what-if stories and project their impact on your plan to create a variety of alternative projections.

Multisegment strategy   Targeting a new, unreached segment of your market.

Need   A basic deficiency that is outside the marketer's control. You may need clothes, but you want to buy the Polo label.

Netiquette   Internet etiquette.

Netizen   Internet citizen.

Objectives   The quantified, measurable versions of your strategies.

Observation   Gathering data by watching people.

OEM   Original Equipment Manufacturer.

Off the record   Not for publication.

On the record   Communication with a journalist that you agree may appear in the media, with direct attribution to the source.

Opinion leader   A person who is part of your reference group who sets the trends for buying behavior for the group.

Organizational marketing   Selling goods and services to consumers who are themselves in need of goods and services to run their own businesses.

Outdoor advertising   A wide variety of advertising, including signs, posters, roadside billboards, and indoor signs, flags, and banners.

Out-of-home advertising   The general outdoor advertising category. This category includes signs, flags, banners, bumper stickers, transit advertising, and even T-shirts, along with the traditional billboard formats.

Packaging   Provides protection, containment, communication and utility for the product.

Parallel pricing   Mirroring competitor's prices.

Patent   This legally protects a design.

Penetration pricing   Accepting a lower profit margin and pricing relatively low in the introduction of a product. It generates higher sales and helps the product get established in the market quickly.

Personal selling   Selling face to face.

Pioneering strategy   Used when the majority of prospects are unfamiliar with the product

Placeholding strategy   Using *product lines* to create clear product niches and hold them for replacement products.

Planogram   Diagrams showing how to lay out and display a store's merchandise.

Point of purchase   The time and place at which the purchase is made.

Point-of-purchase marketing   Doing whatever advertising is necessary to sway the consumer your way at the time and place of their purchase.

Pop-up blocker   Programs to detect and remove tracking cookies.

Pop-ups   Promotional windows that open, especially while you are leaving a site.

Positioning   A strategic management decision that determines the place a product should occupy in a given market — its market niche; designing the company's offering and image to occupy a distinctive place in the target market's mind.

Positioning statement   A detailed (but readable) statement of how you want customers to think and feel about your product.

Positioning strategy   A positioning strategy takes a psychological approach to marketing, by getting people to see your product in a favorable light.

Premium   Any product with a marketing message somewhere on it that you give away to customers or sell at a discount as a reward for doing business with you.

Premium promotion   When you give the customer something extra for buying something

Press release   A short document designed for journalists who want to call to get more information or to arrange an interview about a story.

Prestige pricing   Using a high price to signal quality.

Pretesting   Exposing people to the ad in a controlled setting and measuring their reactions to it.

Price bundling   When you group similar or complementary products and charge a total price that is lower than if they were sold separately.

Price fixing   Business competitors agreeing informally to push the price of a product as high as possible, leading to great profits for all sellers.

Price lining   Keeping pricing consistent with product positions in your product line.

Price sensitivity   The degree to which purchases are affected by price level.

Price signaling   Announcing a planned price increase.

Price squeezing   Setting wholesale prices too high for small-sized orders, which drives independent or small-size retailers out of business.

Primary research   Gathering data by observing people to see how they behave or by asking them for verbal or written answers to questions.

Producers and manufacturers   These firms extract, grow, or make products. Firms range from a one-person operation to a multinational corporation with several thousand people that generates billions of dollars in sales.

Product concept   A synthesis or description of a product idea that reflects the core element of the proposed product.

Product differentiation   The attempt to distinguish your product in some tangible or intangible way from that of all the others in the eyes of customers.

Product lifecycle concept (PLC)   A framework for planning the management of products.

Product line   Any logical grouping of products offered to customers.

Public relations   The active pursuit of publicity for marketing purposes.

Pull or draw   The thing that attracts shoppers to your retail establishment.

Pull power   The ability of a marketing communication to draw people to a place or event.

Qualifying   Gathering enough information about someone or some business to make sure he or she fits a profile of a good customer.

Qualitative research   Research that involves qualitative analysis, to answer the question "why."

Quality strategies   Using quality as your competitive advantage when marketing.

Quantitative research   Research that involves quantitative analysis, to answer the question "what happened."

Rate sheet   A table listing the prices of ads by size of ad and also showing the discount rate per ad if you buy multiple ads instead of just a single one.

Reach   Number of viewers

Rebate   A refund of a fixed amount of money for a specified time.

Redemption rate   The percentage of people who use the coupon.

Reexamination rates   The average number of times viewers bother to read the same outdoor ad.

Reference groups   An informal or formal group of people with whom you identify.

Reminder strategy   A reminder strategy is good when you think people would buy your product if they thought of it — but may not without a reminder.

Repositioning   Changing the market's perceptions of a product or brand so that it can compete more effectively in its present market or in other market segments.

Retailers   Retailing includes all activities necessary to market consumer goods and services to ultimate users who are buying for individual or family needs, as opposed to business, institutional, or industrial use.

Retentive strategy   Used when attracting new customers costs more than keeping old customers.

Roughs   Full-size sketches with headlines and subheads drawn carefully enough to give the feel of a particular font and **style** (the appearance of the printed letters).

Routinization The right products are always found in places where the consumer expects to find them, comparisons are possible, prices are marked, and payment methods are available.

Sales promotion A marketing initiative that's designed to boost sales.

Sales representatives Reps who work on commission.

Saturation When replacement products are being sold.

Schedule Shows when ads for each magazine issue need to be placed and what the topics of future issues will be.

Scrambled merchandising strategy Using unconventional combinations of product lines.

Secondary research Data that has already been collected and published by someone else.

Segmenting markets Targeting your efforts to cover a narrow market

Selective distribution strategy When you target the most desirable areas or members of your market.

Self-liquidating premium A premium that customers end up covering your costs for.

Service mark A service name, which U.S. law treats similarly to a trademark.

Service recovery Repairing a customer service problem.

Shopcart An online shopping cart.

SIC codes Standard Industrial Classification codes, published by the United States government, to classify business firms by the main product or service that they provide.

Signature The company's trademarked version of its name. Often, advertisers use a logo design that features a brand name in a distinctive font and style. The signature is a written equivalent to the trademark's visual identity.

Simplicity marketing This strategy positions a company as simpler, easier to understand, and easier to use or work with than the competition.

Situation analysis   Examines the context, looking at trends, customer preferences, competitor strengths and weaknesses, and anything else that may impact sales.

Skimming the market   Selling the product at such a high price that only the very wealthy or least price-sensitive customers will buy it.

SKU (stock keeping unit)   A unique inventory code for each item you stock.

Slogan   An optional element consisting of a (hopefully) short phrase evoking the spirit or personality of the brand.

Socialization agent   A person who influences you.

Soft bounce-back   An undeliverable message resulting from some kind of temporary problem.

Spam   Junk e-mails.

Special offers   Temporary inducements to make customers buy on the basis of price or price-related factors.

Spyware and adware   Computer code that goes into personal computers and collects information about their users, mainly for marketing purposes.

Stickiness   The term Web marketers use to describe a site that keeps people coming back.

Stopping power   The ability of an advertisement or other marketing communication to stop people in their tracks, to make them sit up and take notice.

Storyboard   A way to show the key visual images of film, using pictures in sequence.

Strategy   A big picture vision of what you are trying to do.

Subhead   The optional addition to the headline to provide more detail, also in large (but not quite as large) print.

Survey research   Asking people what they think.

Sweeps   Quarterly surveys of viewership in major media markets.

Targeting markets   A process by which one or more target markets, or segments, are chosen from the rest.

Thumbnails   The rough sketches designers use to describe layout concepts.

Time-period forecasts   Work by week or month, estimating the size of sales in each time period, and then add these estimates for the entire year. This approach helps when your program or the market isn't constant across the entire year.

Tracking-cookies   Small text files that Web-site operators and third-party companies that do Web advertising place on a user's computer.

Trade discounts   The amount your intermediaries receive out of the total price.

Trademark   A tangible product's legally protected name and/or visual symbol.

Trade name   Protection for a business name or logo.

Traffic   The flow of target customers near enough to the store for its external displays and local advertising to draw them in.

Traffic counts   The number of vehicles per day — or day and night if you illuminate your poster — multiplied by the average occupancy of a vehicle.

Typeface   The distinctive design of letters.

Undifferentiated market   One in which nearly everyone consumes products that are perceived as almost identical.

Unique Selling Proposition (USP)   The feature that makes your product stand out from the competition.

URL   A Web address.

Value-based pricing   When only the customer's perception determines your price.

Vertical marketing system   When a member of the channel, typically the manufacturer, takes a leadership role and coordinates the efforts of the channel so that mutually beneficial goals can be attained.

VIEW   Acronym that stands for Visibility, Information, Emotion, and Workability; a framework for helpful tips when designing a package.

Viral marketing   An inexpensive way of getting word-of-mouth advertising.

Visual   An illustration that makes a visual statement.

Want   What marketers try to influence by trying to get the consumer to choose your product or service instead of someone else's.

Webcast   Similar to a broadcast, but on the Internet rather than television or radio.

Wholesalers   Wholesaling includes all activities required to market goods and services to businesses, institutions, or industrial users who are buying for resale or to produce and market other products and services.

Word of mouth (WOM)   What consumers tell each other about your products or services.

INDEX

A

Abercrombie & Fitch, selling lifestyle, 179
Administered vertical marketing systems (VMS), structure of, 155–56
Advertising
    attracting customers with, 4
    budgeting Web, 298–99
    buying print, 249–50
    designing effective print, 251–54
    generating sales leads with, 240–41
    local, 243
    more vs. less effective styles of, 266
    print, 249
    pull power and, 231
    radio, 263–64
    selecting font and typeface for print, 254–56
    television, 264–66
    verifying efficacy of print, 250–51
    video production tips for, 266–68
Advertising life-cycle model, marketing strategies for, 25–26
Adware
    defined, 317
    regulating/stopping, 313–14
Aelera Corporation (research firm), marketing program efficacy survey, 41
Aftermarket customers
    defined, 90
    segmenting business markets and, 82–83
Aging, marketers response to, 105
Allstate insurance, segmenting car insurance markets, 80
Alternatives
    consumers identifying and evaluating, 61
    price and, 198
American Marine (Grand Bank yachts), marketing problems of, 11–12
Animation, on Web sites, 302–3
Anti-spyware, Internet use and, 314
Appearance, customer retention and, 236
Apple iPod, pricing and, 199
Application, positioning by, 135
Attention step, information processing and, 60
Attitudes
    consumer buying behavior and, 50
    defined, 66, 90
    segmenting consumer markets by, 79–80

Attributes, positioning by, 135
Audience participation, stopping power and, 230
Avon, generating sales leads, 242
Awnings, advertising on, 260

B

Baby Boomers, behavior differences of, 49
Background
    defined, 292
    offering journalists, 280
Backward integration
    in corporate VMS, 156
    defined, 166
Bait, direct mail and, 186
Balanced mix approach
    defined, 14
    overview, 3–4
Banner ads (Web)
    defined, 316
    designing and placing, 315–16
    using carefully, 297
Banners, advertising on, 260
Base sales
    defined, 14
    making marketing program improvements and, 11
Bid rigging, avoiding, 214
Billboards, advertising on, 260–62
Blogs
    defined, 316
    sharing product/service information on, 300
Body copy
    defined, 271
    designing effective print ads and, 252
Boutiques, retailing and, 173
Brand
    defined, 140
    giving personality to, 227–29
    protecting product identity with, 128–29
    Web address and, 306
Brand equity
    defined, 243
    pricing and, 196
    vs. pull power, 231
Branding strategies, types of, 128
Brand loyalty, segmenting consumer markets by, 79

Brand mark
    defined, 140
    protecting product identity with, 128–29
Brand names
    defined, 140
    protecting product identity with, 128–29
Breadth
    defined, 140
    managing product lines and, 126–27
Brochures, *see also* Print ads
    designing, 256–58
    planning and budgeting for, 30
Budget
    planning brochure/informational materials, 30
    planning publicity, 29
    POP allocation and, 182
    Web marketing and, 30, 298–99
Buildup forecasts
    defined, 42
    projecting sales with, 40
Bulk e-mail, sending, 313
Business analysis, screening product development
    ideas with, 122
Business markets, segmenting, 76, 82–85
Business personalities, buying behavior and, 55
Business-to-business marketers
    conducting observation, 97
    informational approach and, 3
Buyer size, segmenting business markets and, 83
Buyer's remorse, consumer decision process and, 62
Buying behavior, *see* Consumer buying behavior;
    Organizational buying behavior
Buying factors, segmenting business markets and, 83
Buying habits, segmenting consumer markets by, 79

C

Call centers
    database access at, 184
    defined, 190
Call to action, direct mail and, 187
Canned presentations, using, 242
Captions
    defined, 271
    designing effective print ads and, 252
Cash basis, projecting on, 39
Catalog shopping, growth of, 157
Category appraisal
    defined, 140
    generating new product ideas and, 121
Chain stores, retailing and, 172
Champions
    defined, 140
    products lacking, 134

Channel captains
    in administered VMS, 155–56
    channel communication and, 158
    defined, 166
Channel-management process, *see* Distribution-
    channel management
Channel-marketing systems, types of, 155–56
Channel members
    evaluating and selecting, 162–64
    evaluating performance of, 164–65
    power plays between, 159
    producers and manufacturers, 148–49
    retailers, 149–50
    roles of, 158
    specifying distribution tasks of, 161–62
    types of, 146
    wholesalers, 150–51
Channel objectives, establishing, 161
Channels, *see* Distribution channels
Characteristics, segmenting by, 76
Chats, adding to Web sites, 304–5
Children
    ethics of marketing to, 4
    interviewing, 102
Claims tables
    defined, 114
    making competitive comparisons with, 105–6
Cleanliness, customer retention and, 236
Coattails strategy
    defined, 140
    replacing products using, 138
Cognitive dissonance, postpurchase anxiety and, 62
Commercialization, screening product development
    ideas with, 123
Communication
    developing sales presentations/consultations,
        242–43
    giving products personalities with, 227–29
    good *vs.* bad, 222
    message clarity and, 222–25
    pull power, 231
    stopping power, 229–31
    using visuals for, 225–27
    writing for, 225
Compensation, for sales reps, 238–39
Competitions, as promotions, 287
Competitive comparisons, using for research, 105–6
Competitive pricing
    defined, 216
    types of, 205–6
Competitive strategy
    defined, 42
    product stages and, 25

Competitor Analysis Table, creating, 32
Competitors
    avoiding imitating, 28–29
    gathering information on, 31–32
    generating new product ideas from, 121
    illegal acts against, 214
    imitating in marketing strategy, 34
    positioning by, 135
    price wars and, 205
    pricing and, 204
    researching comparison with, 100
    skimming the market and, 212
Complaints, converting to purchases, 236
Comps
    defined, 271
    designing effective print ads and, 254
Concentration strategy
    defined, 90
    targeting markets and, 87
Concept
    defined, 190
    retail success and, 178
Consistency, importance of in marketing program,
    11–12
Constructional linguistics, naming products and,
    125–26
Consumer buying behavior, *see also* Organizational
    buying behavior
    external influences on, 51–54
    internal influences on, 48–50
    vs. organizational buying behavior, 55
    understanding influences on, 48
Consumer decision process
    identifying and evaluating alternatives, 61
    information processing, 60–61
    information search, 59–60
    need identification, 58–59
    postpurchase behavior, 62
    product/service/outlet selection, 61–62
    purchase decision, 62
    understanding, 56–58
Consumer markets, methods of
    segmenting, 76
Consumer socialization
    consumer buying behavior and, 49–50
    defined, 66
Contact information, in press releases, 281–82
Contractual vertical marketing systems (VMS), struc-
    ture of, 156
Controls, setting up performance tracking, 41
Conventional channels
    defined, 166
    structure of, 155

Cookies
    defined, 317
    using properly, 314
Cooperative advertising, pricing and, 208
Copy
    defined, 271
    designing effective print tabs and, 252
Copyright
    defined, 140
    protecting product with, 129
Corporate vertical marketing systems (VMS), struc-
    ture of, 156
Cost-based pricing, 210
Cost per thousand readers
    buying print ads and, 250
    defined, 271
Costs
    analyzing marketing program, 36–37
    of coupon programs, 209
    evaluating marketing plan, 28–29
    price and, 202
    projecting for marketing program, 39–41
Coupons
    boosting sales with, 286–88
    defined, 216
    pricing and, 207–8
    redemption rates and costs of, 208–9
Crayola, Web contests, 305
Creative twists, stopping power and, 230
Cross-based pricing, 216
Cross-selling, improving marketing program and, 13
Culture, consumer buying behavior and, 52
Curiosity, stopping power and, 230
Customer, analyzing for distribution process, 160–61
Customer behavior, preparing marketing strategy and,
    33
Customer feedback, inviting on Web sites, 303
Customer focus, marketing program and, 10
Customer perception
    defined, 42
    market-share strategy and, 22–23
Customer profiles, using for research, 105
Customer reactions, researching to understand,
    107–10
Customer records, using for research, 106
Customer retention
    customer satisfaction and, 98
    environment and accessibility and, 235–36
Customers
    consulting on marketing program, 12
    entertaining for research, 100–101
    generating new product ideas with, 121

Continued

Customers (*Continued*)
    price perceptions, 203, 210–11
    reducing distribution channels to, 153–55
    targeting narrow groups of, 21–22
    tracking with databases, 184
    understanding, 2
    ways of attracting, 4–5
Customer satisfaction
    gauging in survey research, 98–99
    importance of, 97
    maintaining, 13
    problems exaggerating in survey research, 98
Customer turnover rate
    defined, 243
    service recovery and, 233–36

D

Databases
    management on Web sites, 303
    telemarketing and, 188
    tracking customers with, 184
Debriefing, dissatisfied customers, 13
Decision influencers
    consumer buying behavior and, 53
    cultivating, 285–286
    defined, 292
Decision-making
    analyzing information needs of, 108
    researching for better, 107
Decision process, *see* Consumer decision process;
        Organizational buying process
Declined stage, 124
Defectors, interviewing, 102
Demand, identifying viable market segments and,
    86–87
Demographic market segments, 78–79
Demographics
    consumer buying behavior and, 51–52
    defined, 66, 114
    using for research, 104–5
Demonstration strategy
    defined, 243
    designing communication and, 224
Department stores
    general merchandise strategy and, 174
    retailing and, 172
Depth
    defined, 140
    managing product lines and, 126–27
Details, importance of in marketing plan, 28
Direct mail
    defined, 190
    using, 186–87

Direct marketing, *see also* Direct mail; Direct-response
        ads
    defined, 190
    overview, 183–84
    telemarketing, 187–88
    tips for successful, 189–90
    tracking customers with databases and, 184
Direct-response ads
    defined, 190, 271
    using, 185–86
    verifying efficacy of print ads and, 250–51
Discount houses, retailing and, 172
Displays, designing POP, 181–82
Distribution-channel management, *see also* Channel
        members
    analyzing consumer and, 160–61
    establishing channel objectives and, 161
    evaluating channel member performance and,
        164–65
    evaluating/selecting intermediaries
        and, 162–64
    overview, 146
    specifying distribution tasks and, 161–62
    steps of, 160
Distribution channels
    communication in, 158
    computing prices and trade discounts in complex,
        200–202
    design strategies, 156–57
    functions of, 146–47
    handling conflict within, 159
    improving efficiency of, 151–52
    member roles in, 158
    reducing, 153–55
    routinization in, 148
    type of channel members, 148–51
    types of channel-marketing systems, 155–56
Distributors, finding, 152–53
Domain name
    selecting, 306–7
    on Web sites, 303
Drama, stopping power and, 230
Draw (pull)
    defined, 191
    retail success and, 178
Drucker, Peter (management guru), defining market-
        ing, 9
Dummy
    defined, 271
    designing effective print ads and, 254
Dumping
    defined, 216
    understanding, 215

E

Economic accessibility, identifying viable market
    segments and, 87
Education, segmenting consumer markets by, 78
E-mail
    conducting primary research via, 101
    understanding etiquette for, 311–14
    using lists for, 312
Emotional appeal
    on packaging or label, 131
    stopping power and, 230
Emotional approach
    defined, 14
    overview, 3
    television advertising and, 265–66
End users
    defined, 90
    segmenting business markets and, 82
E-publishing, using, 314–15
Errors, in press releases, 281
Ethics, of marketing to children, 4
Exclusive distribution
    defined, 166
    evaluating efficacy of, 163
Exclusive distributors brand policy, 128
Executive summary, writing, 34–35
Expenses, *see* Costs
Experimental research
    conducting, 99–100
    defined, 114
Exposure step, information processing and, 60
External influences, on consumer buying behavior,
    51–54
E-zines
    defined, 316
    using, 314–15

F

Fact base
    defined, 271
    designing brochures and, 257
Family, consumer buying behavior and, 54
Family life cycle, segmenting consumer markets by,
    78
Financial data, marketing plan and, 27
Five Ps
    analyzing in marketing program, 38–39
    defined, 14
    understanding, 5–7
Flags, advertising on, 260
Focus groups
    defined, 114
    qualitative research and, 96

Font
    defined, 271
    selecting for print ads, 254
Ford Mustang, name strategy of, 126
Foreign markets, generating new product ideas in, 121
Forward integration, 166
Franchises, retailing and, 172
Free samples, attracting customers with, 4
Frequency
    billboard advertising and, 261–62
    defined, 271
Frequent user/loyalty incentive, as promotions, 287
Functional discounts, setting price and, 200–202

G

Gateway, retail efforts of, 74
General merchandise retailing strategy, 174–75
Geographic mobility, segmenting consumer markets
    by, 78
Geography
    segmenting business markets and, 83
    segmenting consumer markets and, 77
Google, buying search engine visibility with, 307
Government databases, using for research, 103–4
Grand Bank yachts (American Marine), marketing
    problems of, 11–12
Grocery stores, scrambled merchandising strategies
    and, 175–76
Gross rating point (GRP)
    buying television advertising time and, 269–70
    defined, 271
Growth stage, 124

H

Hard bounce-back
    defined, 316
    sending e-mail and, 313
Header block
    defined, 316
    using on Web sites, 309
Headline
    defined, 271
    designing effective print ads and, 252
High-involvement decision
    consumer buying behavior and, 51
    defined, 66
Hooks
    defined, 292
    in direct mail, 187
    generating publicity with, 278–79
Horizontal channel systems
    defined, 166
    structure of, 156

Housing industry, multibase segmentation and, 84–85
Hypermarkets, general merchandise strategy and, 175

I

Ideas
    generating new product, 121–22
    researching for better, 107
    screening product development, 122–23
Image, setting strategic price objectives and, 204
Image strategy
    defined, 243
    designing communication and, 224
Impact, communication and, 222
Impact scenario
    defined, 292
    using premiums and, 288–90
Inbound telemarketing
    defined, 191
    toll-free numbers and, 188
Indicator forecasts
    defined, 42
    projecting sales with, 40–41
Indifference zone
    coupons and, 209
    defined, 216
    pricing and, 203
Influence points
    analyzing for marketing program, 35–36
    defined, 15
    identifying for marketing program, 9
    marketing messages covering, 222–24
Influences
    on consumer buying behavior, 48
    external, on consumer buying behavior, 51–54
    internal, on consumer buying behavior, 48–50
Information
    collecting telemarketing, 187
    industrial buyer sources of, 65
    on packaging, 131
    processing in decision making process, 60–61
    searching for in decision making process, 59–60
    wholesalers offering, 150
Information advantage
    defined, 42
    in situation analysis, 31
Informational approach
    defined, 15
    overview, 3
Informational materials, planning and budgeting for, 30
Information parity
    defined, 42
    in situation analysis, 31

Information strategy
    defined, 243
    designing communication and, 224
Insurance industry, bid rigging and, 214
Intensity
    defined, 166
    evaluating distribution strategy and, 162–63
Intensive distribution strategy, 166
Internal influences, on consumer buying behavior, 48–50
Internet, see also Web sites
    budgeting marketing on, 298–99
    marketing domains on, 299–300
    possibilities of, 297–98
Introduction stage, 124
Inventory control, wholesalers and, 150

J

Johnson & Johnson Tylenol, effective public relations for, 277
Journalists
    creating hooks for, 278–79
    establishing relationships with, 279–80
    preparing press releases for, 281–83
Juicy Fruit gum, using focus groups for, 113

K

Key terms
    defined, 316
    using carefully, 297

L

Legal issues
    e-mail subject line and, 313
    pricing and, 213–15
Levi Strauss & Co., direct-marketing initiative of, 183–84
Licensing, generating new product ideas from, 121
Lifestyle
    consumer buying behavior and, 50
    defined, 66, 90
    retailers selling, 179
    segmenting consumer markets by, 80
Lift
    defined, 191
    POP marketing and, 182
Limited-line retailing
    defined, 191
    overview, 175
Limit pricing
    defined, 216
    understanding, 215

Links, on Web sites, 303
Local advertising
    defined, 243
    pull power and, 231
Location
    billboard advertising and, 262
    marketing mix and, 5–6, 7
    retailing and, 178
Low-involvement decision
    consumer buying behavior and, 51
    defined, 66

M

"Make 7-Up Yours" slogan, 3
Malls, retailing and, 173
Manufacturers, as channel members, 148–49
Manufacturers branding policy, 128
Manufacturing department
    generating new product ideas from, 122
    screening product development ideas with, 122
Market expansion
    defined, 15
    marketing strategies and, 9
Market-expansion strategy
    defined, 42, 90
    understanding, 20–21
Marketing
    defined, 2
    testing, 101–2
Marketing approaches, 3–4
Marketing development, screening product development ideas with, 122
Marketing domains, Internet, 299–300
Marketing mix
    defined, 14
    understanding, 5–7
Marketing plan
    breaking down, 29–30
    clarifying/quantifying objectives for, 30
    common ways of losing money and, 28–29
    core components of, 27–28
    preparing situation analysis and, 31–32
    screening product development ideas with, 123
Marketing program
    analyzing costs of, 36–37
    analyzing details of, 38–39
    analyzing influence points for, 35–36
    defined, 8
    demonstrating consistency in, 11–12
    focusing, 10
    identifying influence points for, 9
    identifying strengths for, 8
        keeping happy/satisfied customers and, 13
        making improvements to, 11
        marketing plan and, 27
        marketing strategy guiding, 24–26
        projecting expenses and revenues for, 39–41
        setting up performance tracking controls in, 41
        ways of maximizing, 12–13
Marketing strategy
    common flaws in, 33–34
    defined, 8, 15
    finding market and, 9
    as hub of marketing activities, 24–26
    marketing plan and, 27
    types of, 20–24
    writing, 32–33
Marketing territory, adjusting, 12
Market offerings
    consumer buying behavior and, 52
    defined, 66
Markets, see also Segmenting markets
    criteria for viable, 72
    defined, 15, 90
    identifying, 9
    segmenting business, 76, 82–85
    segmenting consumer, 76
Market-segmentation strategy, see also Segmenting markets
    defined, 42, 90
    overview, 72
    reasons for using, 75–76
    targeting markets and, 85–86
    understanding, 21–22
Market segments, see also Segmenting markets
    business, 82–85
    concentrating on single area of, 87
    demographic, 78–79
    factors involved in, 77
    gauging worth of, 86–87
    geographic, 77–78
    psychological, 79–81
    selecting target markets from, 88–90
    targeting new, 87–88
    usage, 79
Market share
    defined, 15, 43
    marketing strategies and, 9
    setting strategic price objectives and, 204
    trying to increase, 22–23
Market-share strategy
    defined, 43
    understanding, 22–23
Mary Kay cosmetics, generating sales leads, 242
Maturity stage, 124

Media
    buying print ads from, 249–50
    radio advertising, 263–64
Media data, using for research, 104
Media schedule
    buying television advertising time and, 269–70
    defined, 271
Merchandising strategies
    defined, 191
    general merchandise retailing, 174–75
    implementing, 177
    limited-line retailing, 175
    overview, 174
    price and quality, 176
    scrambled merchandising, 175–76
Merck Vioxx, lawsuits against, 137
Messages, see Communication
META tag
    defined, 316
    using on Web sites, 309
Mixed brand policy, 128
Modified rebuy, organizational buying behavior and, 56
Money, common ways of losing, 28–29
Morphemes
    defined, 140
    naming products with, 125–26
Motivational strategy
    defined, 244
    designing communication and, 224
Motives
    defined, 91
    need to understand consumer, 50
    organizational buyers and, 55
    segmenting consumer markets by, 80
Multibase segmentation
    of business markets, 84–85
    defined, 91
Multiple-scenario forecasts
    defined, 43
    projecting revenue/expenses with, 41
Multisegment strategy
    defined, 91
    targeting markets and, 87–88

N

NAICS (North American Industry Classification
        System) codes
    defined, 91
    segmenting business markets and, 83
Naming, products, 125–26
National origin, segmenting consumer markets by, 78

Needs
    ability to measure market segment, 86
    analyzing research, 106–11
    consumer motivation and, 50
    defined, 66
    identifying consumer, 58–59
    identifying in organizational buying process, 63
    price and, 197
    type of, 57
    vs. wants, 57
Netiquette
    defined, 316
    sending e-mail and, 311–14
Netizen
    being good, 314
    defined, 316
Networking, generating sales leads by, 242
Neuromarketing, controversy of, 60
New product development process, see Product
        development process
Newsletters
    attracting customers with, 4
    on Web sites, 304
New task, organizational buying behavior and, 56
Nielsen Television Index, television advertising time
        and, 269
Nonstore retailing, 173
North American Industry Classification System
        (NAICS) codes
    defined, 91
    segmenting business markets and, 83

O

Objectives
    clarifying/quantifying, 30
    defined, 43
    establishing channel, 161
    setting strategic price, 204–6
    writing marketing strategy and, 32–33
Observation
    conducting, 96–97
    defined, 114
Observation research, conducting, 101
Occupation, segmenting consumer markets by, 78
Odd-even pricing, quality sensitivity and, 210
OEM (original equipment manufacturers)
    defined, 91
    segmenting business markets and, 82
Off the record
    defined, 292
    talking to journalists and, 280
On the record

defined, 292
    talking to journalists and, 280
Opinion leaders
    consumer buying behavior and, 53
    defined, 66
Order processing, wholesalers and, 150
Order-routine specification, organizational buying
        process and, 65
Organizational buying behavior
    ability to predict, 55–56
    vs. consumer buying behavior, 55
    overview, 54
    types of, 56
Organizational buying process
    sources of information for, 65
    understanding, 63–65
Organizational marketing
    defined, 67
    understanding, 54–55
Original equipment manufacturers (OEM)
    defined, 91
    segmenting business markets and, 82
Outdoor advertising
    billboards, 260–62
    defined, 271
    overview, 259
    signs, 259–60
Outlets, consumer decision process about, 61–62
Out-of-home advertising, *see also* Outdoor advertising
    defined, 271
    overview, 259

P

Packaging
    defined, 140
    importance of, 129–31
    making effective, 131–32
Parallel pricing
    defined, 216
    legal issues of, 214
Patent
    defined, 140
    protecting product design with, 129
Patterns, violating expected, 230
Penetration pricing
    defined, 216
    new products and, 212
People, marketing mix and, 6, 7
Perception step, information processing and, 60
Performance review, organizational buying process
        and, 65
Personalities, giving products, 227–29

Personal selling
    defined, 244
    determining value of, 232–33
Pets.com, advertising spending, 251
Photographs, on Web sites, 302
Physical needs, 57
Pioneering strategy
    defined, 43
    product stages and, 25
Place, marketing mix and, 5–6, 7, *see also* Location
Place advantages, creating value through, 197
Placeholding strategy
    defined, 140
    replacing products using, 138
Planning research, 110–11, *see also* Marketing plan
Planograms
    defined, 191
    retailers using, 177
PLC (product life-cycle concept)
    defined, 140
    planning product management with, 124–25
Point-of-purchase (POP)
    defined, 140, 191
    designing displays for, 181–82
    encouraging sales at, 180
    packaging and, 130–31
    understanding, 182–83
Point-of-purchase decision-making process, 130
Point-of-purchase (POP) marketing
    defined, 43
    reminder strategy and, 23
    understanding, 24
Point-of-sale displays, as promotions, 288
Points of contact, marketing program and, 10
Pop-up blockers
    defined, 316
    Internet use and, 314
Pop-ups
    defined, 316
    regulating/stopping, 313–14
Positioning
    defined, 91, 140
    importance of effective, 134–35
    target markets and, 89
Positioning strategy
    communication objectives and, 222–23
    defined, 43, 244
    understanding, 24
Positive response, identifying viable market segments
        and, 87
Postpurchase anxiety, consumer decision process
        and, 62

Precise International, marketing Swiss Army Knife, 24
Predatory pricing, understanding, 215
Premium promotions
    defined, 292
    using/misusing, 288–90
Premiums
    benefits of, 209
    defined, 216, 292
    promoting sales with, 288–90
    quality strategy for, 290–91
Press releases
    defined, 292
    guidelines for writing, 281–83
Prestige pricing
    defined, 216
    using, 196
Pretesting
    defined, 271
    print tabs, 251
Price
    costs and, 202
    customers perceptions of, 210–11
    determining for new products, 212
    general approaches to, 206–7
    impact on sales, 197–98
    marketing mix and, 5, 7
    positioning by, 135
    profits and, 198–99
    as promotions, 287
    retailers setting, 200
    setting competitively, 205–6
    setting strategic objectives for, 204–6
    trade discounts and, 200–202
    understanding customer perception of, 203
    understanding secondary influences on, 203–4
    understanding strategies and trends, 196–97
Price bundling
    customer price perceptions and, 211
    defined, 216
Price fixing
    avoiding, 213
    defined, 216
Price lining
    customer price perceptions and, 210
    defined, 140, 216
    replacing products using, 139
Price promotions, boosting sales with, 286–88
Price sensitivity
    coupon redemption rates and, 208
    defined, 216
    indicators of, 197–98
    penetration pricing and, 212
    product quality and, 210

Price signaling
    avoiding, 213
    defined, 216
Price squeezing
    defined, 216
    understanding, 215
Price wars, competition and, 205
Pricing strategies, 176
Primary research, *see also* Research
    conducting experimental research, 99–100
    conducting observation, 96–97
    conducting survey research, 97–99
    defined, 114
    methods of, 100–102
    understanding, 96
Print ads
    designing brochures, 256–58
    designing effective, 251–54
    overview, 249
    selecting font and typeface for, 254–56
    verifying efficacy of, 250–51
Privacy, e-mail and, 312
Problem recognition, organizational buying process
        and, 63
Problems, common marketing strategy, 33–34
Procter & Gamble
    coupons and, 287
    Vicks 44 POP display, 181
Producers, as channel members, 148–49
Producers and Manufacturers, 166
Product attraction, marketing program and, 10
Product categories
    market-share strategy and, 22
    planning advertising/promotions by, 29
Product class, positioning by, 135
Product concept
    defined, 141
    testing, 122
Product demonstrations, attracting customers with, 4
Product development process
    generating new product ideas, 121–22
    overview, 119–20
    screening product development ideas, 122–23
Product development stage, 124
Product differentiation
    defined, 91
    targeting markets and, 85–86
    in undifferentiated markets, 73–74
Product life-cycle concept (PLC)
    defined, 140
    planning product management with, 124–25
Product-lined placeholding strategy, replacing prod-
        ucts using, 138

Product-line management, pricing and, 204
Product lines
    defined, 141
    designing and managing, 126–27
Product mix strategies
    overview, 133
    positioning, 134–35
    reasons for product modification, 133–34
Product placement, attracting customers
            with, 4
Products
    consumer decision process about, 61–62
    dealing with problems with, 137
    eliminating or replacing, 138–39
    giving personalities, 227–29
    introducing new, 119–25
    marketing mix and, 5, 7
    naming, 125–26
    pricing new, 212
    protecting with branding, 128–29
    reasons for eliminating, 135–37
    reasons for modifying, 133–34
    sharing information on blogs, 300
    understanding customers feelings/thoughts
            about, 2
Product specification, organizational buying process
            and, 63
Product stages, marketing strategies for, 25–26
Product user, positioning by, 135
Professional association meetings, attracting
            customers with, 4
Profits
    setting strategic price objectives and, 204
    ways of boosting, 198–99
Projecting, expenses and revenues for marketing
            program, 39–41
Promotions
    marketing mix and, 6, 7
    projecting for marketing plan, 29
    on Web sites, 303
Proposal solicitation, organizational buying process
            and, 64
Psychological market segments, 79–81
Psychological needs, 57
Publicity
    creating exciting, 283–84
    generating, 278–79
    planning and budgeting, 29
    role of, 277
    word of mouth, 284–86
Public relations (PR)
    cultivating media contacts for, 279–80
    defined, 292

    press releases, 281–83
    role of, 277–78
Pull (draw)
    defined, 191
    retail success and, 178
Pull power
    building traffic with, 231
    defined, 244
Purchase situations
    consumer buying behavior and, 51
    organizational buying behavior and, 56
    segmenting by, 76
    segmenting consumer markets by, 79
Purchasing decisions, informational vs. emotional
            dimensions of, 2

Q

Qualifying
    defined, 244
    generating sales leads and, 239–40
Qualitative research
    defined, 114
    primary research and, 96
Quality, price and, 196
Quality strategy
    defined, 43
    for premiums, 290–91
    retailers and, 176
    understanding, 23
Quantitative research
    defined, 114
    primary research and, 96
Questions, problematical in survey research, 98

R

Race, segmenting consumer markets by, 78
Radio, advertising on, 263–64
Rate sheet
    buying print ads and, 249
    defined, 271
Reach
    billboard advertising and, 261–62
    defined, 272
    of various media, 264
Realty Executives, compensating sales reps, 239
Rebates
    defined, 217
    pricing and, 207–8
Redemption rate
    defined, 217
    evaluating, 208–9

Reexamination rates
    defined, 272
    of outdoor ads, 262
Reference groups
    consumer buying behavior and, 53
    defined, 67
Referrals
    attracting customers with, 4
    improving marketing program and, 12
Religion, segmenting consumer markets by, 78
Reminder strategy
    defined, 43
    understanding, 23
Replacements, packaging selling, 131
Repositioning, 141
Research, *see also* Primary research; Secondary
        research
    activities involved in, 112–13
    analyzing needs of, 106–11
    generating new product ideas from, 122
    planning, 110–11
    type of, 112
Resources, preparing marketing strategy and, 33
Retailers
    as channel members, 149–50
    creative thinking and, 177–78
    defined, 166
    encouraging POP sales, 180
    setting price, 200
    store atmosphere and, 178–79
    types of, 172–73
Retention step, information processing and, 61
Retentive strategy
    defined, 43
    product stages and, 25
Retrieval and application step, information processing
        and, 61
Revenues
    projecting for marketing plan, 29
    projecting for marketing program, 39–41
Risks
    market-expansion strategy and, 20–21
    of product differentiation, 74
Rolling Rock beer, product positioning and, 89
Roughs
    defined, 272
    designing effective print ads and, 253–54
Routinization
    defined, 166
    need for, 148

S
Sales
    impact of pricing on, 197–98
    personal selling, 232–33
    pursuing retail, 177
    service recovery and, 233–36
    setting strategic price objectives and, 204
    wholesalers and, 150
Sales activities, breaking down for marketing
        plan, 29
Sales consultations, developing, 242–43
Sales department, generating new product ideas
        from, 122
Salesforce, organizing, 236–37
Sales leads, generating, 239–41
Sales presentations, developing, 242–43
Sales promotions
    choice of premiums and, 290–91
    defined, 292
    overview, 286
    premiums, 288–90
    using price promotions and coupons,
        286–88
Sales representatives
    compensating, 238–39
    defined, 244
    finding, 237–38
    organizing, 236–37
Sales/service process
    flowchart of, 234
    overview, 233
Saturation
    defined, 141
    eliminating products and, 136
Schedule, *see also* Media schedule
    buying print ads and, 249
    defined, 272
Scrambled merchandising strategy
    defined, 191
    overview, 175–76
Search engines, buying visibility on, 307–8
Secondary research, *see also* Research
    defined, 114
    overview, 103
    using competitive comparisons, 105–6
    using customer profiles, 105
    using customer records for, 106
    using demographic data, 104–5
    using government databases, 103–4
    using media data, 104

Segmenting markets, *see also* Market-segmentation
        strategy; Market segments
    business, 82–85
    defined, 15
    demographically, 78–79
    factors involved in, 77
    geographically, 77–78
    marketing strategies and, 9
    methods of, 76
    psychologically, 79–81
    reasons for, 74
    by usage, 79
Segway Human Scooter, public-relations
        and, 109
Selective distribution strategy
    defined, 167
    evaluating efficacy of, 163
Self-liquidating premiums
    benefits of, 209
    defined, 217
Service mark
    defined, 141
    representing product identity with, 129
Service recovery
    defined, 244
    sales and, 233–36
Services
    consumer decision process about, 61–62
    sharing information on blogs, 300
Services provided, positioning by, 135
7-Up, "Make 7-Up Yours" slogan, 3
Sex, stopping power of, 230–31
Shopping bags, advertising on, 260
Shopping cart
    defined, 316
    including on Web sites, 302
Shopping centers, retailing and, 173
Signature
    defined, 272
    designing effective print tabs and, 252
Signs, creating effective, 259–60
Simplicity marketing
    defined, 43
    understanding, 23
Situation analysis
    defined, 43
    preparing, 31–32
Size
    determining billboard, 261
    selecting print ad, 250

Skimming the market
    defined, 217
    pricing new products and, 212
SKU (stock-keeping unit)
    defined, 191
    retailers using, 177
Slamming, 14
Slogan
    defined, 272
    designing effective print ads and, 252
Social class, consumer buying behavior and, 52–53
Social factors, consumer buying behavior
        and, 52–54
Socialization
    consumer buying behavior and, 49–50
    defined, 66
Socialization agent
    consumer buying behavior and, 49–50
    defined, 67
Soft bounce-back
    defined, 317
    sending e-mail and, 313
Sources, for decision making information search, 59
Spam
    defined, 317
    using e-mail and, 313
Special offers
    defined, 217
    pricing and, 207–8
Specialty shops, retailing and, 173
Spitzer, Eliot (New York State attorney general), bid
        rigging and, 214
Spreadsheet, analyzing marketing program costs
        with, 36–37
Spyware
    defined, 317
    regulating/stopping, 313–14
Start-up firms
    preparing marketing plans, 28
    risk and, 21
State of readiness, segmenting consumer markets
        by, 79
Statistical analysis, quantitative research and, 96
Steppenwolf Theatre, telemarketing campaign of, 188
Stickiness
    defined, 317
    Web site content and, 302
Stock-keeping unit (SKU)
    defined, 191
    retailers using, 177

Stopping power
    communications with, 229–31
    defined, 244
Storyboard
    defined, 272
    television advertising and, 266
Straight rebuy, organizational buying behavior and, 56
Strategy, 43, *see also specific strategies*
Strategy wheel, organizing marketing activities and, 25
Streaming video, on Web sites, 302–3
Strengths
    identifying for marketing program, 8
    market segmentation strategy and, 75
    researching, 101
Subhead
    defined, 272
    designing effective print ads and, 252
Subject line, legal e-mail, 313
Substitute products, price and, 197
Supermarkets, retailing and, 172
Supplier search, organizational buying process and, 63–64
Supplier selection, organizational buying process and, 65
Supply-chain management, distribution and, 152
Surprise, stopping power and, 230
Survey research
    conducting, 97–99, 101
    defined, 114
Surveys, telemarketers abusing, 241–42
Survival, setting strategic price objectives and, 204
Sweeps
    buying television advertising time and, 269
    defined, 272

T
Targeting markets
    concentration strategy and, 87
    defined, 91
    multisegment strategy and, 87–88
    overview, 85–86
    selecting, 88–90
    using direct-response adds, 185–86
Technical development, screening product development ideas with, 122
Technical information, organizational buying behavior and, 55
Telemarketing, avoiding deceptive practices, 241–42
Telephone slamming, 14
Telephone systems, customer retention and, 235–36
Television advertising
    buying time for, 268–70
    using, 264–66
    video production tips for, 266–68

Testmarketing, screening product development ideas with, 123
Thumbnails
    defined, 272
    designing effective print ads and, 253
Tiffany & Company, image and, 206
Time, organizational buying process and, 55
Time advantages, creating value through, 197
Time-period forecasts
    defined, 43
    projecting sales with, 40
Toll-free numbers, inbound telemarketing and, 188
Toyota, using word of mouth, 285
Tracking cookies
    defined, 317
    using properly, 314
Trade discounts
    defined, 217
    setting price and, 200–202
Trademark
    defined, 141
    designing effective print ads and, 252
    representing product identity with, 129
Trade name
    defined, 141
    representing product identity with, 129
Trade secrecy laws, using competitor's ideas and, 121
Trade shows, attracting customers with, 4
Traffic
    building with pull power, 231
    defined, 191
    drawing to Web sites, 306–10
    importance of, 177–78
Traffic counts
    billboard advertising and, 262
    defined, 272
Trait perspective, developing product personality with, 229
Transit ads, using, 260
Transportation, wholesalers and, 150
Travel industry, on Internet, 300
Trend reports, conducting research with, 101
Trends, pricing and, 204
Trial coupons, attracting customers with, 4
T-shirts, advertising on, 260
Typeface
    defined, 272
    selecting for print ads, 254–56

U
Undifferentiated market
    defined, 91
    differentiating products in, 73–74
    strategic approach to, 73

Uniqueness
    market segmentation strategy and, 75
    researching, 101
    Web address and, 307
Unique selling proposition (USP)
    defined, 191
    designing POP displays and, 181
URL
    defined, 317
    selecting, 306–7
    on Web sites, 303
Usage market segments, 79
Users status, segmenting consumer markets by, 79

V

VALS, example of, 81
VALS 2
    consumer segmentation by, 80
    example of, 81
Value-based pricing
    customer price perceptions and, 210–11
    defined, 217
Vertical marketing systems (VMS)
    defined, 167
    structure of, 155–56
Video, on Web sites, 302–3
Video production tips, 266–68
Viral marketing
    defined, 317
    using, 314–15
Virtual packaging, using, 131
Visibility, information, emotion, and workability
    (VIEW)
    defined, 141
    designing packaging with, 131–32
Visuals
    communicating by, 225–26
    defined, 272
    designing effective print tabs and, 252
    television advertising and, 265
    on Web sites, 302
Volkswagen, using emotional appeal, 228
Volvo, customer champions and, 134

W

Wait time, telemarketing and, 187
Wants
    defined, 67
    vs. needs, 57

Warehouse retailing, 172
Warehousing, wholesalers and, 150
Web address
    selecting, 306–7
    on Web sites, 303
Webcasts
    adding to Web sites, 304–5
    defined, 317
Web sites
    attracting customers with, 4
    buying search engine visibility for, 307–8
    creating interesting content for, 302–4
    designing, 301
    designing in placing banner ads on, 315–16
    developing registration-based, 305
    interpreting click rates on, 310
    marketing on, 299–300
    planning and budgeting for, 30
    posting press releases on, 283
    shopping for designers for, 301–2
    tracking visitors on, 308–9
    using header block on, 309
    using META tags on, 309
    virtual packaging and, 131
Webzines
    defined, 316
    using, 314–15
Wenger Swiss Army Knife, marketing, 24
Whiskas cat food, responding to customer feedback,
    102
White papers, on Web sites, 304
Wholesalers
    as channel members, 150–51
    defined, 167
Wm. Wrigley Jr. Company, using focus groups, 113
Word of mouth (WOM)
    creating publicity with, 284–86
    defined, 292
World Wide Web, *see* Internet; Web sites
Writing
    communicating by, 225
    press releases, 281–83
    television advertising and, 265

Y

Yahoo!, buying search engine visibility from, 308